S0-BOC-622

*Where do I go for answers to my travel questions?*

*What's the best and easiest way to plan and book my trip?*

# frommers.travelocity.com

**Frommer's**, the travel guide leader, has teamed up with **Travelocity.com,** the leader in online travel, to bring you an in-depth, easy-to-use resource designed to help you plan and book your trip online.

At **frommers.travelocity.com**, you'll find free online updates about your destination from the experts at Frommer's plus the outstanding travel planning and purchasing features of Travelocity.com. Travelocity.com provides reservations capabilities for 95 percent of all airline seats sold, more than 47,000 hotels, and over 50 car rental companies. In addition, Travelocity.com offers more than 2,000 exciting vacation and cruise packages. Travelocity.com puts you in complete control of your travel planning with these and other great features:

> **Expert travel guidance from Frommer's** - over 150 writers reporting from around the world!

> **Best Fare Finder** - an interactive calendar tells you when to travel to get the best airfare

> **Fare Watcher** - we'll track airfare changes to your favorite destinations

> **Dream Maps** - a mapping feature that suggests travel opportunities based on your budget

> **Shop Safe Guarantee** - 24 hours a day / 7 days a week live customer service, and more!

Whether traveling on a tight budget, looking for a quick weekend getaway, or planning the trip of a lifetime, Frommer's guides and Travelocity.com will make your travel dreams a reality. You've bought the book, now book the trip!

# A New Star-Rating System & Other Exciting News from Frommer's!

In our continuing effort to publish the savviest, most up-to-date, and most appealing travel guides available, we've added some great new features.

Frommer's guides now include a new star-rating system. Every hotel, restaurant, and attraction is rated from 0 to 3 stars to help you set priorities and organize your time.

We've also added seven brand-new features that point you to the great deals, in-the-know advice, and unique experiences that separate travelers from tourists. Throughout the guide look for:

| | |
|---|---|
| *Finds* | Special finds—those places only insiders know about |
| *Fun Fact* | Fun facts—details that make travelers more informed and their trips more fun |
| *Kids* | Best bets for kids—advice for the whole family |
| *Moments* | Special moments—those experiences that memories are made of |
| *Overrated* | Places or experiences not worth your time or money |
| *Tips* | Insider tips—some great ways to save time and money |
| *Value* | Great values—where to get the best deals |

# Frommer's®

## PORTABLE
# Los Cabos
# & Baja

### 2nd Edition

*by Lynne Bairstow*

Hungry Minds™

Best-Selling Books • Digital Downloads • e-Books •
Answer Networks • e-Newsletters • Branded Web Sites • e-Learning
New York, NY • Cleveland, OH • Indianapolis, IN

## ABOUT THE AUTHOR

**Lynne Bairstow** is a writer specializing in travel and the Internet, who has
lived in Puerto Vallarta, Mexico, at least part-time for the past 9 years. She
now lives there year-round, and was assisted in her research for this book
by Claudia Velo. In a previous professional life, Lynne was a vice president
for Merrill Lynch in Chicago and New York. She is the co-author of
*Frommer's Mexico; Frommer's Cancún, Cozumel & the Yucatán; Frommer's
Portable Acapulco, Ixtapa & Zihuatanejo; Frommer's Portable Cancún;* and
*Frommer's Portable Puerto Vallarta, Manzanillo & Guadalajara,* which won
Mexico's Pluma de Plata (Silver Quill) award, given for excellence in for-
eign travel writing about Mexico.

Published by:

## HUNGRY MINDS, INC.

909 Third Avenue
New York, NY 10022

ISBN 0-7645-6434-X
ISSN 1521-5059

Editor: Kelly Regan
Production Editor: Donna Wright
Photo Editor: Richard Fox
Design by Michele Laseau
Cartographer: John Decamillis
Production by Hungry Minds Indianapolis Production Services

## SPECIAL SALES

For general information on Hungry Minds' products and services, please
contact our Customer Care department within the U.S. at 800-762-2974,
outside the U.S. at 317-572-3993 or fax 317-572-4002. For sales inquiries
and reseller information, including discounts, bulk sales, customized editions, and premium sales, please contact our Customer Care department at
800-434-3422.

Manufactured in the United States of America

5  4  3  2  1

# Contents

# List of Maps

## AN INVITATION TO THE READER

In researching this book I have discovered many wonderful places—hotels, restaurants, shops, and more. I'm sure you'll find others. Please tell us about them, so that I can share the information with your fellow travelers in upcoming editions. If you were disappointed with a recommendation, we'd love to know that, too. Please write to:

*Frommer's Portable Los Cabos & Baja,* 2nd Edition
Hungry Minds, Inc. • 909 Third Avenue • New York, NY 10022

## AN ADDITIONAL NOTE

Please be advised that travel information is subject to change at any time—and this is especially true of prices. We therefore suggest that you write or call ahead for confirmation when making your travel plans. The authors, editors, and publisher cannot be held responsible for the experiences of readers while traveling. Your safety is important to us, however, so we encourage you to stay alert and be aware of your surroundings. Keep a close eye on cameras, purses, and wallets, all favorite targets of thieves and pickpockets.

## WHAT THE SYMBOLS MEAN

The following abbreviations are used for credit cards:

| | | | | | |
|---|---|---|---|---|---|
| AE | American Express | DISC | Discover | V | Visa |
| DC | Diners Club | MC | MasterCard | | |

## FROMMERS.COM

Now that you have the guidebook to a great trip, visit our website at www.frommers.com for travel information on nearly 2,000 destinations. With features updated regularly, we give you instant access to the most current trip-planning information available. At Frommers.com, you'll also find the best prices on airfares, accommodations, and car rentals—and you can even book travel online through our travel booking partners. At Frommers.com you'll also find the following:

- Daily Newsletter highlighting the best travel deals
- Hot Spot of the Month/Vacation Sweepstakes & Travel Photo Contest
- More than 200 Travel Message Boards
- Outspoken Newsletters and Feature Articles on travel bargains, vacation ideas, tips & resources, and more!

# Planning a Trip to Baja California

A little advance planning can make the difference between a good trip and a great trip. When should you go? What's the best way to get there? How much should you plan on spending? What festivals or special events will be taking place during your visit? What safety or health precautions are advised? I'll answer these and other questions for you in this chapter.

In addition to these basics, I highly recommend taking some time to learn a little about the culture and traditions of Mexico. It can make the difference between simply "getting away" and truly adding understanding to your experience.

## 1 Baja at a Glance

The Baja Peninsula is part of Mexico—and yet it is not. Attached to the mainland United States and separated from the rest of Mexico by the Sea of Cortez (also called the Gulf of California), the Baja peninsula is longer than Italy, stretching 876 miles from Mexico's northernmost city of Tijuana to Cabo San Lucas at its southern tip. Volcanic uplifting created the craggy desertscape you see today. Whole forests of cardón cactus, spiky Joshua trees, and spindly ocotillo bushes populate this raw, untamed landscape where volcanoes once rumbled.

Culturally and geographically, Baja is set apart from mainland Mexico, and it remained isolated for many years. Now the state of Baja California del Sur has developed into a vacation haven that offers fishing, diving, and whale-watching amidst beautiful settings and posh resorts. Great sportfishing originally centered attention on Los Cabos, and it remains a lure today, although golf has overtaken it as the principle attraction. Once accessible only by water, Baja attracted a hearty community of cruisers, fishermen, divers, and adventurers starting in the late 1940s. By the early 1980s, the Mexican government realized the growth potential of Los Cabos and invested in new highways, airport facilities, golf courses, and modern marine facilities. Expanded airlift and the opening of Transpeninsular Highway 1 in 1973 paved the way for the area's spectacular growth.

**BAJA SUR**   Of the peninsula's three regions, Baja Sur has attracted the most attention and travelers, and is increasingly known as a haven for golfers. Twin towns with distinct personalities sit at the tip of the peninsula: Cabo San Lucas and San José del Cabo. The two Cabos are the center of accommodations and activities.

The road that connects Cabo San Lucas and San José del Cabo is the centerpiece of resort growth. Known as the Corridor, this stretch of four well-paved lanes offers cliff-top vistas but still has no night-time lighting. The area's most deluxe resorts and renowned golf courses are found here, along with a collection of dramatic beaches and coves.

Although Los Cabos often feels like the southern playground of the United States' West Coast, other areas of Baja Sur can seem like the least crowded corners of Mexico. Todos Santos, an artistic com-munity on the Pacific side of the coastal curve, just north of the tip, draws travelers who find that Cabo San Lucas has outgrown them. La Paz, the capital of Baja Sur, remains an easygoing maritime port, with an interesting assortment of small hotels, inns, and a growing diversity of eco- and adventure tours.

**MID-BAJA**   Among the highlights of the mid-Baja region are the east coast towns of Loreto, Mulegé, and Santa Rosalía. Although they have a much richer historic and cultural heritage than Baja Sur's resort towns (as center of the Jesuit Mission movement during the 1700s), they've been eclipsed by the growth of tourism infra-structure and services in the two Cabos. Loreto currently stands at the center of attention of the Mexican government's promotional and investment focus, so expect this quiet town to be growing soon.

This area's natural attractions have made it a center for sea kayak-ing, sportfishing, and hiking—including excursions to view indige-nous cave paintings, which have been named a World Heritage Site by UNESCO. This is also the place to come to if you're interested in whale-watching; many tour companies operate out of Loreto and the smaller neighboring towns. For more information, see "Whale-Watching in Baja: A Primer," in chapter 4.

**BAJA NORTE**   Tijuana has the dubious distinction of being the most visited and perhaps most misunderstood town in all of

# The Baja Peninsula

Bahía de Sebastián Viscaino
Playa San Rafael
B. San Rafael
Bahía Tortugas
**Guerrero Negro**
Pto. Nuevo
Scammon's Lagoon
B. San Carlos
La Trinidad
Bahía Asuncion
B. La Asunción
Guadalupe
**DESIERTO DE**
B. Sta. Ana
*Gulf of California*
Bahía San Hipólito
San Ignacio
**VIZVAINO**
**Santa Rosalía**
Laguna de San Ignacio
**Mulegé**
*Bahía Concepción*
SE. COYOTE
La Purisima
B. San Basílio
San Isidro
*Pacific Ocean*
**Loreto**
Isla Del Carmen
Boca La Soledad
Va. Ignacio Zaragoza
**Pto. Adolfo Lopez Mateos**
Ciudad Insurgentes
*Sea of Cortéz*
**Puerto San Carlos**
B. Sta. María
**Ciudad Constitución**
El Ciruelo
Bahía Magdalena
Isla San José
San Ignacio
B. Coyote
Isla La Partida
Isla Espíritu Santo
Isla Cerralvo
Pichilingue
Las Cruces
**La Paz**
San Pedro
La Ventana
B. de los Muertos
Buena Vista
Los Barriles
B. de Palmas
**Todos Santos**
**La Rivera**
Santiago
Miraflores
Cabo Pulmo
**Cabo San Lucas**
**San José del Cabo**
SIERRA DE LA LAGUNA

Legend
Airport ✈
Beach ↗

0            50 Mi
0            50 Km

3

Mexico. Dog racing, easy tequila, and a sin-city reputation have all been hallmarks of this classic border town, a favored resort for the Hollywood who's who during Prohibition times. New cultural and sporting attractions, extensive shopping, and strong business growth—of the reputable kind—are helping to brighten up Tijuana's image.

Tranquil Rosarito Beach is also reemerging as a viable resort town, given a boost after the movie *Titanic* was filmed here (the set is still in place, turned into a museum of sorts, with plans for a movie-themed amusement park in the works). Further south down the Pacific coast is the lovely port town of Ensenada, also known for its prime surfing and spirited sportfishing. A new and growing attraction are the nearby vineyards—Mexico's wine country.

## 2 Visitor Information, Entry Requirements & Money

### SOURCES OF INFORMATION

The Mexico Hot Line (© 800/44-MEXICO) is an excellent source for general information; you can request brochures on the country and get answers to the most commonly asked questions. If you have a fax, Mexico's Ministry of Tourism also offers Fax-Me-Mexico (© 541/385-9282). Call, key in your fax number, and select from a variety of topics from general destination information to specific accommodations (the service lists 400 hotels), shopping, dining, sports, sight-seeing, festivals, and nightlife. They'll then fax you the materials you're interested in.

More information (15,000 pages worth, they say) about Mexico is available on the Mexico Ministry of Tourism's website: www.visitmexico.com. Also, information still remains on the government's former site (http://mexico-travel.com).

The U.S. State Department (© 202/647-5225 for travel information and Overseas Citizens Services) offers a Consular Information Sheet on Mexico, with a compilation of safety, medical, driving, and general travel information gleaned from reports by official U.S. State Department offices in Mexico. You can also request the Consular Information Sheet by fax (© 202/647-3000). The State Department is also on the Internet; check out http://travel.state.gov/mexico.html for the Consular Information Sheet on Mexico; http://travel.state.gov/travel_warnings.html for other Consular Information sheets and travel warnings; and

**http://travel.state.gov/tips_mexico.html** for the State Department's Tips for Travelers to Mexico.

## MEXICAN GOVERNMENT TOURISM BOARD OFFICES

New Mexico Tourism Promotion Board offices opened in the summer of 2000, using the same locations and phone numbers of the former Mexican Government Tourism Offices. Those operating in North America include the following:

United States: Chicago, IL (✆ **312/606-9252**); Houston, TX (✆ **713/772-2581** ext. 105); Los Angeles, CA (✆ **213/351-2069,** fax 213/351-2074); Miami, FL (✆ **305/718-4095**); New York, NY (✆ **800/446-3942**); and the Mexican Embassy Tourism Delegate, 1911 Pennsylvania Ave., Washington, D.C. 20005 (✆ **202/728-1750**). The Tourism Board offices are combined with Mexican Consulate offices in the same cities, providing one central source for official information on Mexico.

Canada: 1 Place Ville-Marie, Suite 1931, Montréal, QUEB, H3B 2C3 (✆ **514/871-1052**); 2 Bloor St. W., Suite 1502, Toronto, ON, M4W 3E2 (✆ **416/925-2753**); and 999 W. Hastings, Suite 1110, Vancouver, BC, V6C 2W2 (✆ **604/669-2845**).

## ENTRY REQUIREMENTS

**DOCUMENTS**  All travelers to Mexico are required to present proof of citizenship, such as an original birth certificate with a raised seal, a valid passport, or naturalization papers. Those using a birth certificate should also have a current photo identification such as a driver's license or official ID. Those whose last name on the birth certificate is different from their current name (women using a married name, for example) should also bring a photo identification card and legal proof of the name change, such as the original marriage license or certificate. This proof of citizenship may also be requested when you want to reenter either the United States or Mexico. Note that photocopies are not acceptable.

You must also carry a Mexican Tourist Permit (abbreviated in Spanish as FMT), which is issued free of charge by Mexican border officials after proof of citizenship is accepted, and is also provided free of charge by airlines on flights into Mexico. The tourist permit is more important than a passport in Mexico, so guard it carefully. If you lose it, you may not be permitted to leave the country until you can replace it—a bureaucratic hassle that can take anywhere from a few hours to a week. (If you do lose your tourist permit, get a police report from local authorities indicating that your documents were stolen; having one might lessen the hassle of exiting the country without all your identification. Also, make sure to report the loss to your embassy or consulate.)

A tourist permit can be issued for up to 180 days, although your stay south of the border may be shorter than that. Sometimes officials don't ask—they just stamp a time limit, so be sure to say "6 months" (or at least twice as long as you intend to stay). If you should decide to extend your stay, you may request that additional time be added to your permit from an official immigration office in Mexico. In Baja California, immigration laws have changed, and now tourist visas (FMT) are only allowed for a maximum period of 180 days per year, with a maximum of 30 days per visit. This is to encourage the more regular visitors, or those who spend longer periods of time in Mexico, to obtain the proper immigration documents that denote partial residency there.

Note that children under age 18 traveling without parents or with only one parent must have a notarized letter from the absent parent or parents authorizing the travel.

For travelers entering Mexico by car at the border of Baja California, note that tourist permits (FMT) for driving a car into Mexico are issued only in Tijuana, Tecate, Mexicali, Ensenada, and Guerrero Negro. If you travel anywhere beyond the frontier zone without this document, you will be fined $40. Permits for driving a car with foreign plates in Mexico are available only in Tijuana, Ensenada, Tecate, Mexicali, or La Paz.

**Lost Documents**    To replace a lost passport, contact your embassy or nearest consular agent (see "Fast Facts: Baja California," below). You must establish a record of your citizenship and also fill out a form requesting another Mexican tourist permit if it, too, was lost. Without the tourist permit you can't leave the country, and without an affidavit affirming your passport request and citizenship, you may have problems at Customs when you get home. So it's important to clear everything up before you try to leave. Mexican Customs may, however, accept the police report of the loss of the tourist permit and allow you to leave.

**CUSTOMS ALLOWANCES**    When you enter Mexico, Customs officials will be tolerant as long as you have no illegal drugs or firearms. You're allowed to bring in two cartons of cigarettes or 50 cigars, plus a kilogram (2.2 lb.) of smoking tobacco; the liquor allowance is two 1-liter bottles of anything, wine or hard liquor; you are also allowed 12 rolls of film. A laptop computer, camera equipment, and sporting equipment (golf clubs, scuba gear, or a bicycle, for example) that could feasibly be used during your stay are also allowed. The underlying guideline is that you shouldn't bring anything that looks like it's meant to be resold in Mexico.

When you reenter the United States, federal law allows you to bring in up to $400 in purchases duty-free every 30 days. The first $1,000 over the $400 allowance is taxed at 10%. You may bring in a carton (200) of cigarettes, 100 cigars, or 2 kilograms (4.4 lb.) of smoking tobacco, plus 1 liter of an alcoholic beverage (wine, beer, or spirits).

Canadian citizens are allowed $50 in purchases after a 24-hour absence from the country, $300 after a stay of 48 hours, or $750 after a stay of 7 days or more. In addition, Canadian citizens may bring 200 cigarettes or 50 cigars plus 1 kilogram (2.2 lbs.) of chewing tobacco, plus 1.5 liters of hard liquor or wine.

British travelers returning from outside the European Union are allowed to bring in £145 worth of goods, in addition to the following: up to 200 cigarettes, 50 cigars, or 250 grams of tobacco; 2 liters of wine; 1 liter of liquor greater than 22% alcohol by volume; and 60cc/milliliters of perfume. If any item worth more than the limit of £145 is brought in, payment must be made on the full value, not just on the amount above £145.

Citizens of New Zealand are allowed to return with a combined value of up to NZ$1,000 in goods, duty-free.

**Going Through Customs**     Mexican Customs inspection has been streamlined. At most points of entry, tourists are requested to press a button in front of what looks like a traffic signal, which alternates on touch between red and green signals. Green light and you go through without inspection; red light and your luggage or car may be inspected briefly or thoroughly. If you have an unusual amount of luggage or an oversized piece, you may be subject to inspection despite the traffic-signal routine.

## MONEY

**CASH/CURRENCY**     The currency in Mexico is the Mexican peso. Paper currency comes in denominations of 20, 50, 100, 200, and 500 pesos. Coins come in denominations of 1, 2, 5, and 10 pesos, and 20 and 50 *centavos* (100 centavos equal 1 peso). The current exchange rate for the U.S. dollar is around 10 pesos; at that rate, an item that costs 10 pesos would be equivalent to $1.

## Tips  A Few Words About Prices in Mexico

The peso's value continues to fluctuate—at press time it was slightly more than 9 pesos to the dollar. Prices in this book (which are always given in U.S. dollars) have been converted to U.S. dollars at 10 pesos to the dollar. Most hotels in Mexico—with the exception of places that receive little foreign tourism—quote prices in U.S. dollars. Thus, currency fluctuations are unlikely to affect the prices charged by most hotels.

Mexico has a **value-added tax** of 15% (*Impuesto al Valor Agregado,* or IVA, pronounced ee-bah) on most everything, including restaurant meals, bus tickets, and souvenirs. (One of the exceptions is Los Cabos, where the IVA is 10%; as ports of entry, the towns receive a special 5% break on taxes.) Hotels charge the usual 15% IVA, plus a locally administered bed tax of 2% (in many but not all areas), for a total of 17%. In Los Cabos, hotels charge the 10% IVA plus 2% room tax. IVA will not necessarily be included in the prices quoted by hotels and restaurants. You may find that upper-end properties (three or more stars) quote prices without IVA included, while lower-priced hotels include IVA in their quotes. Always ask to see a printed price sheet and always ask if the tax is included.

Getting change continues to be a problem in Mexico. Small-denomination bills and coins are hard to come by, so start collecting them early in your trip and continue as you travel. Shopkeepers everywhere seem always to be out of change and small bills; that's doubly true in a market.

Many establishments that deal with tourists, especially in coastal resort areas, quote prices in dollars. To avoid confusion, they use the abbreviations "Dlls." for dollars and "M.N." (*moneda nacional,* or national currency) for pesos. All dollar equivalencies in this book were based on an exchange rate of 10 pesos per dollar.

**EXCHANGING MONEY**    The rate of exchange fluctuates a tiny bit daily, so you probably are better off not exchanging too much of your currency at once. Don't forget, however, to have enough pesos to carry you over a weekend or Mexican holiday, when banks are closed. In general, avoid carrying the U.S. $100 bill, the bill most commonly counterfeited in Mexico and therefore the most difficult to exchange, especially in smaller towns. Since small bills and coins in pesos are hard to come by in Mexico, the U.S. $1 bill is very useful for tipping. Using U.S. coins for tipping is ineffective, as most Mexicans cannot exchange them—U.S. coins are not accepted in Mexican banks.

The bottom line on exchanging money of all kinds: It pays to ask first and shop around. Banks pay the top rates.

Exchange houses (*casas de cambio*) are generally more convenient than banks because they have more locations and longer hours; the rate of exchange may be the same as a bank or only slightly lower. *Note:* Before leaving a bank or exchange-house window, always count your change in front of the teller before the next client steps up.

Large airports have currency-exchange counters that often stay open whenever flights are arriving or departing. Though convenient, these generally do not offer the most favorable rates. Exchange counters can be found both in the San José del Cabo and the La Paz airports.

A hotel's exchange desk commonly pays less favorable rates than banks; however, when the currency is in a state of flux, higher-priced hotels are known to pay higher than bank rates, in their effort to attract dollars. It pays to shop around, but in almost all cases, you receive a better exchange by changing money first, then paying for goods or services, rather than by paying with dollars directly to an establishment.

**BANKS & ATMs**   Banks in Mexico are rapidly expanding and improving services. New hours tend to be from 9am until 5 or 6pm, with many open for at least a half day on Saturday. The exchange of dollars, which used to be limited until noon, can now be accommodated anytime during business hours in the larger resorts and cities. Some, but not all, banks charge a service fee of about 1% to exchange traveler's checks. However, most purchases can be paid for directly with traveler's checks at the stated exchange rate of the establishment. Don't even bother with personal checks drawn on a U.S. bank—although theoretically they may be cashed, it's not without weeks of delay, and the bank will wait for your check to clear before giving you your money.

### Money Matters

The universal currency sign ($) is used to indicate pesos in Mexico. The use of this symbol in this book, however, denotes U.S. currency.

Travelers to Mexico can also access money from automatic teller machines (ATMs), now available in most major cities and resort areas in Mexico. Universal bankcards (such as the Cirrus and PLUS systems) can be used, and this is a convenient way to withdraw money from your bank and avoid carrying too much with you at any time. There is often a service fee charged by your bank for each transaction (roughly ranging between $1 and $2), but the exchange rate is generally more favorable than the one found at a currency house. Most machines offer Spanish/English menus and dispense pesos, but some offer the option of withdrawing dollars. Be sure to check the daily withdrawal limit before you depart, and ask your bank whether you need a new personal ID number. For Cirrus locations abroad, call ✆ **800/424-7787,** or check out MasterCard's website (www. mastercard.com/atm/). For PLUS usage abroad, call ✆ **800/843-7587,** or visit Visa's website (www.visa.com/atms).

**TRAVELER'S CHECKS**    Traveler's checks are readily accepted nearly everywhere, but they can be difficult to cash on a weekend or holiday or in an out-of-the-way place. Their best value is in replacement in case of theft.

**CREDIT CARDS**    You'll be able to charge most hotel, restaurant, and store purchases, as well as almost all airline tickets, on your credit card. You can get cash advances of several hundred dollars on your card, but there may be a wait of 20 minutes to 2 hours. You generally can't charge gasoline purchases in Mexico; however, with the new franchise system of Pemex stations taking hold, this may change as well. Visa, MasterCard, and American Express are the most accepted cards.

Credit card charges will be billed in pesos, then converted into dollars by the bank issuing the credit card. Generally you receive the favorable bank rate when paying by credit card, but keep in mind that most credit card companies charge a fee of between 1 and 3 percent for processing this foreign-currency transaction. You won't usually see the fee on your statement, since it's factored into the conversion rate.

## 3 When to Go

**SEASONS**    Mexico has two principal travel seasons. High season begins around December 20 and continues to Easter, although in some places high season can begin as early as mid-November; during Christmas and New Year's, it's almost impossible to find a room.

Low season begins the day after Easter and continues to mid-December; during low season, prices may drop 20% to 50%.

The weather in Baja, land of extremes, can be unpredictable. It can be sizzling hot in summer and cold and windy in winter—so windy that fishing and other nautical expeditions may have to be grounded for a few days. Though winter is often warm enough for water sports, bring a wet suit along if you're a serious diver or snorkeler, as well as warmer clothes for unexpectedly chilly weather at night.

# BAJA CALIFORNIA CALENDAR OF EVENTS

*Note:* Banks, government offices, and many stores are closed on days marked as national holidays.

## January

**New Year's Day** (*Año Nuevo*). Parades, religious observances, parties, and fireworks welcome in the New Year everywhere. January 1. National holiday.

## February

**Day of the Constitution** (*Día de la Constitución*). The constitution that currently rules Mexican laws was signed in 1917 as a result of the revolutionary war of 1910. It is sometimes celebrated with parades. February 5. National holiday.

**Carnaval.** Carnaval takes place the 3 days preceding Ash Wednesday and the beginning of Lent. It is celebrated with special zeal in La Paz, with a festive atmosphere and parades. The 3 days preceding Ash Wednesday.

## March

**Holy Week.** Celebrates the last week in the life of Christ from Palm Sunday through Easter Sunday with somber religious processions almost nightly, spoofing of Judas, and reenactments of specific biblical events, plus food and craft fairs. Businesses close during this traditional week of Mexican national vacations.

If you plan on traveling to or around Mexico during Holy Week, make your reservations early. Airline seats on flights into and out of the country will be reserved months in advance. For 2002, March 24 through 29 is Holy Week, Easter Sunday is March 31, and the week following is a traditional vacation period.

## May

**Labor Day,** celebrated nationwide. Workers' parades countrywide, and everything closes. May 1. National holiday.

**Cinco de Mayo,** celebrated nationwide. A national holiday that celebrates the defeat of the French at the Battle of Puebla. May 5.

## June

**Navy Day** (*Día de la Marina*). Celebrated in all coastal towns, with naval parades and fireworks. June 1.

## September

**Independence Day.** Celebrates Mexico's independence from Spain. A day of parades, picnics, and family reunions throughout the country. At 11pm on September 15, the president of Mexico gives the famous independence *grito* (shout) from the National Palace in Mexico City. At least half a million people are crowded into the *zócalo* (town square), and the rest of the country watches the event on TV. September 15 and 16. September 16 is a national holiday.

## November

**Day of the Dead.** What's commonly called the Day of the Dead is actually 2 days, All Saints' Day—honoring saints and deceased children—and All Souls' Day, honoring deceased adults. Relatives gather at cemeteries countrywide, carrying candles and food, often spending the night beside graves of loved ones. November 1 and 2. November 1 is a national holiday.

**Revolution Day.** Commemorates the start of the Mexican Revolution in 1910 with parades, speeches, rodeos, and patriotic events. November 20. National holiday.

## December

**Feast of the Virgin of Guadalupe.** Throughout the country the patroness of Mexico is honored with religious processions, street fairs, dancing, fireworks, and masses. This is one of Mexico's most moving and beautiful displays of traditional culture. The Virgin of Guadalupe appeared to a young man, Juan Diego, in December 1531, on a hill near Mexico City. He convinced the bishop that he had seen the apparition by revealing his cloak, upon which the Virgin was emblazoned. It's customary for children to dress up as Juan Diego, wearing mustaches and red bandannas. December 12.

**Christmas.** Mexicans extend this celebration and leave their jobs, often beginning 2 weeks before Christmas and continuing all the way through New Year's. Many businesses close, and resorts and hotels fill up. On December 23 also there are significant celebrations. December 24 and 25.

**New Year's Eve.** As in the rest of the world, New Year's Eve in Mexico is celebrated with parties, fireworks, and plenty of noise. December 31.

## 4  Active Vacations in Baja

Los Cabos, where several championship tournaments are held each year, has become the preeminent golf destination in Mexico. Tennis, racquetball, squash, water-skiing, surfing, bicycling, and horseback riding are all sports that visitors can enjoy in Baja. Scuba diving is excellent in the Sea of Cortez.

**OUTDOORS ORGANIZATIONS & TOUR OPERATORS**
There's a new association of eco- and adventure tour operators in Mexico called **AMTAVE** (Asociación Mexicana de Turismo de Aventura y Ecoturismo, A.C.). They publish an annual catalog of participating firms and their offerings, all of which must meet certain criteria for security, quality, and training of the guides, as well as for sustainability of natural and cultural environments. For more information, contact them (in Cancún) at ℗/fax **9/884-9580** or 9/884-3667, or check out their website at www.amtave.com.mx; info@amtave.com).

The **American Wilderness Experience** (Globe Travel), P.O. Box 1486, Boulder, CO 80306 (℗ **800/444-3833** or 303/444-2622; dial 0 and ask the operator to connect you to a Baja adventure specialist), leads catered camping, kayaking, biking, and hiking trips in Baja California.

**Baja Expeditions,** 2625 Garnet Ave., San Diego, CA 92109 (℗ **800/843-6967** or 858/581-3311; www.bajaex.com; travel@bajaex.com), offers natural-history cruises, whale-watching, sea kayaking, camping, and scuba-diving trips out of Loreto, La Paz, and San Diego, depending on the trip of your choice. Small groups and special itineraries are their specialty.

**Mountain Travel Sobek,** 6420 Fairmount Ave., El Cerrito, CA 94530 (℗ **800/227-2384** or 510/527-8100), leads groups for kayaking in the Sea of Cortez.

**Naturequest,** 30872 South Coast Highway, Suite 185, Laguna Beach, CA 92651 (℗ **800/369-3033** or 949/499-9561; natureqst@aol.com), specializes in the natural history, culture, and wildlife of the Copper Canyon and the remote lagoons and waterways off Baja California. Baja trips get close to nature with special permits for venturing by two-person kayak into sanctuaries for whales and birds, and slipping among mangroves and into shallow bays, estuaries, and lagoons.

**North Star** (℗ **800/258-8434** or 520/773-9917; fax 520/773-9965; www.adventuretrip.com; Northstar@ AdventureTrip.

com), guides 6-day sea-kayaking trips in the Sea of Cortez, from October to May. Several routes are available, with boat support, traveling along the coast from San José and past the San Francisco Islands and the Sierra de la Giganta. A 10-day trip from Loreto to La Paz is also offered. No prior kayaking experience is necessary, but you have to be in good physical condition. Custom trips for groups of 10 or more can be arranged.

**One World Workforce,** P.O. Box 3188, La Mesa, CA 91944 (© 800/451-9564), has weeklong "hands-on conservation trips" that offer working volunteers a chance to help with sea-turtle conservation at Bahía de Los Angeles, Baja (spring, summer, and fall).

For more than 20 years, Trudi Angell has been guiding sea-kayaking tours in the Loreto area with **Tour Baja,** P.O. Box 827, Calistoga, CA 94515 (© 800/398-6200 or 707/942-4550; fax 707/942-8017; www.tourbaja.com; info@tourbaja.com). This is also her home, so she and her group of guides offer firsthand knowledge of the area, its natural history, and local culture. Her company's kayaking, mountain biking, pack trips, and sailing charters all combine these elements with great outdoor adventures.

By alternating sea-kayaking trips between Alaska and Baja for 19 years, **Sea Trek Sea Kayaking Center** (© 415/488-1000; fax 415/488-1707; www.seatrekkayak.com; paddle@seatrekkayak.com) has gained an intimate knowledge of the remote coastline of Baja. Eight-day trips depart from and return to Loreto; a new 12-day expedition travels from Loreto to La Paz. An optional day excursion to Bahía Magdalena for gray-whale-watching is also available. Full boat support is provided, and no previous paddling experience is necessary.

## 5 Health, Safety & Insurance

### STAYING HEALTHY

Mosquitoes and gnats are prevalent along the coast. Insect repellent (*repelente contra insectos*) is a must, and it's not always available in Mexico. If you'll be in these areas and are prone to bites, bring along a repellent that contains the active ingredient deet. Avon's Skin So Soft also works extremely well. If you're sensitive to bites, pick up some antihistamine cream from a drugstore at home.

Most readers won't ever see a scorpion (*alacrán*). But if you're stung by one, go immediately to a doctor.

**MORE SERIOUS DISEASES**    You shouldn't be overly concerned about tropical diseases if you stay on the normal tourist routes and don't eat street food. However, both dengue fever and cholera have appeared in Mexico in recent years. Talk to your doctor or to a medical specialist in tropical diseases about any precautions you should take. You can also get medical bulletins from the U.S. State Department and the Centers for Disease Control (see "Sources of Information," above). You can protect yourself by taking some simple precautions: Watch what you eat and drink; don't swim in stagnant water (ponds, slow-moving rivers, or wells); and avoid mosquito bites by covering up, using repellent, and sleeping under mosquito netting. The most dangerous areas seem to be on Mexico's west coast, away from the big resorts, which are relatively safe.

**EMERGENCY EVACUATION** For extreme medical emergencies, a 24-hour air-ambulance service from the United States will fly people to American hospitals: **Air-Evac** (© **888/554-9729,** or call collect 510/293-5968). You can also contact the service in Guadalajara (© **01-800/305-9400,** 3/616-9616, or 3/615-2471). There are several other companies that offer air-evacuation services; for a list refer to the U.S. State Department website at http://travel.state.gov/medical.html.

## SAFETY
**CRIME** I have lived and traveled in Mexico for almost a decade, have never had any serious trouble, and rarely feel suspicious of anyone or any situation. You probably will feel physically safer in most Mexican cities and villages than in any comparable place at home.

When traveling anyplace in the world, common sense is essential. A good rule of thumb is that you can generally trust people whom you approach for help, assistance, or directions—but be wary of anyone who approaches you offering the same. The more insistent they are, the more cautious you should be. The crime rate is on the whole much lower in Mexico than in most parts of the United States, and the nature of crimes in general is less violent—most crime is motivated by robbery or jealousy. Random, violent crime or serial crime is essentially unheard of in Mexico. You are much more

### Over-the-Counter Drugs in Mexico
Antibiotics and other drugs that you'd need a prescription to buy in the States are sold over the counter in Mexican pharmacies. Mexican pharmacies also have common over-the-counter cold, sinus, and allergy remedies, although not the broad selection we're accustomed to.

## *Tips* What to Do If You Get Sick

It's called "travelers' diarrhea" or *turista*, the Spanish word for "tourist": the persistent diarrhea, often accompanied by fever, nausea, and vomiting, that used to attack many travelers to Mexico. Some in the United States call this "Montezuma's revenge," but you won't hear it referred to this way in Mexico. Widespread improvements in infrastructure, sanitation, and education have practically eliminated this ailment, especially in well-developed resort areas. Most travelers make a habit of drinking only bottled water, which also helps to protect against unfamiliar bacteria. In resort areas, and generally throughout Mexico, only purified ice is used. Doctors say that *turista* is not caused by just one "bug," but by a combination of factors: consuming different foods and water, upsetting your schedule, being overtired, and experiencing the stresses of travel. Also, be careful of buffets at all-inclusive resorts. Although the food is probably just fine when it is set out initially, be careful to check that serving dishes are kept well-iced (or chafing dishes are hot), and don't eat any seafood that appears to have been out for a period of time. A good high-potency vitamin supplement, or even extra vitamin C, is helpful; the active cultures in yogurt are good for healthy digestion. If you do happen to come down with this ailment, nothing beats Pepto Bismol, readily available in Mexico.

**How to Prevent It:** The U.S. Public Health Service recommends the following measures for preventing travelers' diarrhea:

likely to meet kind and helpful Mexicans than you are to encounter those set on thievery and deceit.

**BRIBES & SCAMS**  As is the case around the world, there are the occasional bribes and scams, targeted at people believed to be naive in the ways of the place—obvious tourists, for example. For years Mexico was known as a place where bribes—called *propinas* (tips) or *mordidas* (bites)—were expected; however, the country is rapidly changing. Frequently, offering a bribe today, especially to a police officer, is considered an insult, and can land you in deeper trouble.

Whatever you do, avoid impoliteness; under no circumstances should you insult a Latin American official. Mexico is ruled by

- *Drink only purified water.* This means tea, coffee, and other beverages made with boiled water; canned or bottled carbonated beverages and water; or beer and wine. Most restaurants with a large tourist clientele use only purified water and ice.
- *Choose food carefully.* In general, avoid salads, uncooked vegetables, and unpasteurized milk or milk products (including cheese). However, salads in a first-class restaurant, or one serving a lot of tourists, are generally safe to eat. Choose food that is freshly cooked and still hot. Peelable fruit is ideal. Don't eat undercooked meat, fish, or shellfish. Again, if you are staying at an all-inclusive resort, only eat buffet food that appears fresh and that has recently been brought out to the serving table.
- In addition, something as simple as clean hands can go a long way toward preventing turista.

Since dehydration can quickly become life threatening, the Public Health Service advises that you be especially careful to replace fluids and electrolytes (potassium, sodium, and the like) during a bout of diarrhea. Do this by drinking Pedialyte, a rehydration solution available at most Mexican pharmacies, or glasses of natural fruit juice (high in potassium) with a pinch of salt added. Or you can try a glass of boiled pure water with a quarter teaspoon of sodium bicarbonate (baking soda) added.

extreme politeness, even in the face of adversity. In Mexico, gringos have a reputation for being loud and demanding. By adopting the local custom of excessive courtesy, you'll have greater success in negotiations of any kind. Stand your ground, but do it politely.

## INSURANCE

There are three kinds of travel insurance: trip cancellation, medical, and lost-luggage coverage. Trip-cancellation insurance is a good idea if you have paid a large portion of your vacation expenses up front. The other two types of insurance, however, don't make sense for most travelers. Rule number one: check your existing policies before you buy any additional coverage.

Your existing health insurance should cover you if you get sick while on vacation (although if you belong to an HMO, you should check whether you are fully covered when away from home). If you need hospital treatment, most health insurance plans and HMOs will cover out-of-country hospital visits and procedures, at least to some extent. Most make you pay the bills up front at the time of care, however; you'll get a refund after you've returned home and filed all the paperwork. Members of Blue Cross/Blue Shield can now use their cards at select hospitals in most major cities worldwide (call ℂ **800/810-BLUE** or check www.bluecares.com/health-travel/worldwide_hospitals.html for a list of hospitals). For independent travel health insurance providers, see below.

Your homeowner's insurance should cover stolen luggage. The airlines are responsible for $1,250 on domestic flights if they lose your luggage; if you plan to carry anything more valuable than that, keep it in your carry-on bag.

The differences between travel assistance and insurance are often blurred, but in general the former offers on-the-spot assistance and 24-hour hot lines (mostly oriented toward medical problems), whereas the latter reimburses you for travel problems (medical, travel, or otherwise) after you have filed the paperwork. The coverage you should consider will depend on how much protection is already contained in your existing health insurance or other policies. Some credit and charge-card companies may insure you against travel accidents if you buy plane, train, or bus tickets with their cards. Before purchasing additional insurance, read your policies and agreements carefully. Call your insurers or credit/charge-card companies if you have any questions.

Some credit cards (American Express and certain gold and platinum Visa and MasterCards, for example) offer automatic flight insurance against death or dismemberment in case of an airplane crash.

If you'll be driving in Mexico, see "Getting There/By Car" and "Getting Around/By Car" below for information on collision, damage, and personal-accident insurance.

**Health Care Abroad,** Wallach and Co. Inc., 107 W. Federal St. (P.O. Box 480), Middleburg, VA 20118 (ℂ **800/237-6615** or 540/687-3166), and **World Access,** 6600 W. Broad St., Richmond, VA 23230 (ℂ **800/628-4908** or 804/285-3300), offer medical and accident insurance as well as coverage for trip cancellation. Always read the fine print on the policy to be sure that you're getting the coverage you want.

## 6  Tips for Travelers with Special Needs

**FOR FAMILIES**   I can't think of a better place to introduce children to the exciting adventure of exploring a different culture. Among the best destinations for children in Mexico is La Paz (see chapter 3). The larger hotels in Los Cabos can often arrange for a baby-sitter. Some hotels in the moderate-to-luxury range have small playgrounds and pools for children and hire caretakers with special activity programs during the day. Few budget hotels offer these amenities.

Before leaving, you should check with your doctor to get advice on medications to take along. Disposable diapers cost about the same in Mexico but are of poorer quality. You can get Huggies Supreme and Pampers identical to the ones sold in the United States, but at a higher price. Gerber's baby foods are sold in many stores. Dry cereals, powdered formulas, baby bottles, and purified water are all easily available in midsize and large cities or resorts.

Cribs, however, may present a problem—only the largest and most luxurious hotels provide them. Rollaway beds, however, are often available for children staying in the room with parents. Child seats or high chairs at restaurants are common, and most restaurants will go out of their way to accommodate the comfort of your child.

Because many travelers to Baja will rent a car, it is advisable to bring your car seat. Leasing agencies in Mexico do not have car seats for rent.

**FOR GAY & LESBIAN TRAVELERS**   Mexico is a conservative country, with deeply rooted Catholic religious traditions. Public displays of same-sex affection are rare and still considered shocking for men, especially outside of urban or resort areas. Women in Mexico frequently walk hand in hand, but anything more would cross the boundary of acceptability. However, gay and lesbian travelers are generally treated with respect and should not experience any harassment, assuming the appropriate regard is given to local culture and customs. The **International Gay & Lesbian Travel Association** (IGLTA) (© **800/448-8550** or 954/776-2626; fax 954/776-3303; www.iglta.org), can provide helpful information and additional tips. The **Travel Alternative Group** (TAG) (© **415/ 437-3800;** info@mark8ing.com) maintains a database and publishes the *Gay-Friendly Accommodations Guide*. **Arco Iris** is a gay-owned, full-service travel agency and tour operator specializing in Mexico packages and special group travel. Contact them by phone ((© **800/795-5549**) or through their website, www.arcoiristours.com.

**FOR TRAVELERS WITH DISABILITIES**    Mexico may seem like one giant obstacle course to travelers in wheelchairs or on crutches. At airports, you may encounter steep stairs before finding a well-hidden elevator or escalator—if one exists. Airlines will often arrange wheelchair assistance for passengers to the baggage area. Porters are generally available to help with luggage at airports and large bus stations, once you've cleared baggage claim.

In addition, escalators (there aren't many in the country) are often out of operation. Few restrooms are equipped for travelers with disabilities, or when one is available, access to it may be via a narrow passage that won't accommodate someone in a wheelchair or on crutches. Many deluxe hotels (the most expensive) now have rooms with baths for people with disabilities. Those traveling on a budget should stick with one-story hotels or those with elevators. Even so, there will probably still be obstacles somewhere. Stairs without handrails abound in Mexico. Generally speaking, no matter where you are, someone will lend a hand, although you may have to ask.

**FOR SENIORS**    Mexico is a popular country for retirees. For decades, North Americans have been living indefinitely in Mexico by returning to the border and recrossing with a new tourist permit every 6 months. Mexican immigration officials have caught on, and now limit the maximum time in the country to 6 months within any year. This is to encourage even partial residents to comply with the proper documentation.

*AIM,* Apdo. Postal 31–70, 45050 Guadalajara, Jalisco, Mexico, is a well-written, candid, and very informative newsletter on retirement in Mexico. Subscriptions are $18 to the United States and $21 to Canada. Back issues are three for $5.

Members of the **American Association of Retired Persons (AARP),** 601 E. St. NW, Washington, D.C. 20049 (© **800/ 424-3410;** www.aarp.com) receive discounts at hotel chains such as Best Western, Holiday Inn, and Marriott, as well as car rentals from companies like Avis and Hertz.

In addition, most of the major U.S.-based airlines, including American, United, Continental, and US Airways, all offer discount programs for senior travelers—ask whenever you book a flight.

*The Mature Traveler,* a monthly newsletter on senior citizen travel, is a valuable resource. It is available by subscription ($30 a year); for a free sample send a postcard with your name and address to GEM Publishing Group, Box 50400, Reno, NV 89513 (mature-trav@aol.com). Another helpful publication is *101 Tips for the*

*Mature Traveler,* available from Grand Circle Travel, 347 Congress St., Suite 3A, Boston, MA 02210 (© **800/221-2610;** www.gct.com).

Grand Circle Travel is also one of the literally hundreds of travel agencies that specialize in vacations for seniors. But beware: many of them are of the tour-bus variety, with free trips thrown in for those who organize groups of 20 or more. Seniors seeking more independent travel should probably consult a regular travel agent. **SAGA International Holidays,** 222 Berkeley St., Boston, MA 02116 (© **800/343-0273**), offers inclusive tours and cruises for those 50 and older.

**FOR WOMEN**    As a female traveling alone, I can tell you firsthand that I feel safer traveling in Mexico than in the United States. But I use the same common-sense precautions I follow traveling anywhere else in the world and am alert to what's going on around me.

Mexicans in general, and men in particular, are nosy about single travelers, especially women. If taxi drivers or anyone else with whom you don't want to become friendly asks about your marital status, family, etc., our advice is to make up a set of answers (regardless of the truth): "I'm married, traveling with friends, and I have three children." Saying you are single and traveling alone may send out the wrong message about availability. Movies and television shows exported from the United States have created an image of sexually aggressive North American women. If someone bothers you, don't try to be polite—just leave or head into a public place.

## 7 Getting There

### BY PLANE

The airline situation in Mexico is changing rapidly, with many new regional carriers offering flights to areas previously not served. In addition to regularly scheduled service, charter service direct from U.S. cities to resorts is making Mexico more accessible.

**THE MAJOR INTERNATIONAL AIRLINES**    The main airlines operating direct or nonstop flights from the United States to points in Baja include **AeroCalifornia** (© 800/237-6225), **Aeromexico** (© 800/237-6639), **Alaska Airlines** (© 800/426-0333), **America West** (© 800/235-9292), **American** (© 800/433-7300), **Continental** (© 800/231-0856), **Lacsa** (© 800/225-2272), **Mexicana** (© 800/531-7921), **Northwest/KLM** (© 800/225-2525), **United** (© 800/241-6522), and **US Airways** (© 800/428-4322). **Southwest Airlines** (© 800/435-9792) serves San Diego, on the U.S. border.

The main departure points in North America for international airlines are Atlanta, Chicago, Dallas/Fort Worth, Denver, Houston, Los Angeles, Miami, New Orleans, New York, Orlando, Philadelphia, Raleigh/Durham, San Antonio, San Francisco, Seattle, Toronto, Tucson, and Washington, D.C.

## BY CAR

Consider renting a car for touring around a specific region once you arrive in Mexico. Rental cars in Mexico are now generally new, clean, and very well maintained. Although pricier than in the United States, discounts are often available for rentals of a week or longer, especially when arrangements are made in advance from the United States. (See "Car Rentals," below, for more details.)

If, after reading the section that follows, you have any additional questions or you want to confirm the current rules, call your nearest Mexican consulate, Mexican Government Tourist Office, or AAA.

**CAR DOCUMENTS**   To drive your car into Mexico, you'll need a temporary car-importation permit, which is granted after you provide a strictly required list of documents (see below). The permit can be obtained either through Banco del Ejército (Banjercito) officials, who have a desk, booth, or office at the Mexican Customs (Aduana) building after you cross the border into Mexico. Or you can obtain the permit before you travel, through Sanborn's Insurance or the American Automobile Association (AAA), each of which maintains border offices in Texas, New Mexico, Arizona, and California. These companies may charge a fee for this service, but it will be worth it to avoid the uncertain prospect of traveling all the way to the border without proper documents for crossing. Even if you go through Sanborn's or AAA, however, your credentials may be reviewed again by Mexican officials at the border—you must take them all with you, since they are still subject to questions of validity.

The following requirements for border crossing were accurate at press time:

- A **valid driver's license,** issued outside of Mexico.
- Current, original **car registration** and a copy of the **original car title.** If the registration or title is in more than one name and not all the named people are traveling with you, then a notarized letter from the absent person(s) authorizing use of

## (Tips Carrying Car Documents

You must carry your temporary car-importation permit, tourist permit (see "Entry Requirements," earlier in this chapter), and, if you purchased it, your proof of Mexican car insurance (see below) in the car at all times. The temporary car-importation permit papers will be issued for between 6 months to a year, while the tourist permit is usually issued for 30 days. It's a good idea also to overestimate the time you'll spend in Mexico, so that if something unforeseen happens and you have to (or want to) stay longer, you'll avoid the hassle of getting your papers extended. Whatever you do, don't overstay either permit. Doing so invites heavy fines and/or confiscation of your vehicle, which will not be returned. Remember also that 6 months does not necessarily work out to be 180 days—be sure that you return before whichever expiration date comes first.

the vehicle for the trip is required; have it ready just in case. The car registration and your credit card (see below) must be in the same name.

- A **valid international major credit card.** With a credit card, you are required to pay only an $11.50 car-importation fee. The credit card must be in the same name as the car registration. If you do not have a major credit card (Visa, MasterCard, American Express, or Diners Club) you will have to post a bond or make a deposit equal to the value of the vehicle. Check cards are not accepted.

- **Original immigration documentation.** This will either be your tourist permit (FMT), or the original immigration booklet, FM2 or FM3, if you hold this more permanent status.

- A signed declaration promising to return to your country of origin with the vehicle. This form (*Carta Promesa de Retorno*) is provided by AAA or Sanborn's before you go or by Banjercito officials at the border. There's no charge. The form does not stipulate that you must return through the same border entry you came through on your way south.

- **Temporary Importation Application.** Upon signing this form, you are stating that you are only temporarily importing the car for your personal use, and will not be selling the vehicle.

For up-to-the-minute information, a great source is the Customs office in Nuevo León (Módulo de Importación Temporal de Automóviles, Aduana Nuevo León; ☎ 8/712-2071).

*Important reminder:* Someone else may drive the car, but the person (or relative of the person) whose name appears on the car-importation permit must always be in the car at the same time. (If stopped by police, a nonregistered family-member driver driving without the registered driver must be prepared to prove familial relationship to the registered driver—no joke.) Violation of this rule makes the car subject to impoundment and the driver to imprisonment and/or a fine. You can only drive a car with foreign license plates if you have an international (non-Mexican) driver's license.

**MEXICAN AUTO INSURANCE**   Auto insurance is now legally required in Mexico. U.S. insurance is invalid in Mexico; to be insured in Mexico, you must purchase Mexican insurance. Any party involved in an accident and who has no insurance may be sent to jail and his or her car impounded until all claims are settled. This is true even if you just drive across the border to spend the day. U.S. companies that broker Mexican insurance are commonly found at the border crossings, and several will quote daily rates.

Car insurance can also be purchased through **Sanborn's Mexico Insurance,** P.O. Box 52840, 2009 S. 10th, McAllen, TX 78505-2840 (☎ **800/222-0158** or 956/686-3601; fax 956/686-0732; www.sanbornsinsurance.com; info@sanbornsinsurance.com). The company has offices at all the border crossings in the United States. Its policies cost the same as the competition's do, but with Sanborn's you get legal coverage (attorney and bail bonds, if needed) and a detailed mile-by-mile guide for your proposed route. Most of Sanborn's border offices are open Monday through Friday, and a few are staffed on Saturday and Sunday. The American Automobile Association (AAA) also sells insurance.

**RETURNING TO THE UNITED STATES WITH YOUR CAR**
The car papers you obtained when you entered Mexico must be returned when you cross back with your car or at some point within 180 days. (You can cross as many times as you wish within the 180 days.) If the documents aren't returned, heavy fines are imposed ($250 for each 15 days late), and your car may be impounded and confiscated or you may be jailed if you return to Mexico. You can only return the car documents to a Banjercito official on duty at the Mexican Customs building before you cross back into the United

**See Baja by Boat: Cruising the Sea of Cortez**

John Steinbeck made this journey famous, a 4,000-mile expedition during which he collected marine specimens and recorded his observations and philosophies in the 1951 classic, *The Log from the Sea of Cortez.* These days, a few companies are offering small-ship cruises from Cabo San Lucas north to the French-colonial town of Santa Rosalía, an ideal way to sample the best of Baja. Any travel agent can price or book Sea of Cortez cruises.

**Cruise West** (© 800/888-9378 or 206/441-8687 in the U.S.; fax 206/441-4757; www.cruisewest.com), offers several voyages that explore the interior Baja coast. Along the way, the ship pulls into small, pristine coves where passengers can participate in nature walks, hiking, snorkeling, and kayaking. One itinerary has stops at Loreto, Santa Rosalía, Mulegé, La Paz, and an overland side trip to Bahía Magdalena for a day of whale-watching. There are two ships: the 217-foot *Spirit of Endeavor,* with 51 cabins, all with double accommodations and full facilities; and the 192-foot *Spirit of '98,* with 48 double cabins with full facilities. Prices range from $2,095 to $4,695 per person (based on double occupancy) for the 7-night cruise; all meals and activities are included. This cruise is oriented toward a slightly older passenger; there's an exceptional educational orientation aimed at learning about the areas explored, especially the regional flora and fauna. Photography-themed cruises also are available.

**Voyager Cruise Line** (© 800/451-5952 in the U.S.; www.voyagercruiseline.com) offers a similar cruise program and itinerary at slightly lower costs, with a more active, adventurous traveler in mind. Their two ships offer 43 staterooms in four categories, with prices starting at $1,795 per person (based on double occupancy) per 7-night cruise, all meals and activities included.

**Baja Expeditions,** 2625 Garnet Ave., San Diego, CA 92109 (© 800/843-6967 or 858/581-3311; www.bajaex. com; travel@bajaex.com), offers natural-history cruises, whale-watching, sea kayaking, and scuba-diving trips out of La Paz.

States. Some border cities have Banjercito officials on duty 24 hours a day, but others do not; some also do not have Sunday hours. On the U.S. side, Customs agents may or may not inspect your car from stem to stern.

## BY SHIP

Numerous cruise lines serve Mexico, with many ships (including specialized whale-watching trips) originating in California and traveling down to the Baja Peninsula. If you don't mind taking off at the last minute, several cruise-tour specialists arrange substantial discounts on unsold cabins. One such company is **The Cruise Line,** 150 NW 168 St., North Miami Beach, Miami, FL 33169 (© **800/ 777-0707** or 305/521-2200).

## 8 Planning Your Trip Online

With a mouse, a modem, and a certain do-it-yourself determination, Internet users can tap into the same travel-planning databases that were once accessible only to travel agents. Sites such as **Travelocity, Expedia,** and **Orbitz** allow consumers to comparison shop for airfares, book flights, learn of last-minute bargains, and reserve hotel rooms and rental cars.

But don't fire your travel agent just yet. Although online booking sites offer tips and hard data to help you bargain shop, they cannot endow you with the hard-earned experience that makes a seasoned, reliable travel agent an invaluable resource, even in the Internet age. And for consumers with a complex itinerary, a trusty travel agent is still the best way to arrange the most direct flights to and from the best airports.

The benefits of researching your trip online can be well worth the effort:

- **Last-minute specials,** known as "E-savers," such as weekend deals or Internet-only fares, are offered by airlines to fill empty seats. Most of these are announced on Tuesday or Wednesday and must be purchased online. They are only valid for travel that weekend, but some can be booked weeks or months in advance. Sign up for weekly e-mail alerts at airline websites (see below) or check mega-sites that compile comprehensive lists of E-savers, such as Smarter Living (smarterliving.com) or WebFlyer (www.webflyer.com).

- Some sites will send you **e-mail notification** when a cheap fare becomes available to your favorite destination. Some will also tell you when fares to a particular destination are lowest.
- The best of the travel-planning sites are now **highly personalized;** they track your frequent-flier miles, and store your seating and meal preferences, tentative itineraries, and credit card information, letting you plan trips or check agendas quickly.
- All major airlines offer **incentives**—bonus frequent-flier miles, Internet-only discounts, sometimes even free cell phone rentals—when you purchase online or buy an e-ticket.
- Advances in mobile technology provide business travelers and other frequent travelers with **the ability to check flight status, change plans,** or **get specific directions** from handheld computing devices, mobile phones, and pagers. Some sites will e-mail or page a passenger if a flight is delayed.

## TRAVEL-PLANNING & BOOKING SITES

The best travel-planning and booking sites cast a wide net, offering domestic and international flights, hotel and rental car bookings, plus news, destination information, and deals on cruises and vacation packages. Keep in mind that free (one-time) registration is often required for booking. Because several airlines are no longer willing to pay commissions on tickets sold by online travel agencies, be aware that these online agencies will either charge a $10 surcharge if you book a ticket on that carrier—or neglect to offer those air carriers' offerings.

The sites in this section are not intended to be a comprehensive list, but rather a discriminating selection to get you started. Recognition is given to sites based on their content value and ease of use and is not paid for—unlike some website rankings, which are based on payment. *Remember:* This is a press-time snapshot of leading websites—some undoubtedly will have evolved or moved by the time you read this.

- **Travelocity** (www.travelocity.com or www.frommers.travelocity.com) and **Expedia** (www.expedia.com) are the most long-standing and reputable sites, each offering excellent selections and searches for complete vacation packages. Travelers search by destination and dates coupled with how much they are willing to spend.

*Tips* **Frommers.com: The Complete Travel Resource**

For an excellent travel planning resource, we highly recommend **Arthur Frommer's Budget Travel Online** (www.frommers.com). Among the special features are: **"Ask the Expert"** bulletin boards, where Frommer's authors answer your questions via online postings; **Arthur Frommer's Daily Newsletter**, for the latest travel bargains and inside travel secrets; and Frommer's **Destinations Archive**, where you'll get expert travel tips, hotel and dining recommendations, and advice on the sights to see for more than 200 destinations around the globe. Once your research is done, the **Online Reservation System** (www.frommers.com/booktravelnow) takes you to Frommer's favorite sites for booking your vacation at affordable prices.

- The latest buzz in the online travel world is about **Orbitz** (www.orbitz.com), a site launched by United, Delta, Northwest, American, and Continental airlines. It shows all possible fares for your desired trip, offering fares lower than those available through travel agents.
- **Qixo** (www.qixo.com) is another powerful search engine that allows you to search for flights and hotel rooms on 20 other travel-planning sites (such as Travelocity) at once. Qixo sorts results by price, after which you can book your travel directly through the site.

## AIRLINE WEBSITES

Below are the websites for the major airlines that service Mexico. These sites offer schedules and booking, and most of the airlines have E-saver alerts for weekend deals and late-breaking bargains.

- **Aeromexico.** www.aeromexico.com
- **Alaska Airlines.** www.alaskaair.com
- **America West.** www.americawest.com
- **American Airlines.** www.aa.com
- **Continental Airlines.** www.continental.com
- **Delta.** www.delta.com
- **Mexicana.** www.mexicana.com

- **Northwest Airlines.** www.nwa.com
- **United Airlines.** www.ual.com
- **US Airways.** www.usairways.com

## 9 Choosing a Package Tour

Package tours are not the same thing as escorted tours. They are simply a way of buying your airfare, accommodations, and other pieces of your trip (usually airport transfers, and sometimes meals and activities) at the same time.

For popular destinations like the Los Cabos beach resorts, package tours are often the smart way to go, because they can save you a ton of money. In many cases, a package that includes airfare, hotel, and transportation to and from the airport will cost you less than just the hotel alone if you booked it yourself. You can buy a package at any time of year, but the best deals usually coincide with low season—May to early December—when room rates and airfares plunge. Packages vary widely. Some offer a better class of hotels than others. Some offer the same hotels for lower prices. Some offer flights on scheduled airlines, while others book charters. Each destination usually has some packagers that are better than the rest because they buy in even bigger bulk. Not only can that mean better prices, but it can also mean more hotels to choose from.

### WHERE TO BROWSE

- For one-stop shopping on the Web, go to **www. vacationpackager.com**, an extensive search engine that'll link you up with more than 30 packagers offering Mexican beach vacations—and even let you custom design your own package.
- Check out **www.2travel.com** and find a page with links to a number of the big-name Mexico packagers, including several of the ones listed here.

### RECOMMENDED PACKAGERS

- **Aeromexico Vacations** (© 800/245-8585; www.aeromexico. com) offers year-round packages for Los Cabos. Aeromexico has a large selection of resorts in a variety of price ranges. The best deals are from Houston, Dallas, San Diego, Los Angeles, Miami, and New York, in that order.
- **Alaska Airlines Vacations** (© 800/426-0333; www. alaskair.com) sells packages to Los Cabos. Alaska flies direct to Mexico from Los Angeles, San Diego, San Jose, San Francisco, Seattle, Vancouver, Anchorage, and Fairbanks.

- **American Airlines Vacations** (© 800/321-2121; www. aavacations.com) has various travel packages to Los Cabos, year-round. You don't have to fly with American if you can get a better deal on another airline; land-only packages include hotel, airport transfers, and hotel room tax. American's hubs to Mexico are Dallas/Fort Worth, Chicago, and Miami, so you're likely to get the best prices—and the most direct flights—if you live near those cities.
- **America West Vacations** (© 800/356-6611; www. americawestvacations.com) has deals to Los Cabos, mostly from its Phoenix gateway. Golfers can book golf vacations to Los Cabos through their specialized site at www.awagolf.com or by calling 888/AWA-GOLF.
- **Apple Vacations** (© 800/365-2775) offers inclusive packages and has the largest choice of hotels (14 in Los Cabos). Scheduled carriers booked for the air portion include AeroCalifornia, Aeromexico, Alaska Airlines, American, Delta, Mexicana, Reno Air, TWA, United, and US Airways. Apple perks include baggage handling and the services of an Apple representative at the major hotels.
- **Continental Vacations** (© 800/634-5555 and 888/ 989-9255; www.continental.com) has year-round packages available, and the best deals are from Houston; Newark, NJ; and Cleveland. With Continental, you've got to buy air from the carrier if you want to book a room.
- **Funjet Vacations** (bookable through travel agents, with information only available online at www.funjet.com), one of the largest vacation packagers in the United States, has packages to Los Cabos. You can choose a charter or fly on Aeromexico, Alaska Air, American, Continental, Delta, TWA, United, or US Airways.
- **Mexicana Vacations** (or MexSeaSun Vacations) (© 800/ 531-9321; www.mexicana.com) offers getaways, buttressed by Mexicana's daily direct flights from Los Angeles to Los Cabos.

## REGIONAL PACKAGERS

- **From the West Coast: Suntrips** (© 800/357-2400 or 888/888-5028 for departures within 14 days, www.suntrips.com) is one of the largest packagers for Mexico on the West Coast, arranging regular charters to Los Cabos from San Francisco and Denver, paired with a large selection of hotels.

## 10 Getting Around

*An important note:* If your travel schedule depends on an important connection, say a plane trip between points, or a ferry or bus connection, use the telephone numbers in this book or other information resources mentioned here to find out whether the connection you are depending on is still available. Although we've done our best to provide accurate information, transportation schedules can and do change.

### BY PLANE

To fly from point to point within Mexico, you'll rely on Mexican airlines. Mexico has two privately owned large national carriers: **Mexicana** (℡ **800/366-5400**) and **Aeromexico** (℡ **800/021-4000**), in addition to several up-and-coming regional carriers. Mexicana and Aeromexico both offer extensive connections to the United States as well as within Mexico.

**AIRPORT TAXES**    Mexico charges an airport tax on all departures. Passengers leaving the country on an international departure pay $17.25 (in dollars or the peso equivalent). It has become a common practice to include this departure tax in your ticket price, but double-check to make sure so you're not caught by surprise at the airport upon leaving. Taxes on each domestic departure you make within Mexico cost around $12.50, unless you're on a connecting flight and have already paid at the start of the flight, in which case you shouldn't be charged again. A new tourist departure tax of $15 per person, in place of a visa fee, was instituted in July 1999. It may or may not be included in your package tour or airline ticket price, so check to be sure.

### BY CAR

Most Mexican roads are not up to U.S. standards of smoothness, hardness, width of curve, grade of hill, or safety marking. Driving at night is dangerous—the roads aren't good and are rarely lit; trucks, carts, pedestrians, and bicycles usually have no lights; and you can hit potholes, animals, rocks, dead ends, or bridges out with no warning.

The "spirited" style of Mexican driving sometimes requires super vision and reflexes. Be prepared for new customs, as when a truck driver flips on his left-turn signal when there's not a crossroad for miles. He's probably telling you the road's clear ahead for you to pass—after all, he's in a better position to see than you are. Another custom that's very important to respect is how to make a left turn. Never turn left by stopping in the middle of a highway with your left signal on. Instead, pull off the highway onto the right shoulder, wait for traffic to clear, and then proceed across the road.

**GASOLINE**   There's one government-owned brand of gas and one gasoline station name throughout the country—Pemex (*Petroleras Mexicanas*). There are two types of gas in Mexico: *magna,* an 87-octane unleaded gas, and the newer, premium 93-octane. In Mexico, fuel and oil are sold by the liter, which is slightly more than a quart (40 liters equals about 10½ gal.). There is a new trend toward franchise Pemex stations, many of which have bathroom facilities and convenience stores—a great improvement over the old ones. *Important note:* No credit cards are accepted for gas purchases.

**BREAKDOWNS**   If your car breaks down on the road, help might already be on the way. Radio-equipped green repair trucks operated by uniformed English-speaking officers patrol the major highways during daylight hours to aid motorists in trouble. These Green Angels (*Angeles Verdes*) will perform minor repairs and adjustments for free, but you pay for parts and materials.

To find a mechanic on the road, look for a sign that says *taller mecánico.*

Flat tires are repaired at places called *vulcanizadora* or *llantera;* it is common to find such places open 24 hours a day on the most traveled highways. Even if the place looks empty, chances are you will find someone who can help you fix a flat.

**MINOR ACCIDENTS**   When possible, many Mexicans drive away from minor accidents or try to make an immediate settlement to avoid involving the police. If the police arrive while the involved persons are still at the scene, everyone may be locked in jail until blame is assessed. In any case, you have to settle up immediately, or be faced with days of red tape. Foreigners who don't speak fluent Spanish are at a distinct disadvantage when trying to explain their side of the event. Three steps may help the foreigner who doesn't wish to do as the Mexicans do: If you are in your own car, notify your Mexican insurance company, whose job it is to intervene on your behalf; if you are in a rental car, notify the rental company immediately and ask how to contact the nearest adjuster (you did buy insurance with the rental, right?); finally, if all else fails, ask to contact the nearest Green Angel, who may be able to explain to officials that you are covered by insurance. See also "Mexican Auto Insurance" in "Getting There," above.

**CAR RENTALS**    You'll get the best price if you reserve a car a week in advance in the United States. U.S. car-rental firms include **Avis** (© 800/331-1212 in the U.S., 800/TRY-AVIS in Canada), **Budget** (© 800/527-0700 in the U.S. and Canada), **Hertz** (© 800/654-3131 in the U.S. and Canada), and **National** (© 800/CAR-RENT in the U.S. and Canada). For European travelers, **Kemwel Holiday Auto** (© 800/678-0678) and **Auto Europe** (© 800/223-5555) can arrange Mexican rentals, sometimes through other agencies. You'll find rental desks at airports, all major hotels, and many travel agencies.

Car-rental costs are high in Mexico because cars are more expensive there. The condition of rental cars has improved greatly over the years, however, and clean, comfortable, new cars are the norm. The basic cost of a 1-day rental of a Volkswagen Beetle, with unlimited mileage (but before 15% tax and $15 daily insurance), was $48 in Los Cabos. Renting by the week gives you about a 15% lower daily rate. Rental prices may be considerably higher around a major holiday.

Car-rental companies usually write up a credit card charge in U.S. dollars.

**Deductibles**    Be careful—these vary greatly in Mexico; some are as high as $2,500, which comes out of your pocket immediately in case of car damage. Hertz's deductible is $1,000 on a VW Beetle; Avis' is $500 for the same car.

**Insurance**    Insurance is offered in two parts: Collision and damage insurance covers your car and others if the accident is your fault, and personal accident insurance covers you and anyone in your car. Read the fine print on the back of your rental agreement and note that insurance may be invalid if you have an accident while driving on an unpaved road.

**Damage**    Always inspect your car carefully and note every damaged or missing item, no matter how minute, on your rental agreement, or you may be charged.

**Trouble Number**    It's advisable to carefully note both the rental company's trouble number, and the direct number of the agency where you rented the car.

## BY TAXI

Taxis are the preferred way to get around in almost all the resort areas of Mexico, but are very expensive in the Los Cabos area. One-way travel between Cabo San Lucas and San José del Cabo averages $35. Short trips within towns are generally charged by preset zones

> **Travel Tip**
> Little English is spoken at bus stations, so come prepared with your destination written down, then double-check the departure.

and are quite reasonable compared with U.S. rates. For longer trips or excursions to nearby cities, taxis can generally be hired for around $10 to $15 per hour, or for a negotiated daily rate. Even drops to different destinations can be arranged. A negotiated one-way price is usually much less than the cost of a rental car for a day, and service is much faster than travel by bus. For anyone who is uncomfortable driving in Mexico, this is a convenient, comfortable alternative. An added bonus is that you have a Spanish-speaking person with you in case you run into any car or road trouble. Many taxi drivers speak at least some English. Your hotel can assist you with the arrangements.

## BY BUS

Bus service is not as well developed in the Baja peninsula as in other parts of the country, although it is available between principle points. Travel class is generally labeled second (*segunda*), first (*primera*), and deluxe (*ejecutiva*). The deluxe buses often have fewer seats than regular buses, show video movies en route, are air-conditioned, and make few stops; some have complimentary refreshments. Many run express from origin to the final destination. They are well worth the few dollars more that you'll pay. In rural areas, buses are often of the school-bus variety, with lots of local color.

 **FAST FACTS: Baja California**

**Abbreviations** Dept. (apartments); Apdo. (post office box); Av. (*Avenida*; avenue); c/ (*calle*; street); Calz. (*Calzada*; boulevard). C on faucets stands for *caliente* (hot), and F stands for *fría* (cold). PB (*planta baja*) means ground floor, and most buildings count the next floor up as the first floor (1).

**Business Hours** In general, businesses in larger cities are open between 9am and 7pm; in smaller towns many close between 2 and 4pm. Most are closed on Sunday. Bank hours are Monday through Friday from 9 or 9:30am to 3 or 5pm. Increasingly, banks are offering Saturday hours for at least a half-day (10am 2pm).

*Cameras/Film* Film costs about the same as in the United States.

*Customs* See "Visitor Information, Entry Requirements & Money," earlier in this chapter.

*Doctors/Dentists* Every embassy and consulate is prepared to recommend local doctors and dentists with good training and modern equipment; some of the doctors and dentists speak English. See the list of embassies and consulates under "Embassies/Consulates," below. Hotels with a large foreign clientele can often recommend English-speaking doctors. Almost all first-class hotels in Mexico have a doctor on call.

*Drug Laws* To be blunt, don't use or possess illegal drugs in Mexico. Mexican officials have no tolerance for drug users, and jail is their solution, with very little hope of getting out until the sentence (usually a long one) is completed or heavy fines or bribes are paid. Remember, in Mexico the legal system assumes you are guilty until proven innocent. *Important note:* It isn't uncommon to be befriended by a fellow user, only to be turned in by that "friend," who's collected a bounty. Bring prescription drugs in their original containers. If possible, pack a copy of the original prescription with the generic name of the drug.

U.S. Customs officials are also on the lookout for diet drugs sold in Mexico but illegal in the U.S., possession of which could land you in a U.S. jail. If you buy antibiotics over the counter (which you can do in Mexico)—say, for a sinus infection—and still have some left, you probably won't be hassled by U.S. Customs.

*Drugstores* See "Pharmacies" below.

*Electricity* The electrical system in Mexico is 110 volts AC (60 cycles), as in the United States and Canada. In reality, however, it may cycle more slowly and overheat your appliances. To compensate, select a medium or low speed for hair dryers.

*Embassies/Consulates* They provide valuable lists of doctors and lawyers, as well as regulations concerning marriages in Mexico. Contrary to popular belief, your embassy cannot get you out of a Mexican jail, provide postal or banking services, or fly you home when you run out of money. Consular officers can provide you with advice on most matters and problems, however. Most countries have a representative embassy in Mexico City, and many have consular offices or representatives in the provinces.

The **Embassy of Australia** in Mexico City is at Ruben Darío 55 Col. Polanco (✆ **5/531-5225**; fax 5/531-9552); it's open Monday through Friday from 9am to 1pm.

The **Embassy of Canada** in Mexico City is at Schiller 529, in Polanco (✆ **5/724-7900**); it's open Monday through Friday from 9am to 1pm and 2 to 5pm. (At other times the name of a duty officer is posted on the embassy door.) There is a **consular agency** in Tijuana (✆ **6/684-0461**). Visit their website at www.canada.org.mx for a complete listing of the addresses of the consular agencies in Mexico.

The **Embassy of New Zealand** in Mexico City is at José Luis Lagrange 103, 10th floor, Col. Los Morales Polanco (✆ **5/281-5486**); it's open Monday through Thursday from 9am to 2pm and 3 to 5pm, and Friday from 9am to 2pm.

The **Embassy of the United Kingdom** in Mexico City is in Río Lerma 71, Col. Cuauhtemoc (✆ **5/207-2089** or 5/207-7672; www.embajadabritanica.com.mx); it's open Monday through Friday from 8:30am to 3:30pm.

The **Embassy of Ireland** is located on Cerrada Blvd. Avila Camacho 76, 3rd floor, Col. Lomas de Chapultepec in Mexico City (✆ **5/520-5803**); it's open Monday through Friday from 9am to 3pm.

The **South African Embassy** in Mexico City is on Andres Bello 10, 9th floor, Col. Polanco (✆ **5/282-9260**). Open Monday through Friday from 8am to 4pm.

The **Embassy of the United States** in Mexico City is next to the Hotel María Isabel Sheraton at Paseo de la Reforma 305, at the corner of Río Danubio (✆ **5/209-9100**). Visit www.usembassy-mexico.gov for a list of all the street addresses of the U.S. consulates inside Mexico. There is a **U.S. Consulate General** in Tijuana, Tapachula 96 (✆ **6/681-7400**). In addition, the U.S. has a consular agency in Cabo San Lucas (✆ **1/143-3566**).

*Emergencies* Dial ✆ **060** to reach police in most cities. They can usually assist in getting an ambulance or fire department, but most operators do not speak English. You should also contact the closest consular office in case of an emergency.

*Internet Access* In the bigger resort areas and cities, a growing number of five-star hotels offer business centers with Internet access. As a general rule of thumb, the number of cybercafes in a town is directly proportional to the number of business travelers or the size of the foreign community. Note that many ISPs will automatically cut off your Internet connection after a specified period of time (say, 10 minutes) because telephone lines are at a premium.

*Legal Aid* **International Legal Defense Counsel**, Located at 111 S. 15th St., 24th Floor, Packard Building, Philadelphia, PA 19102 (© **215/977-9982**), this law firm specializes in legal difficulties of Americans abroad. See also "Embassies/ Consulates" and "Emergencies," above.

*Liquor Laws* The legal drinking age in Mexico is 18, but it is extremely rare that anyone will be asked for ID or denied purchase (often, children are sent to the stores to buy beer for their parents). If you look 18, you will likely be able to buy liquor easily. Authorities are beginning to target drunk drivers more aggressively.

*Mail* Postage for a postcard or letter is 59¢; it may arrive anywhere between 1 to 6 weeks after it's mailed. A registered letter costs $1.90. To send a package can be quite expensive—the Mexican postal service charges $8 per kilo (2.2 lbs.)—and unreliable; it takes between 2 and 6 weeks, if indeed it arrives at all—packages are frequently lost within the Mexican postal system, although the situation has improved in recent years. The recommended way to send a package or important mail continues to be through DHL, Federal Express, UPS, or any other reputable international mail service.

*Newspapers/Magazines* In southern Baja, a number of local English-language papers are available, including *Baja Life*, *Baja Sun*, and the irreverent, entertaining *Gringo Gazette*.

*Pharmacies Farmacias* will sell you just about anything you want, with a prescription or without one. Most drugstores are open Monday through Saturday from 8am to 8pm. Generally, one or two 24-hour pharmacies are now located in the major resort areas. If you are in a smaller town and need to buy medicines after normal hours, ask for the name of the nearest

24-hour pharmacy; they are becoming more common in Mexico.

*Police* Especially in the tourist areas, most officers are very protective of international visitors.

*Taxes* There's a 15% IVA (*Impuesto al Valor Agregado*, or value-added tax) on goods and services in most of Mexico, and it's supposed to be included in the posted price. This tax is 10% in Los Cabos. (However, at press time, new legislation was being reviewed to set IVA at 15% in the whole country, except for the border towns and cities.) An exit tax of around $17.25 is imposed on every foreigner leaving the country; it's usually included in the price of airline tickets.

*Telephone/Fax* For Directory Assistance, dial **040**, but remember that it is common for businesses to be listed under the name of the owner, rather than the name of the establishment. And it's unlikely you'll get an English-speaking operator.

Many fax numbers are also regular telephone numbers; you have to ask the person who answers your call for the fax tone ("*tono de fax, por favor*").

The country code for Mexico is **52**. International long-distance calls to the United States or Canada are accessed by dialing ℂ **001** and then the area code and seven-digit number. You can reach an AT&T operator by dialing ℂ **01-800-288-2872,** MCI by dialing ℂ **01-800-021-8000,** Sprint by dialing ℂ **001-800-877-8000,** and British Telecom (BT) by dialing ℂ **01-800-123-0244** (pay phones may sometimes require a coin deposit). To make a person-to-person or collect call to outside of Mexico, dial ℂ **090.** For other international dialing codes, dial the operator at ℂ **040.** Other international long distance calls to Europe, Africa, and Asia are accessed by dialing ℂ **00,** then the country code, the city code, and the number. For further assistance dial ℂ **090.**

*Time Zone* Central Standard Time prevails throughout most of Mexico. The state of Baja California Norte is on Pacific Time, but Baja California Sur is on Mountain Time. Mexico observes Daylight Savings Time from mid-May until September, but this might change by 2002, as Mexico's federal government is currently reviewing the country's policy regarding time changes and adhering to the practice of Daylight Savings Time.

*Tipping* Most service employees in Mexico count on tips to make up the majority of their income—especially bellboys and waiters. Bellboys receive the equivalent of 50¢ to $1 per bag; waiters generally receive 10% to 20% of the bill, depending on the level of service. In Mexico, it is not customary to tip taxi drivers, unless they are hired by the hour or provide touring or other special services.

*Water*  Most hotels have decanters or bottles of purified water in the rooms; the better hotels have either purified water from regular taps, or special taps marked *agua purificada*. Some hotels will charge for in-room bottled water. Virtually any hotel, restaurant, or bar will bring you purified water if you specifically request it, but you'll usually be charged for it. Bottled purified water is sold widely at drugstores and grocery stores (popular brands include Santa María, Ciel, and Bonafont).

 ## Phone Number Changes Announced

As this book went to press, Mexico had announced a sweeping change in the country's long-distance dialing codes, to take effect at the end of 2001. (It will affect every phone number in this book.) The new plan, in most cases, will replace the current one-digit area code with a three-digit area code. Keep in mind that in Baja, the area code 1 will be replaced with a three-digit number that begins with 6. The exceptions to this three-digit area code change are three of the country's largest cities; Mexico City, Guadalajara, and Monterrey will get a two-digit area code, followed by an eight-digit local number. Mexico City's new area code is 55, Guadalajara's is 33, and Monterrey's is 81.

The following table supplies new area codes for some of the major destinations in this book.

| City | present area code | new area code |
|------|-------------------|---------------|
| Cabo San Lucas | 1 | 624 |
| La Paz | 1 | 612 |
| San Jose del Cabo | 1 | 624 |
| Tijuana | 6 | 666 |
| Todos Santos | 1 | 612 |

# 2

# Los Cabos

The most popular destinations in Baja Sur are the twin towns at the peninsula's tip: Cabo San Lucas and San José del Cabo. Collectively they are known as Los Cabos (The Capes), although they couldn't be more different. Cabo San Lucas is an extension of American-styled Southern California, with luxury accommodations, ubiquitous golf courses, endless shopping, franchise restaurants, and a spirited nightlife. San José del Cabo, however, remains rooted in the traditions of a quaint Mexican town, although it's rapidly becoming gentrified.

Eighteen miles of smooth highway known as the Corridor lie between the two Cabos. It is along this stretch that the major new resorts and residential communities, including some of the world's finest golf courses, have been developed. And what has always been here continues to beckon: dozens of pristine coves and inlets with a wealth of marine life just offshore.

Golf has overtaken sportfishing as Los Cabos' main draw, with five championship courses open for play. Still more activities to keep you busy are sea kayaking, whale-watching, diving, surfing, and hiking, as well as the chance to explore ancient cave paintings and to camp on isolated, wild beaches.

The Los Cabos area has earned a deserved reputation for being much higher priced than other Mexican resorts. Although there has been a boom in new hotel construction, these have all been luxury resorts, only solidifying Los Cabos' higher average room prices, and not adjusting prices downward with the added supply of rooms. The other factor driving up prices is that compared to mainland Mexico, there's little agriculture in Baja; most foodstuffs (and other daily required items) must be shipped in. U.S. dollars are the preferred currency here, and it's not uncommon to see price listings in dollars rather than pesos.

With more than 20 miles separating the two Cabos and numerous attractions in between, you should consider renting a car, even if only for a day. Transportation by taxi is expensive here, and if you are at all interested in exploring, a rental car is your most economical

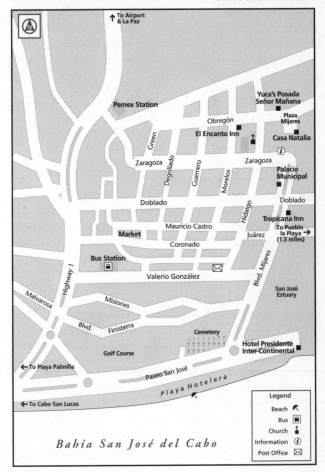

To Airport
& La Paz

Pemex Station

Obregón

Yuca's Posada
Señor Mañana

Plaza
Mijares

El Encanto Inn

Casa Natalia

Green

Zaragoza

Degollado

Guerrero

Morelos

Zaragoza

Palacio
Municipal

Doblado

Doblado

Hidalgo

Tropicana Inn

Mauricio Castro

To Pueblo
la Playa
(1.3 miles)

Market

Juárez

Coronado

Bus Station

Valerio González

Malvarosa

Highway 1

Misiones

Blvd.

Finisterra

San José
Estuary

Cemetery

Hotel Presidente
Inter-Continental

← To Playa Palmilla

Golf Course

Blvd. Mijares

Paseo San José

Playa Hotelera

← To Cabo San Lucas

*Bahía San José del Cabo*

| Legend | |
|---|---|
| Beach | ⌐ |
| Bus | 🚏 |
| Church | ⛪ |
| Information | ⓘ |
| Post Office | ✉ |

option. Because of the distinctive character and attractions of each of these two towns and the Corridor between, they are treated separately here. It is common to stay in one and make day trips to the other two.

## 1 San José del Cabo ★★★

122 miles SE of La Paz; 22 miles NE of Cabo San Lucas; 1,100 miles SE of Tijuana

San José del Cabo, with its pastel cottages and flowering trees lining the narrow streets, retains the air of a provincial Mexican town.

Originally founded in 1730 by Jesuit missionaries, it remains the seat of the Los Cabos government and the center of its business community. The main square, adorned with a wrought-iron bandstand and shaded benches, faces the cathedral, which was built on the site of an early mission.

San José is becoming increasingly sophisticated, with a collection of noteworthy cafes, art galleries, and intriguing small inns adding a newly refined flavor to the central downtown area. Still, this is the best choice for those who want to travel to this paradoxical landscape but still be aware that they're in Mexico.

## ESSENTIALS
### GETTING THERE & DEPARTING

**BY PLANE**   **AeroCalifornia** (© **800/237-6225** in the U.S., 1/143-3700 or 1/143-3915; crc@aerocalifornia.uabcs.mx), has nonstop or direct flights from Los Angeles and Phoenix; **Aeromexico** (© **800/237-6639** in the U.S., or 1/146-5098; www.aeromexico.com), flies nonstop from San Diego, and has connecting flights from Houston, Dallas, New York, Tucson, Guadalajara, and Mexico City. **Alaska Airlines** (© **800/426-0333** in the U.S., or 1/146-5101; www.alaskaair.com) flies from Los Angeles, San Diego, Seattle, and San Francisco; **America West** (© **800/235-9292** in the U.S.; www.americawestvacations.com) makes connecting flights through Phoenix; **Continental** (© **800/231-0856** in the U.S., or 1/142-3840; www.continental.com) flies from Houston; **Mexicana** (© **800/531-7921** in the U.S., 1/143-5352, or 1/143-5353; www.mexicana.com; geventassid@ mexicana. com.mx), has direct or connecting flights from Denver, Guadalajara, Los Angeles, Mexico City, Puerto Vallarta, and Mazatlán.

**BY CAR**   From La Paz, take Highway 1 south, a scenic route that winds through foothills and occasionally skirts the eastern coastline; the drive takes 3 to 4 hours. From La Paz, you can also take Highway 1 south just past the village of San Pedro, then take Highway 19 south (a less winding road than Highway 1) through Todos Santos to Cabo San Lucas, where you pick up Highway 1 east to San José del Cabo; this route takes 2 to 3 hours. From Cabo San Lucas, it's a half-hour drive.

**BY BUS**   The bus station (*terminal de autobuses*) on Valerio González, a block east of Highway 1 (© **1/142-1100**), is open daily from 5:30am to 7pm, although buses can arrive and depart later. Buses between Cabo San Lucas and La Paz run almost hourly during the day. For points farther north you usually change buses in La Paz. The trip to Cabo San Lucas takes 40 minutes; to La Paz, 3 hours. Buses also go to Todos Santos on the Pacific; the trip takes around 3 hours.

## ORIENTATION

**ARRIVING**   The one airport that serves both Cabos and the connecting Corridor is 7½ miles northwest of San José del Cabo and 22 miles northeast of Cabo San Lucas. Upon arrival at the airport, buy a ticket inside the building for a *colectivo* (minivan) or a taxi, which can be shared by up to four passengers. Colectivo fares run about $7 for up to eight passengers and are only available from the airport. A private van for up to five passengers is $35. Taxis charge about $6 to San José. Time-share resorts have booths in the arrival/baggage area of this airport. The promoters hook visitors with a free ride to their hotel in return for listening to their sales presentation.

The major car-rental agencies all have counters at the airport, open during flight arrivals: **Avis** (© **800/331-1212** from the U.S., or 1/146-0201; avissjd@avis.com.mx; open 7am to 9pm); **Budget** (© **800/527-0700** from the U.S., or 1/143-4190; open 8am to 7pm); **Hertz** (© **800/654-3131** from the U.S., or 1/142-0375; open 8am to 8pm); and **National** (© **800/328-4567** from the U.S., or 1/142-2424; open 8am to 8pm). Advance reservations are not always necessary.

If you arrive at the bus station, it's too far from the hotels to walk with luggage. A taxi from the bus station to either area costs $2 to $4.

**VISITOR INFORMATION**   The **city tourist information office** (© **1/142-0465**) is in the old post office building on Zaragoza at Mijares. It offers maps, free local publications, and other basic information about the area. It's open Monday through Friday from 8am to 3pm.

**CITY LAYOUT**   San José del Cabo consists of two zones: downtown, where sophisticated inns as well as traditional budget hotels are located, and the hotel zone along the beach.

Zaragoza is the main street leading from the highway into town; Paseo San José runs parallel to the beach and is the principal boulevard of this hotel zone. The mile-long Blvd. Mijares connects the two areas.

## GETTING AROUND

There is no local bus service between downtown and the beach; a taxi is the only means of getting there.

For day trips to Cabo San Lucas, catch a bus (see "Getting There & Departing," above) or a cab. **Tourcabos** (℅ 1/142-0982; fax 1/142-2050), in the Plaza Los Cabos on Paseo San José, offers a day tour to Cabo San Lucas for around $35. The tour leaves at 9am and returns around 4pm. Their office is in the Plaza Los Cabos, across from the Fiesta Inn on the malecón. Bicycles rent for $3 an hour and $15 a day from **Baja Bicycle Club** (℅ 1/142-2828), at the Brisa del Mar Trailer Park on the highway just south of town. Ask them about special offers; they also offer surfboards, boogie boards, and snorkel equipment. They are open daily from 9:30am to 8pm.

---

 **FAST FACTS: San José del Cabo**

**Area Code** The local telephone prefix is 114. Calls between San José del Cabo and Cabo San Lucas are toll calls, so you must use the area code.

**Banks** Banks exchange currency during business hours, generally Monday through Friday from 8:30am to 6pm and Saturday from 9am to 2pm. There are two major banks on Zaragoza between Morelos and Degollado.

**Emergencies** You can try 060, but generally, there will be no answer. The local city hall number is **1/142-0361**.

**Hospital** Hospital General, Retorno Atunero s/n, Col. Chamizal (℅ **1/142-0013**).

**Internet Access** Cabo Online, at Malvarrosa and Gobernadora (℅ 1/142-2905; www.caboonline.com.mx), is open Monday through Friday from 9am to 2pm and 4 to 6pm and Saturday from 9am to 2pm. Cost is $2 for 15 minutes, $3 for 30 minutes. **Trazzo Internet,** located a block from the central plaza, at the intersection of Zaragoza and Morelos, charges $2.50 for 30 minutes or less, with high-speed access.

**Pharmacy** Farmacia ISSTE, Km 34 Carretera Transpeninsular, Plaza California (℅ 1/142-2645), and **Farmacia Plaza Dorada,** Km 29 Carretera Transpeninsular, Plaza Dorada (℅ **1/142-0140**), are the two major pharmacies in the area.

---

*Post Office* The *correo,* at Blvd. Mijares 1924 at Valerio González (*©* **1/142-0911**), is open Monday through Friday from 8am to 4pm and Saturday from 9am to 1pm.

## BEACHES & OUTDOOR ACTIVITIES

The relaxed pace of San José del Cabo makes it an ideal place to unwind and absorb authentic Mexican flavor. Beach aficionados who want to explore the beautiful coves and beaches along the 22-mile coast between the two Cabos should consider renting a car for a day or so ($45 to $65 per day and up). Frequent bus service between San José del Cabo and Cabo San Lucas makes it possible to take in the pleasures of both towns (see "Getting There & Departing," above).

### BEACHES

The nearest beach safe for swimming is **Pueblo la Playa** (also called La Playita), located about 2 miles east of town: From Blvd. Mijares, turn east at the small sign PUEBLO LA PLAYA and follow the dusty dirt road through cane fields and palms to a small village and beautiful beach where a number of *pangas* (skiffs) belonging to local fishermen are pulled ashore. The La Playita Resort and its adjacent restaurant (see "Where to Stay," below) offer the only formal sustenance on the beach. There are no shade *palapas.*

**Estero San José,** a nature reserve with at least 270 species of birds, is located between Pueblo la Playa and the Presidente Inter-Continental Hotel. The estuary is a protected ecological reserve. A building at the edge of the water is a small cultural center (*©* **1/142-1504**), with changing exhibitions such as revolutionary photos and geological artifacts. It's open Tuesdays through Sundays, from 9am to 5pm. A $1 donation is suggested. Just beside it is a pathway to enter the estuary on foot.

A fine swimming beach with beautiful rock formations, **Playa Palmilla,** 5 miles west of San José, is located near the Spanish colonial-style Hotel Palmilla—an elegant place to stay or to eat lunch or dinner. To reach Playa Palmilla, take a taxi to the road that leads to the Hotel Palmilla grounds, then take the fork to the left (without entering the hotel grounds) and follow signs to Pepe's restaurant on the beach.

## Moments  Festivals & Special Events in Los Cabos

The feast of the patron saint of San José del Cabo is cele-brated on March 19 with a fair, music, dancing, feasting, horse races, and cockfights. June 19 is the festival of the patron saint of San Bartolo, a village 62 miles north. July 25 is the festival of the patron saint of Santiago, a village 34 miles north.

For a list of other nearby beaches worth exploring if you have a rental car, see "Beaches & Outdoor Activities" under "Cabo San Lucas" later in this chapter.

## CRUISES

Both daytime and sunset cruises are featured. Boats depart from Cabo San Lucas; the cruises vary in prices and offerings, but gener-ally include music, open bar, and snacks for between $30 and $40 per person. Arrange cruises through a travel agency, or call **Xplora Adventours,** located in the Sierra Madre store on the plaza, Bvld. Mijares at Zaragoza (© **1/142-3537** or 1/142-9000, ext. 8050). Xplora handles all tour providers in the area and can give unbiased information on the full selection available. It's open daily from 8am to 10pm.

## LAND SPORTS

**ADVENTURE TOURS**   A variety of land- and water-based adventure and nature tours are available through **Tio Sports** (© **1/143-3399;** www.tiosports.com), including the popular ATV tours to Candelaria, and parasailing at $40 single or $70 tandem. Kayak, catamaran, snorkeling, and diving trips are also offered.

**GOLF**   Los Cabos is rapidly becoming a major golf destination, with several new courses open and others under construction. The most economical greens fees are at the nine-hole **Club Campo de Golf San José** (© **1/142-0901** or 1/142-0905), on Paseo Finisterra across from the Howard Johnson Hotel. The course is open daily from 7am to 4pm (to 4:30pm in summer). Club guests can also use the swimming pool. The green fee is $15 for nine holes. Carts cost $30. For more information about playing golf in Los Cabos, see "The Lowdown on Golfing in Cabo" later in this chapter.

**HORSEBACK RIDING**   Horses can be rented near the Presidente Inter-Continental, Fiesta Inn, and Palmilla hotels at $15 to $20 per hour. Most people choose to ride on the beach.

**TENNIS**   You can play tennis at the two courts of the **Club Campo de Golf Los Cabos,** Paseo Finisterra no. 1 (© 1/142-0905), for $10 an hour during the day, $20 an hour at night. Club guests can use the swimming pool. Tennis is also available at the **Hotel Palmilla** (two lit courts) and the **Presidente Inter-Continental** (two lit courts); see "Where to Stay," below.

## WATER SPORTS

**FISHING**   The least expensive way to enjoy deep-sea fishing is to pair up with another angler and charter a *panga,* a 22-foot skiff used by local fishermen from Playa la Puebla. Several panga fleets offer 6-hour sportfishing trips, usually from 6am to noon, for $25 per hour (there's a 3-hr. minimum.) The cost can be divided between two or among three people. For information, contact the fisherman's cooperative in Pueblo la Playa, or **Victor's Aquatics** (© 949/496-0960 in the U.S., or 1/142-1092; fax 1/142-1093; victor@1cabonet.com.mx), at the Hotel Posada Real, open from 9am to 7pm. Victor's has a full fishing fleet with both pangas ($165 for 6 hr.) and cruisers ($380 to $495). Outfitters supply the boat and tackle, and the client buys the bait, drinks, and snacks.

**SEA KAYAKING**   Fully guided, ecologically oriented Ocean Kayak Tours are available through **Cabo Travel Advisors,** Plaza José Green, Local 6-C, in San José (© 1/142-4444; cta@1cabonet.com.mx). The tour runs from 8:30 to 11:30am, and includes breakfast and beverages for a price of $55. No previous experience is necessary, as complete instruction is given at the start of the tour. Kayaks are the most popular and practical way to explore the pristine coves that dot this shoreline.

**SNORKELING/DIVING**   Trips start around $50 per person and can be arranged through **Xplora Adventours,** (© 1/142-3537 or

---

### *Tips* Swimming Safety

Although the area is ideal for water sports, occasional strong currents and undertow sometimes make swimming dangerous at Playa Hotelera, the town beach—check conditions before entering the surf. Swimming is generally safe at Pueblo la Playa (see "Beaches," above).

1/142-9000, ext. 8316; open from 7:30am to 10pm); **Cabo Travel Advisors,** (✆ **1/142-4444;** ecta@1cabonet.com.mx); or **Amigos del Mar** in Cabo San Lucas (✆ **1/143-0505**).

**SURFING**    **Playa Costa Azul,** at Km 29 on Highway 1 just south of San José, is the most popular surfing beach in the area. There are a few bungalows available for rent here, or surfers can camp on the beach. Surfboards can also be rented by the day at Costa Azul, along with surf racks for your rental car, but it's generally better to bring your own. Spectators can watch from the highway lookout point at the top of the hill south of Costa Azul.

When summer hurricanes spin off the southern end of the peninsula, huge surf is sent northward at beaches like Zippers, Punta Gorda, and Old Man's. People have compared Zippers (near the Brisa del Mar Trailer Park and the Costa Azul surf shop outside San José del Cabo) with places like Pipeline, on the north Shore of Oahu. That may be a bit of an exaggeration, but there are great waves nonetheless.

**WHALE-WATCHING**    From January through March, whales congregate offshore. Fishermen at Pueblo la Playa will take small groups out to see the whales; a 4-hour trip runs about $45 per person. Another option is **Cabo Travel Advisors** (✆ **1/142-4444;** cta@1cabonet.com.mx), which arranges whale-watching for groups of four or more people; the 2½-hour trip costs $45 per person, and includes snacks and beverages. For more, see "Whale-Watching in Baja: A Primer," in chapter 4.

## SHOPPING

The town has a growing selection of unique design shops, hip boutiques, and collections of fine Mexican *artesanía* (handcrafts) clustered around Blvd. Mijares and Zaragoza, the main street. The municipal market on Mauricio Castro and Green sells edibles and utilitarian wares. Highlights include:

**ADD (Arte, Diseño y Decoración)**    This shop sells creative home accessories and furnishings, mostly made of rustic wood, pewter, and Talavera ceramics. Shipping is available. Zaragoza at Hidalgo. ✆1/142-2777.

**Copal**    Traditional and contemporary Mexican artesanía and silver jewelry are the specialties in this former residence, tastefully converted into a contemporary shop. Plaza Mijares 10. ✆**1/142-3070.** Daily 9am-10:30pm.

**Escape**    This store features designer and casual sportswear and accessories, including designer jeans, leather bags, belts, and a trendy selection of sunglasses. There's also a new interior decor shop by the same name next door, with a small cafe and espresso bar in the connecting courtyard. Plaza Florentine, Zaragoza, across from the cathedral. No phone.

**Sierra Madre**    Here you'll find nature-inspired gifts, books, and collectibles, with a conservationist theme. Xplora Adventours has a location inside the shop. Zaragoza, on the plaza. ✆ 1/142-3537. Daily 9am-10pm.

## GALLERIES

San José has a growing number of art galleries—mainly artist studios, open to the public—as the town's creative ambience blossoms. The most notable is **Galeria Wentworth Porter,** Av. Obregón 20 (✆ 1/142-3141), which features a selection of original fine art, along with prints and art cards by local artists. As the name implies, locally popular artist Dennis Wentworth Porter's work figures prominently. Open Monday through Saturday from 10am to 5pm.

## WHERE TO STAY

There's more demand than supply for hotel rooms in Baja Sur, so prices tend to be higher than equivalent accommodations in other parts of Mexico. San José has only a handful of budget hotels, so it's best to call ahead for reservations if you want economical accommodations. A new trend here is toward smaller inns, or bed-and-breakfasts, offering stylish accommodations in town. The beachfront hotel zone often offers package deals that bring room rates down to the moderate range, especially during summer months. Check with your travel agent.

### EXPENSIVE

**Casa Natalia** 𝓕𝓕𝓕 *(Finds)*    This recently opened boutique hotel is exquisite. Owners Nathalie and Loic have transformed a former residence into a beautiful amalgam of palms, waterfalls, and flowers that mirrors the beauty of the land. The inn itself is a completely renovated historic home, which now combines modern architecture with traditional Mexican touches. Each of the rooms has a name that reflects the decor, such as Conchas (seashells), Azul (blue), or Talavera (ceramics); all have sliding glass doors that open onto small private terraces with hammocks and chairs, shaded by bougainvillea and bamboo. The two spa suites each have a private terrace with a

Jacuzzi and hammock. A small courtyard pool is surrounded by 39 tall California palms; the terraces face this view. Casa Natalia offers its guests privacy, style, and romance, and welcomes children 13 and older. It's in the heart of the Blvd. Mijares action, just off of the central plaza.

Blvd. Mijares 4, 23400 San José del Cabo, B.C.S. © **888/277-3814** in the U.S., or 1/142-5100. Fax 1/142-5110. www.casanatalia.com. 16 units, including 2 spa suites. High season $220 standard; $345 spa suite. Low season $180 standard; $295 spa suite. AE, MC, V. **Amenities:** Exceptional gourmet restaurant (see "Where to Dine," below), bar; heated swimming pool with waterfall and palapa swim-up bar; spa services upon request; concierge; room service; in-room massage; laundry service. *In room:* A/C, TV, dataport, coffeemaker, hair dryer, safe-deposit boxes.

**Hotel Presidente Inter-Continental** 𝓡𝓡    Serenity, seclusion, and luxury are the hallmarks of the Presidente, set on a long stretch of beach next to the Estero San José. Low-rise, Mediterranean-style buildings frame the beach and San José's largest swimming pool, which has a swim-up bar. If possible, select a ground-floor oceanfront room, as the lower level offers spacious terraces as an alternative to a tiny balcony on upper-level units. The rooms have satellite TV and large bathrooms; suites include a separate sitting area. The all-inclusive nature of this resort makes it a good choice for those who want to principally stay put at one place and enjoy it; it's also popular with families.

Blvd. Mijares s/n, 23400 San José del Cabo, B.C.S. © **800/327-0200** in the U.S., or 1/142-0211. Fax 1/142-0232. 240 units. $442 double standard room; $410 double oceanfront room; $570 double suite. Rates include all meals, beverages, and many sports. AE, DC, MC, V. **Amenities:** 3 restaurants, garden café, plus theme-night buffet dinners. The largest swimming pool in San José (actually 2 pools joined together), plus a separate pool for children; golf clinics; tennis; gym; bicycles; horseback riding; tour desk; twice-daily shuttle to Cabo San Lucas for a fee; room service; laundry. *In room:* A/C, TV, hair dryer, makeup mirrors, safe-deposit boxes.

## MODERATE
**El Encanto Inn** 𝓡𝓡 *Value*    Located on a quiet street in the historic downtown district, this charming small inn borders a grassy courtyard with fountain, offering a very relaxing alternative to busy hotels. Rooms are all attractively decorated—each unique—with rustic wood and contemporary iron furniture. The nice-sized bathrooms have colorful tile accents. Rooms have two double beds, while suites have king-size beds and an added sitting room. El Encanto's welcoming owners, Cliff and Blanca, can also help arrange fishing packages, as well as golf and diving outings. Blanca is a lifelong resident of San José, so she's a great resource

for information and dining tips. It's best for couples or singles looking for a peaceful place from which to explore historic San José.
Continental breakfast at Jazmin's restaurant, half a block away, is
included with room rates. It's located between Obregón and
Comonfort, half a block from the church.

Morelos 17, 23400 San José del Cabo, B.C.S. © 1/142-0388. www.elencanto.com.
elencant@prodigy.net.mx. 19 units. $69 double; $99 suite, including breakfast.
Limited street parking available. AE, MC, V. **Amenities:** Tour and fishing service. *In
room:* A/C, TV.

**La Playita Resort**    Removed from even the slow pace of San José,
this older yet impeccably clean and friendly courtyard hotel is ideal
for fishermen and those looking for something removed from a traditional hotel vacation. It's the only hotel on San José's only beach
that's safe for swimming. Just steps from the water and the lineup of
fishing pangas, the two stories of sunlit rooms frame a patio with a
swimming pool just large enough to allow you to swim laps. Each
room is spacious, with high ceilings, high-quality if basic furnishings, screened windows, and nicely tiled bathrooms, plus cable TV.
Two large suites on the second floor have small refrigerators. If you
catch a big one, there's a fish freezer for storage. Services include coffee every morning and golf-cart shuttle to the beach. Next door, the
hotel's La Playita Restaurant is open from 12am to 10pm and serves
a great mix of seafood and standard favorites, plus occasional live
jazz or tropical music. To find the hotel from Blvd. Mijares, follow
the sign pointing to PUEBLO LA PLAYA, taking a dirt road for about 2
miles to the beach. The hotel is on the left, facing the water and at
the edge of the tiny village of Pueblo la Playa.

Pueblo la Playa, Apdo. Postal 437, 23400 San José del Cabo, B.C.S. © 888/
288-8137 from the U.S., or ©/fax 1/142-4166. www.mexonline.com/playita/. 26
units. High season $75 double. Low season $65 double. MC, V. Free parking.
**Amenities:** Adjoining restaurant; swimming pool; fish freezer; morning coffee service. *In room:* A/C, cable TV.

**Tropicana Inn** ⪡    This handsome colonial-style hotel has been a
long-standing favorite in San José and welcomes many repeat visitors. Set just behind (and adjacent to) the Tropicana Bar and Grill,
it frames a plant-filled courtyard with a graceful arcade bordering
the rooms and inviting swimming pool. Each nicely furnished,
medium-size room in the L-shaped building (which has a two- and
a three-story wing) comes with tile floors, two double beds, a window looking out on the courtyard, a brightly tiled bathroom with
shower, and a coffee pot. Each morning, freshly brewed coffee,

delicious sweet rolls, and fresh fruit are set out for the hotel guests. There's room service until 11pm from the adjacent Tropicana Bar and Grill (owned by the hotel). The inn is located behind the restaurant, a block south of the town square.

Blvd. Mijares 30, 23400 San José del Cabo, B.C.S. ℂ **1/142-0907** or 1/142-1580. Fax 1/142-1590. 38 units. High season $85 double. Low season $70 double. AE, MC, V. Free limited parking in back. **Amenities:** Restaurant/bar; small pool; tour desk; room service; laundry service. *In room:* A/C, TV, minibar, coffeemaker.

## INEXPENSIVE
**Posada Señor La Mañana**   This comfortable two-story guest house, set in a grove of tropical fruit trees, offers basic rooms with tile floors and funky furniture, and an abundance of hammocks strewn about the property. Guests have cooking privileges in a large, fully equipped common kitchen, set beside two palapas. Ask about discounts and weekly rates. It's next to the Casa de la Cultura, behind the main square.

Obregón 1, 23400 San José del Cabo, B.C.S. ℂ/fax **1/142-1372.** sr_manana@ 1cabonet.net.mx. 18 units. $30–$45 double. No credit cards. **Amenities:** Small swimming pool.

# WHERE TO DINE
## EXPENSIVE
**Damiana** 𝔞   SEAFOOD/MEXICAN   This casually elegant restaurant in an 18th-century hacienda is decorated in the colors of a Mexican sunset: deep-orange walls, and tables and chairs clad in bright rose, lavender, and orange cloth. Mariachis play nightly from 8 to 9pm (mid-Dec through Mar) in the tropical courtyard, where candles flicker under the trees and the bougainvillea. For an appetizer, try the mushrooms diablo—a moderately zesty dish. For a main course, the ranchero shrimp in cactus sauce or grilled lobster tail are flavorful choices. You can also enjoy brunch almost until the dinner hour. There is an interior dining room, but the courtyard is the most romantic dining spot in San José. It's located on the east side of the town plaza.

San José town plaza. ℂ**1/142-0499** or 1/142-2899. Fax 1/142-3027. damiana@ 1cabonet.com.mx. Reservations recommended during Christmas and Easter holidays. Lunch $7.50–$20; main courses $30–$40. AE, MC, V. Daily 11am–10:30pm.

**Mi Cocina** 𝔞𝔞𝔞   NUEVELLE MEXICAN/EURO CUISINE   Without a doubt, this is currently the best dining choice in the entire Los Cabos area. From the setting to the service, a dinner at Mi Cocina is sure to be unforgettable. The plant-filled courtyard, with its towering palms and exposed brick walls, accommodates alfresco dining. But it's not just the romance of the setting—the food is creative and consistently superb. Notable starters include the *patoludo*—cured duck breast served on organic greens with grapes and apples, or the vol-u-vent puff pastry filled with shrimp, scallops, mushrooms, and basil *beurre blanc*. Among the favorite main courses are the provençal-style rack of lamb served on a potato cake with onion marmalade, or the jumbo shrimp sautéed with rosemary, olive oil, and sun-dried tomatoes. Save room for dessert; choices range from chocolate eclairs to fresh-fruit-filled meringue discs topped with chantilly cream. The full-service palapa bar offers an excellent selection of wines, premium tequilas, and single-malt scotches, as well as an extensive array of specialty drinks.

Blvd. Mijares, inside Casa Natalia. ⓒ 1/142-5100. www.mi-cocina.com. Main courses $15–$20. AE, MC, V. Open daily to hotel guests only from 7am–4pm, and to the public for dinner 6:30–11pm.

**Tequila** 𝒜𝒜 MEXICAN/ASIAN    The contemporary Mexican cuisine with a light and flavorful touch is the star attraction here, although the garden setting is lovely, with rustic equipal (leather and twine) furniture and lanterns scattered among palms and giant mango trees. Start with a heavenly version of the traditional *chiles en nogada*, stuffed with couscous, raisins, and papaya and seasoned with cinnamon. Grilled tuna with ginger sauce arrives perfectly seared; the whole-grain bread is fresh and hot. Jazz and attentive service complement the fine meal. An added touch: Cuban cigars and an excellent selection of tequilas are available.

M. Doblando s/n. ⓒ1/142-1155. Main courses $10–$45. AE. Daily 11am–3pm and 6–10:30pm.

## MODERATE

**Tropicana Bar and Grill** SEAFOOD/MEAT    The Tropicana remains a popular mainstay, especially for tourists. The bar has a steady clientele day and night and often features special sporting events on satellite TV. The dining area is in a garden (candlelit in the evening) with a tiled mural at one end. Cafe-styled sidewalk dining is also available, but made less romantic by a twirling, brightly lit dessert display. The menu is too extensive to lay claim to any specialty; it aims to please everyone. All meats and cheeses are imported, and dinners include thick steaks and shrimp fajitas. Paella is the Sunday special. The restaurant is 1 block south of the Plaza Mijares.

Blvd. Mijares 30. ⓒ 1/142-1580. Breakfast $4–$6; main courses $8–$20. AE, MC, V. Daily 6am–11pm.

**Zipper's** *&* BURGERS/MEXICAN/SEAFOOD    Mike Posey
and Tony Magdeleno own this popular casual hangout. Sitting at
the far south end of the beach heading toward Cabo San Lucas and
fronting the best surfing waters, it's become popular with gringos in
search of American food and TV sports. Burgers have that back-
home flavor—order one with a side of spicy curly fries. Steaks, lobster, beer-batter shrimp, deli sandwiches, and Mexican combination
plates round out the menu, which is printed with dollar prices.

Playa Costa Azul just south of San José. No phone. Burgers and sandwiches
$7–$10; main courses $7–$18. No credit cards. Daily 8am–10pm.

## SAN JOSÉ AFTER DARK

San José's nightlife is nonexistent outside of the restaurant and hotel
bars. Of particular note are the bars at Casa Natalia and
Tropicana—the former catering to sophisticated romantics, the latter to those in search of rowdier good times. On some weekends,
Tropicana will even bring in a live Cuban band for dancing. Several
of the larger hotels along the beach have Mexican fiestas and other
weekly theme nights that include a buffet (usually all-you-can-eat),
drinks, live music, and entertainment for $25 to $35 per person.
There's also a large disco on Mijares that seems to be under different ownership each year—it was closed at press time, but with a
REOPENING SOON sign on its door. Those intent on real "nightlife"
will find it in Cabo San Lucas (see below).

**Tropicana Bar and Grill**    This is definitely the most popular
place in town. Patrons hang out in leather barrel chairs in the large
bar where, during the day, they tune in to American sports events
on the big-screen TV. Come evening, guitarists play Mexican
boleros and other traditional music from 6 to 11pm. After 9pm on
some nights, a band plays Americanized rock and pop for those
inclined to dance. The Tropicana is open daily from 7am to 1am.
Drinks go for $3 and up. Blvd. Mijares 30. ℂ1/142-0907. No cover.

## 2 The Corridor: Between the Two Cabos *&&*

The Corridor between the towns of San José del Cabo and Cabo
San Lucas contains some of Mexico's most lavish resorts, designed as
self-contained dream getaways. Most growth at the tip of the peninsula is occurring along the Corridor, which has already become a
major international locale for championship golf. The three major
resort areas are Palmilla, Cabo Real, and Cabo del Sol, each a self-
enclosed community with golf courses, elegant hotels, and million-
dollar homes.

If you plan to explore the region while staying at a Corridor hotel, you'll need a rental car for at least a day or two; cars are available at the hotels. Even if you're not staying here, the beaches and dining options are worth visiting. Hotels—all of which qualify as "very expensive" selections—are listed in the order in which you'll encounter them as you drive from San José to Cabo San Lucas. Rates listed are for the high season (winter); typically they'll be 20% lower in the summer. Golf and fishing packages are available at most resorts.

## WHERE TO STAY

### Casa del Mar ★★ (Finds)    A little-known treasure, this intimate resort is one of the best values along the Corridor. The hacienda-style building offers guests luxury accommodations in an intimate setting, as well as an on-site spa and nearby golf facilities. Located within the Cabo Real development, it's convenient to the 18-hole championship Cabo Real golf course. Gentle waterfalls lead to the adults-only pool area and a flowered path takes you further along, to the wide, sandy stretch of beach with a clear surf break. There's even a "quiet area" on the lawn for those looking for a siesta.

Guest rooms have a clean, bright feel to them, with white marble floors, light wicker furnishings, separate sitting area, and a large Jacuzzi tub, plus separate shower on the raised bathroom level. Balconies have oversized chairs, with a view of the ocean beyond the pool. It's a romantic hotel for couples and honeymooners, known for its welcoming, personalized service.

Km 19.5 on Hwy. 1, 23410 Cabo San Lucas, B.C.S. © 800/221-8808 in the U.S., or 1/144-0030. Fax 1/144-0034. www.mexonline.com/casamar.htm. 56 units. High season $396 double; $477 suite. Low season $220 double; $275 suite. AE, MC, V. **Amenities:** Restaurant and lobby bar; adults-only swimming pool and hot tub, plus pool bar; beach club with snack bar; Cabo Real Golf Club privileges; 2 lit Astroturf tennis courts; full service Avanti Spa, plus a small but well-equipped workout room; tour desk; room service; in-room massage; baby-sitting; laundry and dry cleaning services. *In room:* A/C, cable TV, dataport, minibar, safe-deposit boxes, bathrobes.

### Hotel Palmilla ★★★    One of the most comfortably luxurious hotels in Mexico, the Palmilla is the grand dame of Los Cabos resorts. Though it is the oldest property along the Corridor, constant upgrades mean that the rooms and facilities surpass even the newest luxe resorts built in the area. The feeling here is one of classic resort-style comfort. The Palmilla has become renowned as a location for destination weddings or anniversary celebrations with a renewal of vows; ceremonies take place in its small, signature chapel

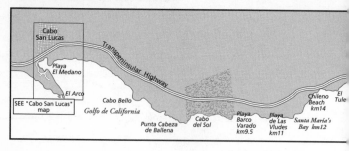

that graces a sloped hillside. Perched on a clifftop above the sea, the resort is a series of white buildings with red-tile roofs, towering palms, and flowering bougainvillea. Talavera vases, carved dressers and headboards, heavy-weave drapes and spreads, and bathrooms walled in hand-painted tiles give the rooms a colonial Mexico feeling. Private balconies have extra comfortable, overstuffed chairs. TVs have built-in VCRs with a wide selection of movies available at the concierge office. Standard amenities include fresh juice, coffee, and croissants delivered after your wake-up call. They also have available a five-bedroom villa for rent, Casa Cristina, with its own private pool. The hotel automatically adds a 15% service charge to all rates, which is included in the rates quoted below.

Km 27.5 on Hwy. 1, 23400 San José del Cabo, B.C.S. © 800/637-2226 in the U.S., or 1/144-5000. Fax 1/144-5100. www.palmillaresort.com. 114 units, 1 villa. High season $450 double; $690–$2,750 suites and villas. Low season $230–$260 double; $435–$2,000 suites and villas. AE, MC, V. **Amenities:** 1 restaurant, pool lunch and snack service, Friday night Mexican fiestas, and the Neptuno Bar, known for both its views and margaritas; swimming pool; across the highway, the resort's championship golf course, designed by Jack Nicklaus, is available for guests; 2 lit tennis courts; small fitness center; croquet court; 2 volleyball courts; horseback riding; hotel-owned fishing boats; on-premises dive shop with dive and snorkel equipment rentals; tour desk; car-rental; salon; room service; in-room massage service; baby-sitting; laundry. boutiques. *In room:* A/C, TV, dataport, minibar, hair dryer, safe-deposit boxes, bathrobes.

## Westin Regina ☆☆ *Kids*  Architecturally dramatic, the Westin Regina sits at the end of a long paved road atop a seaside cliff. Vivid terra-cotta, yellow, and pink walls rise against a landscape of sandstone, cacti, and palms, with fountains and gardens lining the long pathways from the lobby to the rooms. Electric carts carry guests and their luggage through the vast property. The rooms are gorgeous, with both air-conditioning and ceiling fans, private

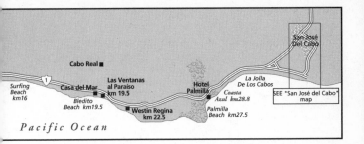

Cabo Real ■

Las Ventanas
al Paraíso
km 19.5

La Jolla
De Los Cabos

Surfing
Beach
km16

Casa del Mar

Hotel
Palmilla

Bledito
Beach km19.5

Coasta
Azul km28.8

SEE "San José del Cabo"
map

Westin Regina
km 22.5

Palmilla
Beach km27.5

San José
del Cabo

Pacific Ocean

balconies, satellite TV, and walk-in showers separate from the bath-
tubs. This is probably the best choice among our selections for families vacationing along the corridor, for the wealth of activities
available for children.

Km 22.5 on Hwy. 1, Apdo. Postal 145, 23400 San José del Cabo, B.C.S.
ⓒ800/228-3000 in the U.S., or 1/142-9000. Fax 1/142-9010. 295 units. $308 dou-
ble with partial oceanview; $347 double with full oceanview; $436–$705 suite.
Rates drop 20% in low season. AE, DC, MC, V. **Amenities:** 6 restaurants, 2 bars;
3 swimming pools; the Palmilla and Cabo Real golf courses are nearby; 2 tennis
courts; beach club, full fitness center; Xplora Adventour services; children's activities; concierge; car-rental desk; business services; salon; room service; baby-sitting;
laundry service. *In room:* A/C, TV, minibar, hair dryer, safe.

**Las Ventanas al Paraíso** 𝕽𝕽𝕽   Las Ventanas is known for its
unerring offering of luxury accommodations and attention to detail.
The architecture, with adobe structures and rough-hewn wood
accents, provides a soothing complement to the desert landscape.
The only burst of color comes from the dazzling windows (*ventanas*)
of pebbled rainbow glass—handmade by regional artisans—that
reflect the changing positions of the sun. Richly furnished,
Mediterranean-style rooms are large (starting at 1,000 sq. ft.) and
appointed with every conceivable amenity, from wood-burning fireplaces to computerized telescopes for stargazing or whale-watching
in your own room. Fresh flowers and tequila setups welcome each
guest, and room standards include satellite TV with VCRs, stereos
with CD players, and dual-line phones. Sizable Jacuzzi tubs overlook the room but may be closed off for privacy. Larger suites offer
pampering extras like rooftop terraces, sunken Jacuzzis on a private
patio, or a personal pool. The Spa is known as among the best in
Mexico—particularly notable is its Sea and Stars nighttime massage
for two, a relaxing aromatherapy massage with two therapists that

takes place on the rooftop terrace of your private suite. With a staff that outnumbers guests by four to one, this is the place for those who want (and can afford) to be seriously spoiled.

Km 19.5 on Hwy. 1, 23410 San José del Cabo, B.C.S. ℂ **888/525-0483** in the U.S., or 1/144-0300. Fax 1/144-0301. www.rosewood-hotels.com. 61 suites. $550 double with partial oceanview; $675 double with full oceanview; $775 split-level suite with rooftop terrace. 1- and 2-bedroom luxury suites $2,200–$3,500. Special spa and golf packages available, as are inclusive meal plans. AE, DC, MC, V. Complimentary valet parking. **Amenities:** Ocean-view gourmet restaurant with wine cellar, adjoining terrace bar with live classical music; seaside casual-dining grill, plus fresh-juice bar; access to adjoining championship Cabo Real golf course; deluxe European Spa with complete treatment and exercise facilities; availability of sportfishing and luxury yachts; water sports; tour services; car rental, shuttle services; 24-hour room service; laundry; meeting rooms. *In room:* A/C, TV, dataport, minibar, hair dryer, iron, safe-deposit boxes; bathrobes.

## WHERE TO DINE

**Pitahayas** 𝓡𝓡𝓡 PACIFIC RIM   Pitahayas' beachfront setting in the Hacienda del Mar resort offers gourmet dining under a grand palapa or on open-air terraces, under a starlit sky. Master chef Volker Romeike has assembled a creative—if not slightly pretentious—menu that blends Pacific Rim cuisine with Mexican native herbs and seasonings. Notable sauces include mango, black bean, and curry. The rotisserie-barbecued duck is a house specialty, along with mesquite grill and wok cooking—all prepared in an impressive exhibition kitchen. A dessert pizza with fresh fruit, chocolate, and marzipan makes a fitting finish to a stunning meal. Pitahayas also boasts the largest wine cellar in Los Cabos with vintages from around the world, housed in an underground *cava*. Formal resort attire is requested, and reservations are an absolute must during high season.

At Hacienda del Mar, Km 10 on Hwy. 1, Cabo del Sol. ℂ **1/145-8010**. Main courses $12–$30. AE, MC, V. Daily 7–11pm.

## 3 Cabo San Lucas 𝓡𝓡

110 miles S of La Paz; 22 miles W of San José del Cabo; 1,120 miles SE of Tijuana

The hundreds of luxury hotel rooms along the corridor to the north of Cabo San Lucas have transformed the very essence of this formerly rustic and rowdy outpost. Although it still retains a boisterous nightlife that belies the pampered services that surround it, Cabo San Lucas is no longer the simple town Steinbeck wrote about and enjoyed. Once legendary for the big-game fish that lurk beneath the deep blue sea, Cabo San Lucas now draws more people for its

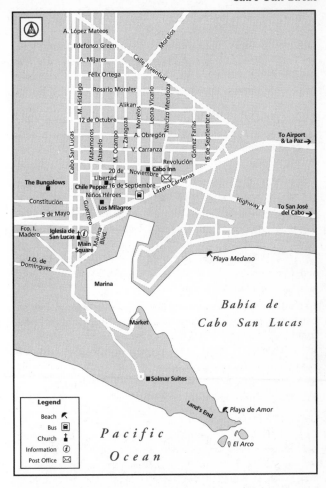

Legend

Beach ↖
Bus 🚍
Church ⛪
Information ⓘ
Post Office ✉

nearby fairways and greens—and the world-class golf being played on them. Today, it caters to a traveler getting away for a long weekend or indulgent stay of sport and relaxation. Cabo San Lucas has become Mexico's most elite resort destination.

Travelers here enjoy a growing roster of adventure-oriented activities, and playtime doesn't end when the sun goes down. The nightlife here is as hot as the desert in July, and oddly casual, having grown up away from the higher-end hotels. It remains the raucous, playful party scene that helped put Cabo on the map. A collection of popular restaurants and bars, spread along Cabo's main street, stay open and active until the morning's first fishing charters head out to sea. Despite the growth in diversions, Cabo remains more or less a "one stoplight" town, with most everything located along the main strip, within easy walking distance.

If you're driving from La Paz, you'll pass through the village of Todos Santos, which has beautifully restored historic buildings and makes a great stop for a meal—try the renowned Café Santa Fe, which draws diners from Los Cabos with its fresh fish and fine Italian cuisine.

## ESSENTIALS
### GETTING THERE & DEPARTING
**BY PLANE**    For arrival and departure information see "Getting There & Departing," earlier in the chapter under "San José del Cabo." Local airline numbers are as follows: **AeroCalifornia** (© 1/143-3700); **Alaska Airlines** (© 1/146-5104 at the airport); and **Mexicana** (© 1/146-5001, or 1/142-0606 at the airport; geventassjd@ mexicana.com.mx).

**BY CAR**    From La Paz, the best route is to take Highway 1 south past the village of San Pedro, then Highway 19 south through Todos Santos to Cabo San Lucas, a 2-hour drive.

**BY BUS**    The bus terminal (© 1/143-5020) is on Niños Héroes at Morelos; it is open daily from 6am to 7pm. Buses go to San José del Cabo about every hour between 6:30am and 8:30pm, and to La Paz every 90 minutes between 6am and 6pm.

### ORIENTATION
**ARRIVING**    At the airport, either buy a ticket for a colectivo from the authorized transportation booth inside the building (about $10) or arrange for a rental car, the most economical way to explore the area. Private taxis can be shared by up to four people, and cost about $60 between the airport and Cabo San Lucas.

It is not too far to walk with light luggage from the bus station to most of the budget hotels, but taxis are readily available.

**VISITOR INFORMATION**    The Secretary of Tourism functions as the information office in Cabo. It's on Madero between Hidalgo and Guerrero (© 1/142-0446; fax 1/142-0260). The English-language *Los Cabos Guide, Los Cabos News, Cabo Life, Baja Sun,* and the irreverent and extremely entertaining *Gringo Gazette* are distributed free at most hotels and shops and have up-to-date information on new restaurants and clubs. *Note:* The many visitor-information booths along the street are actually time-share sales booths, and their staffs will pitch a visit to their resort in exchange for discounted tours, rental cars, or other giveaways.

**CITY LAYOUT**    The small town spreads out north and west of the harbor of Cabo San Lucas Bay, edged by foothills and desert mountains to the west and south. The main street leading into town from the airport and San José del Cabo is Lázaro Cárdenas; as it nears the harbor, Marina Boulevard branches off from it and becomes the main artery that curves around the waterfront.

## GETTING AROUND

Taxis are easily found but are expensive within Cabo, in keeping with the high cost of everything else. Expect to pay about $15 or $25 for a taxi between Cabo and the Corridor hotels.

For day trips to San José del Cabo, catch a bus (see "Getting There & Departing" under "San José del Cabo" above) or a cab. You'll see car-rental specials advertised in town, but before signing on, be sure you understand the total price after insurance and taxes have been added. Rates can run between $40 and $75 per day, with insurance an extra $10 per day. One of the best and most economical car-rental agencies locally is **Advantage Rent-A-Car** (ⓒ **1/143-0909;** tel/fax 1/143-0466; advantage@1cabonet. com.mx), conveniently located in downtown Cabo on Lázaro Cárdenas, between Leona Vicario and Morelos. VW sedans rent for $48 per day, and weekly rentals receive one free day. Collision damage waiver will add $14 per day to the rental price. If you pick up the car downtown, you can return it to the airport at no extra charge.

 *FAST FACTS:* Cabo San Lucas

*Area Code*    The telephone area code is **14,** and local phone numbers begin with 14. Calls between Cabo San Lucas, San José del Cabo, and northern Corridor hotels are toll calls, so you must use the area code.

*Beach Safety*    Before swimming in the open water here, it's important to check whether the conditions are safe. Undertows and large waves are common. Medano Beach, close to the marina and town, is the principal beach safe for swimming; it has several lively beachfront restaurant-bars. It's also easy to find water-sports equipment for rent here. The Hotel Melia Cabo San Lucas, on Medano Beach, has a roped-off swimming area to protect swimmers from jet skis and boats. Colored flags signaling swimming safety aren't generally used in Cabo, and neither are lifeguards.

*Currency Exchange* Banks exchange currency during normal business hours, generally Monday through Friday from 9am to 6pm and Saturday from 10am to 2pm. Currency-exchange booths, found all along Cabo's main tourist areas, aren't as competitive but they're more convenient. ATMs are widely available and even more convenient, dispensing pesos—and in some cases dollars—at bank exchange rates.

*Emergencies/Hospital* See "Fast Facts: San José Del Cabo," above.

*Internet Access* Access is available through **Dr. Z's Internet Café & Bar,** Lazaro Cardenes no. 7, edificio Posada, across from the Pemex gas station (℡ **1/143-5390**). Access costs $5 for 15 minutes, $7 for 30 minutes, or $8 for an hour. Open 9am to 6pm, Monday through Saturday.

*Pharmacy* A long-standing drugstore in town, with a wide selection of toiletries as well as medicines, is **Farmacia Aramburo,** in Plaza Aramburo, on Cárdenas at Zaragoza (no phone); open daily from 7am to 9pm. Also try **Farmacia Faro Viejo,** L. Cardenas and Hidalgo #4 (℡ **1/143-3655**), open daily from 9am to 9pm.

*Post Office* The correo is at Cárdenas and Francisco Villa, on the highway to San José del Cabo, east of the bar El Squid Roe (℡ **1/143-0048**). It's open Monday through Friday from 9am to 1pm and from 3 to 6pm, and Saturday from 9am to noon.

## BEACHES & OUTDOOR ACTIVITIES

Although superb sportfishing put Cabo San Lucas on the map, there's more to do here than drop your line and wait for the Big One. For most cruises and excursions, try to make fishing reservations at least a day in advance; keep in mind that some trips require a minimum number of people. Most sports and outings can be

## ⌒Moments  Festivals & Events in Cabo San Lucas

The Bisbee International Marlin Fishing Tournament is held in October with a huge dollar prize for the winner. October 12 is the festival of the patron saint of Todos Santos, a town about 65 miles north. October 18 is the feast of the patron saint of Cabo San Lucas, celebrated with a fair, feasting, music, dancing, and other special events.

arranged through a travel agency; fishing can also be arranged directly at one of the fishing-fleet offices at the far south end of the marina.

Besides fishing, there's kayaking ($60 for a sunset kayak around the Arches rock formation; $40 for morning kayak trips) and boat trips to Los Arcos or uninhabited beaches. All-inclusive daytime or sunset cruises are provided on a variety of boats, including a replica of a pirate ship. Many of these trips include snorkeling; serious divers have great underwater venues to explore. Horseback riding to Los Arcos and to the Pacific (very popular at sunset) costs $50 for 2 hours.

Whale-watching, between January and March, has become one of the most popular local activities. Guided ATV (all-terrain vehicle) tours take you down dirt roads and through a desert landscape to the old Cabo lighthouse or an ancient Indian village. And then, of course, there's the challenge of world-class golf, now a major attraction of Los Cabos.

For a complete rundown of what's available, contact **Xplora Adventours** at ℂ **1/142-9000,** ext. 8316. They offer all tours from all local companies, rather than working with only a select few. Xplora has tour desks in the Westin Regina hotel, the Sierra Madre store on Lázaro Cárdenas, and at the Cabo Wabo Beach Club at Medano Beach.

**ATV TRIPS**  Expeditions on ATVs to visit Cabo Falso, an 1890 lighthouse, and La Candelaria, an Indian pueblo in the mountains, are available through travel agencies. The 3-hour tour to Cabo Falso includes a stop at the beach, a look at some sea-turtle nests (without disturbing them) and the remains of a 1912 shipwreck, a ride over 500-foot sand dunes, and a visit to the lighthouse. Guided tours cost around $45 per person on a single bike, or $60 for two riding on one ATV. The vehicles are also available for rent at $35 for 3 hours.

La Candelaria is an isolated Indian village in the mountains 25 miles north of Cabo San Lucas. Described in *National Geographic*, the old pueblo is known for the white and black witchcraft still practiced here. Lush with palms, mango trees, and bamboo, the settlement is watered by an underground river that emerges at the pueblo. The return trip of the tour travels down a steep canyon, along a beach (giving you time to swim), and past giant-sea-turtle nesting grounds. Departing at 9am, the La Candelaria tour costs around $80 per person or $100 for two on the same ATV. A 440-pound weight limit per two-person vehicle applies to both tours.

## BEACHES

All along the curving sweep of sand known as **Medano Beach,** on the east side of the bay, you can rent snorkeling gear, boats, WaveRunners ($70 per hr.), kayaks, pedal boats, and windsurf boards. You can also take windsurfing lessons. This is the town's main beach; it's a great place for safe swimming as well as for people-watching from one of the many outdoor restaurants along its shore.

Beach aficionados may want to rent a car (see "Getting Around," above) and explore the five more remote beaches and coves between the two Cabos: **playas Palmilla, Chileno, Santa María, Barco Varado,** and **Vista del Arcos.** Palmilla, Chileno, and Santa María are generally safe for swimming—but always be careful. The other beaches should not be considered safe. Experienced snorkelers may very well wish to check them out, but other visitors should go for the view only. Always check at a hotel or travel agency for directions and swimming conditions. Although a few travel agencies run snorkeling tours to some of these beaches, there's no public transportation: Your only option for beach exploring is to rent a car at a cost of $50 per day and up.

## CRUISES

Glass-bottom boats leave from the town marina every 45 minutes daily between 9am and 4pm. They cost upwards of $10 for an hour's tour past sea lions and pelicans to see the famous El Arco (Rock Arch) at Land's End, where the Pacific and the Sea of Cortez meet. Most boats make a brief stop at Playa de Amor or drop you off there if you ask; you can use your ticket to catch a later boat back (be sure to check what time the last boat departs).

There are a number of daylong and sunset cruises, on a variety of boats and catamarans. They vary in price—from $30 to $45 depending on the boat, duration of cruise, and amenities. A sunset cruise on the 42-foot catamaran *Pez Gato* (© 1/143-3797 or 1/143-2458; pezgato@1cabonet.com.mx) departs from the Plaza las Glorias Hotel dock at 5pm. The 2-hour cruise costs $35, which includes margaritas, beer, and sodas. Similar boats leave from the marina and the Plaza las Glorias Hotel. Check with travel agencies or hotel tour desks.

## LAND SPORTS

**GOLF** Los Cabos has become Mexico's golf mecca, and though the courses are principally located along the Corridor, people look to Cabo San Lucas for information about this sport in Baja Sur. The Los Cabos golf master plan calls for a future total of 207 holes of golf. Fees listed below are for 18 holes of play, including golf cart, water, club service, and tax. Summer rates are about 25% lower, and many hotels offer special golf packages. (For specifics on the playability of the various courses, see "The Lowdown on Golfing in Cabo," below.)

The 27-hole course at the **Palmilla Golf Club,** part of the Palmilla resort (© 800/386-2465 in the U.S., or 1/144-5250; open 7am to 7pm), was the first Jack Nicklaus Signature layout in Mexico, built in 1992 on 900 acres of dramatic oceanfront and desert. The 27-hole course offers your choice of two back-nine options, with high-season greens fees of $214.50. Just a few miles away is another Jack Nicklaus Signature course, the 18-hole Ocean Course at **Cabo del Sol,** at the Cabo del Sol resort development in the Corridor (© 800/386-2465 in the U.S., or 1/145-8200). The 7,100-yard course is known for its challenging three finishing holes. Greens fees are $208 to $228. The 18-hole, 6,945-yard course at **Cabo Real,** by the Melia Cabo Real Hotel in the Corridor (© 1/144-0232; caborealgolf@1cabonet.com.mx; open 6:30am to 6pm) was designed by Robert Trent Jones Jr., and features holes that sit high on mesas overlooking the Sea of Cortez. Fees run $190 for 18 holes. **El Dorado Golf Course** (© 1/144-5451; www.caboreal.com) is a Jack Nicklaus Signature course at Cabo Real that lies next to the Westin Regina hotel. The course is open daily from 7am until dusk. Eighteen holes are $225; after 2pm a twilight special offers a round for $150. Carts are included; caddies are $40.

Located in Cabo San Lucas is the 18-hole course designed by Roy Dye at the **Cabo San Lucas Country Club** (© 800/854-2314 in the U.S., or 1/143-4653; fax 1/143-5809). The entire course

## *Tips* **The Lowdown on Golfing in Cabo**

Los Cabos, now considered one of the world's finest golf destinations, offers an ample and intriguing variety of courses to challenge golfers of all levels.

It's not just the selection, quality, and beauty of the courses in Los Cabos; the reason so many choose to play here is the very reliable weather. The courses highlighted below compare to the great ones in Palm Springs and Scottsdale, with the added beauty of the ocean views, as well as the wider variety of desert cacti and flowering plants.

**Palmilla Golf Club**   The original Cabo course is now a 27-hole course. The original 18 holes are known as the Arroyo, with the new holes known as the Ocean Nine. It's a bit of a misnomer, though—although these newer holes lie closer to the water, only one of the holes has a true oceanview—with a spectacular play directly down to the beach. You must play the Arroyo for your first nine holes, then you choose between Mountain and Ocean for your back nine. If you play this course only once, choose the Mountain back nine, as it offers better ocean views. A mountaintop club house provides spectacular views.

It's beautiful, playable, and well maintained, and throughout the course are unadulterated views of desert mountains and the cobalt ocean, without any interfering construction. Bermuda short-cut grass makes putting fast, and the signature hole is the Mountain 5; you hit over a canyon, then down to the greens below over a forced carry. This is target golf, and as a Jack Nicklaus course, was constructed with strategy in mind.

**Cabo del Sol**   This is the second Jack Nicklaus course to be constructed in Los Cabos. Its dramatic finishing oceanside holes have earned it the nickname "the Pebble Beach of Baja." The course is overseen by pro Brad Wheatly, previously of the Palmilla course. Compared to the Palmilla course, this is much more difficult, with less room for error. Seven of the holes are set along the water.

This is very challenging target golf, with numerous forced carries—even from the red tees. The signature hole here is 17, which runs by the water, with a forced carry. Don't be fooled by the wide and welcoming 1st hole.

**Cabo Real**   This Robert Trent Jones Jr.–designed course is known for its holes along the Sea of Cortez that sit high on mesas overlooking the sea; exceptional among these is the frequently photographed 12th hole. Jones designed the course to test low handicappers, but multiple tees make it enjoyable for average players as well. The par-72 layout is 6,945 yards long, and was designed with professional tournament play in mind. The most famous hole is the 14th, which sits right on the beach near the Melia resort.

**The Cabo San Lucas Country Club**   The front and back nines were planned by different designers in the Dye family, so the course plays like two different courses. Characteristic of Dye design courses, it has deep waste bunkers, subtle terracing up hillsides, and holes built into the natural desert terrain. The most challenging hole is the extremely long, 607-yard, par-five 7th hole around a lake; it's the longest hole in Mexico. The course is designed to offer a variety of play options, from a short course played on front tees to a super-long course with numerous bunkers and hazards.

**El Dorado Golf Course**   A Jack Nicklaus Signature course at Cabo Real, El Dorado is a links-style course in the Scottish tradition. The layout is challenging—seven holes border the Sea of Cortez and 12 are carved out of two pristine canyons. The oceanview holes are not the only water you'll see on this course, as manmade lakes are also a part of the scenery. El Dorado bills itself as the "Pebble Beach of Baja"—but then again, so does Cabo del Sol—you decide.

The newest course to open is **Querencia** (© **1/145-6670**, www.loscabosquerencia.com), a Tom Fazio–designed course. However, it is a strictly private club, with play limited to property owners and Golf Club members, with no provision for resort guests.

The golf offerings in Los Cabos will continue to expand, with another five courses currently under various phases of construction. All courses generally offer 50% off rates if you play after 2 or 2:30pm. This actually is a great time to play, as the temperature is cooler, and play is generally faster. Course fees are high in Cabo—generally over $200 per round, but these are true world-class courses, worth the world-class price to play them.

overlooks the juncture of the Pacific Ocean and Sea of Cortez, including the famous Land's End rocks. It includes the 607-yard, par-five 7th hole—the longest hole in Mexico. Greens fees are $176 and a twilight game is $121. The most economical greens fees in the area are found at the public nine-hole **Club Campo de Golf San José** (℗ 1/142-0900 or 1/142-0905), in San José del Cabo (see above). Greens fees are just $45 for nine holes and $75 for 18 holes, with carts an additional $30 for nine holes and $45 for 18 holes.

**OTHER SPORTS**    Bicycles, boogie boards, snorkels, surfboards, and golf clubs are available for rent at **Cabo Sports Center** in the Plaza Náutica on Blvd. Marina (℗ 1/143-4272); the center is open Monday through Saturday from 9am to 9pm and Sunday from 9am to 5pm.

You can rent horses at the **Hacienda Hotel** (℗ 1/143-0123) or the Melia San Lucas, through **Rancho Colin** (℗ 1/143-3652), for around $20 to $30 per hour. They offer guided beach rides and sunset tours to El Faro Viejo (the Old Lighthouse) for $30 to $45 per person and to the Pacific for sunset riding on the beach. They are open 8am to 6pm.

## WATER SPORTS

**SNORKELING/DIVING**    Several companies offer snorkeling; a 2-hour cruise to sites around El Arco costs $30, and a 4-hour trip to Santa María costs $55, including gear rental. Among the beaches visited on different trips are Playa de Amor, Santa María, Chileno, and Barco Varado. Snorkeling gear rents for $10 to $15. For scuba diving, contact **Amigos del Mar** (℗ 800/344-3349 in the U.S. or fax 213/545-1622 in the U.S.; 1/143-0505 or fax 1/143-0887 in Mexico; sealion@cabotel.com.mx; open 8am to 4:30pm) at the marina. Here diving specialist Ricardo Sevilla has the Cabo diving answers. Dives are made along the wall of a canyon in San Lucas Bay, where you can see a "sandfalls" that even Jacques Cousteau couldn't figure out—no one knows its source or cause. There are also scuba trips to Santa María Beach and places farther away, including the Gordo Banks and Cabo Pulmo. Dives start at $55 for a one-tank dive and $70 for two tanks; trips to the coral outcropping at Cabo Pulmo start at $115. Two hours from Cabo San Lucas, Cabo Pulmo is rated for beginners and up. Gordo Banks, for advanced divers, is an underwater mountain about 5 miles offshore with a black-coral bottom and schools of game fish and manta rays. Resort courses cost $90 per person and open-water certification costs around $400. April through November is the best time to dive, although diving is busiest from October to mid-January—it's important to make reservations in advance if you're planning to dive then. You'll need a wet suit for winter dives.

**SPORTFISHING**   Go to the town marina on the south side of the harbor. There, you'll find several fleet operators with offices near the docks. The best deals are offered by the **panga fleets,** where 5 hours of fishing for two or three people costs $150 to $200. To choose one, take a stroll around the marina and talk with the captains—you may arrive at an economical deal. Try **ABY Charters** (℘ 1/143-0831 or 1/143-0874; abcabo@prodigy.net.mx; MC, V accepted), or the **Picante/Blue Water Sportfishing Fleet** (℘ 1/143-2474; open 6:30am to 8pm; AE, MC, V accepted). Both have booths located at the sportfishing dock at the far south end of the marina. The going rate for a day on a fully equipped cruiser with captain and guide (many of the larger hotels, like the Solmar, have their own fleets) starts at around $700 for up to four people. These have bathrooms aboard. For deluxe trips with everything included aboard a 40-foot boat, you'll have to budget $1,250. (See also "Active Vacations in Baja" in chapter 1 for companies that can arrange fishing in advance.) If you've traveled down in your own vessel, you'll need a fishing permit. Depending on the size of the boat, it will cost $15 to $45 per month. Daily permits, ranging from $4 to $10, and annual permits are also available.

The fishing really lives up to its reputation: Bringing in a 100-pound marlin is routine. Angling is good all year, though the catch varies with the season: Sailfish and wahoo are best from June through November; yellowfin tuna, from May through December; yellowtail, from January through April; black and blue marlin, July through December; and striped marlin are prevalent year-round.

**SURFING**   Good surfing can be found from March through November all along the beaches west of town, and there's a famous

---

**⟨Tips⟩ Don't Sweat the One that Got Away**

"Catch and release" is strongly encouraged in Los Cabos. Anglers reel in their fish, which are then tagged and released unharmed into the sea. The angler gets a certificate and the knowledge that there will still be billfish in the sea when he or she returns.

right break at Chileno Beach, near the Cabo San Lucas Hotel east of town. (Also see "Surfing" in "San José del Cabos," above, for details on Playa Costa Azul and Zippers.) Other good surfing beaches along the corridor are Acapulquito, El Tule, and La Bocana.

The Pacific Coast has yet to face the onslaught of development that's so rapidly changed the east cape. An hour-long drive up the coast to the little towns of Pescadero and Todos Santos can be a great surf journey. There are a couple good point breaks near here.

Playa San Pedrito is reached via the dirt road that begins 7.4 kilometers (4.5 miles) south of the Todos Santos town limits. Follow the signs for SAN PEDRITO CAMPGROUND. The point is very rocky and sharp, but it's a wonderful wave on the right swell direction and tide (NW swell, rising tide). Another stretch down the road will lead you to Playa los Cerritos (12.8km [8 miles] south of Todos Santos), a lovely beach with a surfable point break off a big headland.

Other beach breaks are rideable at various times, but much of the beach around Todos Santos is characterized by a vicious shorebreak and strong undertow. While the unruliness of the ocean has helped keep industrial tourism at bay, it also means you have to hunt a little harder to find playful waves.

**WHALE-WATCHING**    Whale-watching cruises are not to be missed when gray whales migrate to the Los Cabos area between January and March. The sportfishing boats, glass-bottom boats, and cruise catamarans all offer whale-watching trips ranging from $35 to $60 for a half-day trip. You can also spot the whales from shore; good whale-watching spots include the beach by the Solmar Suites hotel on the Pacific and the beaches and cliffs along the Corridor. The ultimate whale excursion is an all-day trip to Magdalena Bay, an hour's plane ride away. In a small skiff you get close enough to touch the whales. The cost for the 4-hour trip, including air transportation, is $380.

## EXPLORING CABO SAN LUCAS
### HISTORIC CABO SAN LUCAS

Sports and partying are Cabo's main attractions, but there are also a few cultural and historical points of interest. The stone Iglesia de San Lucas (Church of San Lucas) on Calle Cabo San Lucas close to the main plaza was established in 1730 by the Spanish missionary Nicolás Tamaral; a large bell in a stone archway commemorates the completion of the church in 1746. Tamaral was eventually killed by the Pericúe Indians, who reportedly resisted his demands that they practice monogamy. Buildings on the streets facing the main plaza are gradually being renovated to house restaurants and shops, and the picturesque neighborhood promises to have the strongest Mexican ambience of any place in town.

## NEARBY DAY TRIPS

Day trips to the city of La Paz can be booked through a travel agency or through **Cabo Travel Advisors** (✆ 1/142-4444) for around $55, including beverages and a tour of the countryside along the way. Usually there's a stop at the weaving shop of Fortunato Silva, who spins his own cotton and weaves it into wonderfully textured rugs and textiles. CTA also offers a day trip to Todos Santos for $60, with a guided walking tour of the Cathedral Mission, museum, Hotel California, and various artists' homes. For more information, see chapter 3, "La Paz: Peaceful Port Town." For more on Todos Santos, see "Todos Santos: A Creative Oasis," below.

## SHOPPING

A popular tourist shopping stop is the open-air market on Plaza Papagayo on Blvd. Marina opposite the entrance to Pueblo Bonito. However, it mainly has trinkets and traditional souvenirs—little in the way of real craftwork. Be sure to bargain. Most shops are on or within a block or two of Blvd. Marina and the plaza.

**Casa Maya**   Unusual decorative items for the home, at excellent prices. Tin lamps, colored glass, and rustic wood furnishings. Open Monday through Saturday from 9am to 7pm. AE accepted. Calle Morelos between Rev. and 20 de Noviembre. ✆/fax: **1/143-3197.**

**El Callejon**   This, the most eclectic shop in Los Cabos, features antiques, unique gifts, paintings, and home furnishings. The one-of-a-kind items are mostly made by local artists. It's open Monday through Saturday from 10am to 8pm. AE, MC, and V are accepted. Vicente Guerrero s/n, between Cárdenas and Madero. ✆ **1/143-1139,** fax 1/143-3188.

**Galería Gattamelata**   In the Medano Beach area, this handsome gallery specializes in antiques and colonial-style furniture. Open daily from 9am to 8pm. AE, MC, and V are accepted. Hacienda Rd. ✆ **1/143-1166.**

**Rostros de México**   Walls of wooden masks and carved religious statues are the draw at this gallery, whose name means "Faces of Mexico." Open Monday through Saturday from 10am to 7pm, Sunday from 10am to 2pm. No credit cards accepted. Cárdenas at Matamoros. ✆ **1/143-0558.**

## WHERE TO STAY

All hotel prices listed here are for the high season, in effect from November through Easter; summer rates are about 20% less. Several Cabo San Lucas hotels offer package deals that significantly lower the nightly rate; ask your travel agent for information.

Budget accommodations are scarce in Cabo San Lucas, but there is a growing number of small inns and B&Bs, with several notable ones having opened in the past year. As most of the larger hotels are well maintained, with packages available through travel agents, we will focus on the smaller, more unique accommodations available in Cabo San Lucas.

### VERY EXPENSIVE

**Solmar Suites** 🏖🏖    Set against sandstone cliffs at the very tip of the Baja Peninsula, the Solmar is beloved by those seeking seclusion, comfort, and easy access to Cabo's diversions. The suites are in two-story white stucco buildings along the edge of a broad beach and have either a king or two double beds, satellite TV, separate seating areas, and private balconies or patios on the sand. Guests gather by the pool and on the beach at sunset and all day long during the winter whale migration. Advance reservations are necessary almost year-round. A small time-share complex adjoins the Solmar; some units are available for nightly stays. Rates below include the hotel's mandatory 10% service charge.

Av. Solmar 1, 23410 Cabo San Lucas, B.C.S. ℂ **1/143-3535.** Fax 1/143-0410 www.solmar.com. (Reservations: Box 383, Pacific Palisades, CA 90272; ℂ **800/ 344-3349** or 310/459-9861; fax 310/454-1686.) 194 units. $165–$433 suite. AE, MC, V. **Amenities:** 1 restaurant, with a Mexican fiesta held each Saturday night; 3 pools, 1 with a swim-up bar facing the palapa-covered beach bar; the Solmar has one of the best sportfishing fleets in Los Cabos, including the deluxe *Solmar V* used for long-range diving, fishing, and whale-watching expeditions; concierge, tour desk, car-rental desk, salon, room service; laundry and dry cleaning services. *In room:* A/C, TV, dataport, minibar, coffeemaker, hair dryer, safe-deposit boxes.

### MODERATE

**The Bungalows** 🏖🏖    One of the most special places to stay in Los Cabos, each "bungalow" is a charming retreat decorated with authentic Mexican furnishings. Terra-cotta tiles, hand-painted sinks, wooded chests, blown glass, and other creative touches make you feel as if you're a guest at a friend's home, rather than in a hotel. Each room has a minikitchenette, plus private bath, purified water, TV with VCR, and designer bedding. The varied rooms, which include 8 one-bedroom suites, 2 one-bedroom deluxe suites, and 6 two-bedroom bungalows, surround a lovely heated pool with cushioned lounges and tropical gardens. Fountains and flowers are found throughout the grounds, and a brick-paved breakfast nook serves a complete gourmet breakfast daily, complemented by fresh-ground coffee and fresh juices—it's also where guests become friends, and share travel tips and experiences. Under owner Steve's warm and welcoming management, this is Cabo's most spacious, comfortable, full-service inn, with service that is exceptionally helpful. A 100% smoke-free environment, it is located 5 blocks from downtown Cabo.

Miguel A. Herrera s/n, in front of Lienzo Charro, 23410 Cabo San Lucas, B.C.S. ℂ/fax **1/143-5035**, or 1/143-0585. www.cabobungalows.com. 16 units. $90 double; $100–$110 suites. Rates include complimentary breakfast. Ask for summer promotions. AE. Street parking available. **Amenities:** Breakfast room (included); pool; concierge; tour desk. *In room:* A/C, TV, dataport, minifridge, coffeemaker.

**Los Milagros** ⟁   The elegant white two-level buildings that contain the 11 suites and rooms of Los Milagros (The Miracles) border either a grassy garden area or small pool. Rooms are each different, but all are decorated with contemporary iron beds with straw headboards, buff-colored tile floors, and artistic details. Some units have kitchenettes, and the master suite has a sunken tub. E-mail, fax, and telephone service are available through the office only, and there's coffee service in the mornings on the patio. Evenings are romantic, as the garden is lit with candles, and classical music plays. Request a room in one of the back buildings, as conversational noise is less intrusive. It's located just a block and a half from the Giggling Marlin and Cabo Wabo.

Matamoros 116, 23410 Cabo San Lucas, B.C.S. ℂ/fax **1/143-4566.** www. losmilagroshotel.com. 11 units. $75 double; ask for summer discounts, group rates, and long-term discounts. No credit cards. Limited street parking. **Amenities:** Small pool. *In-room:* A/C.

## INEXPENSIVE

**Cabo Inn** ⟁⟁ *(Finds)*   This three-story hotel on a quiet street is a real find, and keeps getting better. It's a rare combination of low rates, extra-friendly management, and great, funky style—not to mention extra clean. Rooms are basic and very small; although this was a bordello in a prior incarnation, everything is new, from the mattresses to the minirefrigerators that are found in the rooms on the lower level. Muted desert colors add a spark of personality, and rooms come with either two twin beds or one queen bed. The rooms surround a courtyard where you can enjoy satellite TV, a barbecue grill, and free coffee. The third floor has a rooftop terrace with palapa and a small swimming pool. Also on this floor is Juan's Love Palace, a.k.a. the honeymoon suite. It's a colorful, palapa-topped, open-air room with hanging *tapetes* (woven palm mats) for additional privacy. A large fish freezer is available, as are kitchenettes in most rooms. The hotel's just 2 blocks from downtown and the marina. A lively restaurant next door will even deliver pitchers of margaritas and dinner to your room.

20 de Noviembre and Leona Vicario, 23410 Cabo San Lucas, B.C.S. ©/fax 1/143-0819. www.mexonline.com/caboinn.htm. 20 units. $58 double; $330 double weekly, low season only. No credit cards. Street parking available. **Amenities:** Communal TV and barbecue; small rooftop pool. *In room:* A/C.

### Chile Pepper Inn ★ *Value*    This bright-yellow stucco building contains simple but very tasteful rooms surrounding a common courtyard. One of the best values in town, Chile Pepper is for those who only need a room for sleeping, but want that room to be clean, stylish, and well-appointed. Light wood furnishings are of the hand-carved, rustic variety so popular in Mexico. Palm mats line the floors, and muslin curtains cover the windows that open onto the courtyard. The beds have top-quality orthopedic mattresses and colorful cotton designer bedding, while the bathrooms, although small, are decorated in painted tiles with Talavera sinks. Individual air-conditioning units are new and quiet, the in-room phones offer free local calls, and DirecTV has a large variety of U.S. channels for viewing. The one suite has two queen beds in an L-shaped room. It's located on a quiet street, but still close to Cabo's nightlife action.

16 de Septiembre and Abasolo, 23410 Cabo San Lucas, B.C.S.; ©/fax 1/143-0510 or 1/143-8611. www.chilepepperinn.com. 9 units including 1 master suite. $59 double; $85 suite. AE, MC, V. Street parking available. *In-room:* A/C, TV.

### Siesta Suites    Reservations are a must at this immaculate small inn, which opened in early 1994. The rooms have white tile floors and white walls, kitchenettes with seating areas, refrigerators, and sinks. The mattresses are firm, and the bathrooms are large and sparkling clean. Rooms on the fourth floor have two queen beds each. The accommodating proprietors offer free movies and VCRs, and a comfortable lobby with TV. They can also arrange fishing trips. Weekly and monthly rates are available. The hotel is 1½ blocks from the marina, where parking is available.

Zapata at Hidalgo, 23410 Cabo San Lucas, B.C.S. ©/fax 1/143-2773. siesta@1cabonet.net.mx. 20 suites (15 with kitchenette). $55 double. No credit cards. **Amenities:** Tour desk; VCR and movie library. *In room:* A/C, TV.

# WHERE TO DINE

It's not uncommon to pay a lot for mediocre food in Cabo, so try to get a couple of unbiased recommendations before settling in for a meal. If people are only drinking and not dining, take that as a clue, since many seemingly popular places are long on party atmosphere but short on food. Prices decrease the farther you walk inland from the waterfront. Streets to explore for other good restaurants include Hidalgo and Cárdenas, plus the Marina at the Plaza Bonita. The expected U.S. franchise chains (Kentucky Fried Chicken, Subway, Pizza Hut, etc.) proliferate downtown. Note that many restaurants automatically add the tip to the bill.

## VERY EXPENSIVE

**Casa Rafael's** ✿ INTERNATIONAL  Looking for a little romance? Casa Rafael's, although overpriced, is considered among the most romantic places in Cabo. The chef produces innovative specialties that have become a mainstay of repeat visitors to Los Cabos. Dine in one of the candlelit rooms and alcoves (air-conditioned) of this large house, or outside beside the small swimming pool. Piano music plays in the background while you enjoy a leisurely meal; the courses are timed not to rush you. To start, try the sublime smoked dorado paté, or perhaps the hearts of palm with a raspberry vinaigrette dressing. House specialties—a tasty combination of selections from the meat, seafood, and pasta menus—include the Chicken Parmesan Sonia and scampi with pasta. Steaks are made from black Angus cattle imported from the United States; the lamb comes from New England. The rich desserts may make you wish you'd seen them first before stuffing yourself on the entrees. Wine and aperitif menus are extensive. To find Casa Rafael's, follow Hacienda Road toward the ocean; when you top the hill, look left and turn left when you see the rosy-pink château with arched front and patio with caged birds and fountain.

Calle Medano and Camino el Pescador. ✆ 1/143-0739. www.allaboutcabo.com. casarafa@cabonet.net.mx. Reservations suggested. Main courses $19–$52. Menu prices do not include 10% tax or 15% tip. AE, MC, V. Daily 6–10pm.

## EXPENSIVE

**Nick-San** ✿✿✿ JAPANESE/SUSHI  Exceptional Japanese cuisine and sushi are the specialties in this air-conditioned restaurant with a clean, minimalist decor. A rosewood sushi bar with royal-blue-tiled accents welcomes diners to watch the master sushi chef at work. An exhibition kitchen behind him demonstrates why this place has been honored with a special award for cleanliness.

Blvd. Marina, Plaza de la Danza, Local no. 2. ℂ 1/143-4484. Reservations recommended. Main courses $12–$25; sushi $3.50 and up. MC, V. Tues–Sun
11:30am–10:30pm.

**Peacocks** 𝓡𝓡 INTERNATIONAL    One of Cabo's most exclusive patio-dining establishments, Peacocks emphasizes fresh seafood,
creatively prepared. Start off with the house paté or a salad of feta
cheese with cucumber, tomato, and onion. For a main course, try
one of the pastas—linguini with grilled chicken and sun-dried
tomatoes is a good choice. More filling entrees include steaks,
shrimp, and lamb, all prepared several ways.

Paseo del Pescador s/n, corner of Melia Hotel. ℂ1/143-1858. Reservations recommended. Main courses $15–$30. AE, MC, V. Daily 6–10:30pm.

## MODERATE

**La Dolce** 𝓡𝓡 ITALIAN    This Cabo restaurant is the offspring of
Puerto Vallarta's La Dolce Vita, with authentic Italian thin-crust,
brick-oven pizzas and other specialties. The food is some of the best
you'll find in the Baja Peninsula, and the fact that 80% of their business is from local customers underscores the point. Partner Stefano
(a dead-ringer for Michaelangelo's *David,* albeit with pants) keeps
the service attentive and welcoming, and the food up to the high
standards it's known for. The simple menu also features sumptuous
pastas and calzones, plus great salads. This is the best late-night dining option.

M. Hidalgo y Zapata s/n. ℂ 1/143-4122. Main courses $8–$14. No credit cards.
Mon–Sat 6pm–midnight. Closed Sept.

**Mi Casa** 𝓡 MEXICAN/NOUVELLE MEXICAN    The building's vivid cobalt-blue facade is your first clue that this place
celebrates Mexico; the menu confirms that impression. This is one
of Cabo's most renowned gourmet Mexican restaurants. Traditional
specialties such as *manchamanteles* (literally, "tablecloth stainers"),
*cochinita pibil,* and *chiles en nogada* are everyday menu staples. Fresh
fish is prepared with delicious seasonings and recipes from throughout Mexico. Especially pleasant at night, the restaurant's tables, scattered around a large patio, are set with colorful cloths, traditional
pottery, and glassware. It's across from the main plaza.

Calle Cabo San Lucas at Madero. ℂ 1/143-1933. Reservations recommended.
Main courses $15–$25. AE, MC, V. High season Mon–Sat noon–10:30pm; low season Mon–Sat 5–10pm.

## INEXPENSIVE

**Cafe Canela** COFFEE/PASTRY/LIGHT MEALS This cozy, tasty cafe and bistro is a welcome addition to the Cabo Marina boardwalk. Espresso drinks or a fruit smoothie and a muffin are good eye-openers for early risers. Enjoy a light meal or a tropical drink either inside or on the bustling waterfront terrace. The appealing menu also offers breakfast egg wraps, salads (curried chicken salad with fresh fruit), sandwiches (blue-cheese quesadillas with smoked tuna and mango), and pastas, all reasonably priced. There's full bar service, also.

On the Marina boardwalk, below Plaza Las Glorias hotel. Local 32 y 33. ℂ1/143-3435. Main courses $4–$9; coffee $1.75–$3.50. AE, MC, V. Daily 7am–4:30pm.

**Felix's** 𝕣𝕣 MEXICAN This colorful, friendly family-run place has grown up since opening in 1958, from just serving tacos to offering a full array of tasty Mexican and seafood dishes—among the best eats in Cabo. Everything's fresh and homemade, including the corn tortillas and the numerous and varied salsas—more than 30!—served from their own salsa bar. Fish tacos made with fresh dorado are superb, as are any of their shrimp dishes—especially tasty are the honey-mustard shrimp. Don't leave without someone at your table sampling Felix's original recipe for Mexican bouillabaisse, a rich stew of shrimp, crab, sea bass, scallops, Italian sausage, and savory seasonings. Mexican specialties include carne asada with a chile verde sauce and chimichangas. A year back, Felix's combined space with the family's other Cabo dining institution, Mama Royal's, and now offers a casual dining area and outdoor shaded patio. They offer full bar service, but their specialties are their fresh-fruit margaritas and daiquiris, just $2.50 each.

Hidalgo and Zapata s/n, in the same location as Mama's Royal Café (its name for breakfast service). ℂ 1/143-4290. Main courses $8–$15. MC, V. Mon–Sat 3–10pm.

**Mama's Royale Café** 𝕣𝕣 BREAKFAST What a great place to start the day! The shady patio decked with cloth-covered tables and the bright, inviting interior dining room are both comfortable places to settle in. And the food's just as appetizing. Effrain and Pedro preside over this dining mecca with well-prepared breakfast selections that include grilled sausage, French toast stuffed with cream cheese and topped with pecans, strawberries, and orange liqueur; several variations of eggs Benedict, home fries, fruit crepes, and, of course, traditional breakfasts, plus free coffee refills. The orange juice is fresh squeezed, and there usually is live marimba or mariachi music, performed by a regular group of strolling musicians, to get your morning off to a lively start.

Hidalgo at Zapata. © 1/143-4290. Breakfast special $2.50; breakfast a la carte $2.50–$10. MC, V. Wed–Mon 7:30am–1pm.

**Mocambo's** 𝒜𝒜 SEAFOOD    The new location of this long-standing Cabo favorite is not much to inspire dining—it's basically a large cement building—but the food obviously does. The place is always packed, and generally with local diners tired of high prices and small portions. Ocean-fresh seafood is the order of the day here, and their specialty platter can easily serve the healthy appetites of four people. The restaurant is a block and a half inland from Lázaro Cárdenas.

Leona Vicario and 20 de Noviembre. © 1/143-6070. Main courses $5–$23. No credit cards. Daily 1:30am–10pm.

## CABO SAN LUCAS AFTER DARK

Cabo San Lucas is the nightlife capital of Baja and a contender within resort Mexico. After-dark fun is centered around the party ambience and camaraderie found in the casual bars and restaurants on Blvd. Marina or facing the marina, rather than around a flashy disco scene. You can easily find a happy hour with live music and a place to dance, or a Mexican fiesta with mariachis.

**MEXICAN FIESTAS & THEME NIGHTS**    Some of the larger hotels have weekly Fiesta Nights, Italian Nights, and other buffet-plus-entertainment theme nights that can be fun as well as a good buy. Check travel agencies and the following hotels: the **Solmar** (© 1/143-3535), the **Finisterra** (© 1/143-0000), the **Hacienda** (© 1/143-0123), and the **Melia San Lucas** (© 1/143-0420). Prices range from $16 (drinks, tax, and tips are extra) to $35 (which covers everything, including an open bar with national drinks).

**SUNSET WATCHING**    At twilight, check out Land's End, where the two seas meet, and watch the sun sink into the Pacific.

**WHALE WATCHER'S BAR**    This is Los Cabo's premier place for sunset watching. Its location at Land's End—where the two seas meet—offers a truly world-class view of the sun sinking into the Pacific. The high terrace offers vistas of both sea and beach, as well as magical glimpses of whales from January to March. Mariachis play on Friday, from 6:30 to 9pm. The bar is open daily from 10am to 11pm. "Whale margaritas" cost $4; beer, $3. There are two-for-one drinks during happy hour from 4 to 6pm. In the Hotel Finisterra. ☎1/143-3333. Fax 1/143-0590. AE, DC, MC, V.

**HAPPY HOURS & HANGOUTS**    If you shop around, you can usually find an *hora alegre* (happy hour) somewhere in town between noon and 7pm. On our last visit, the most popular places to drink and carouse until all hours were the Giggling Marlin, El Squid Roe, and the Cabo Wabo Cantina.

Two places to enjoy live music in a more "adult" setting are the **Sancho Panza Wine Bistro** (☎ 1/143-3212; see description below), and the new **Jazz on the Rocks** restaurant and live jazz bar, on Zaragoza at the corner of Niños Heroes (☎ 1/143-8999). Both offer classic jazz in more of a club-style atmosphere, accommodating of conversations.

**El Squid Roe**    El Squid Roe is one of the late Carlos Anderson's inspirations, and it still attracts wild, fun-loving crowds of all ages with its two stories of nostalgic decor and eclectic food that's far better than you'd expect from such a party place. As fashionable as blue jeans, this is a place to see and see what can be seen—women's tops are known to be discarded with regularity here, as the dancing on tables moves into high gear. There's also a patio out back for dancing when the tables, chairs, and bar spots have all been taken. Open daily from noon to 2am. Blvd. Marina, opposite Plaza Bonita. ☎ 1/143-0655. No cover.

**Giggling Marlin**    Live music alternates with recorded tunes to get the happy patrons dancing—and occasionally jumping up to dance on the tables and bar. A contraption of winches, ropes, and pulleys above a mattress provides entertainment as couples literally string each other up by the heels—just like a captured marlin. The food is only fair here; stick with nachos and drinks. There is live music Wednesday through Sunday from 9pm to midnight during high season. The Giggling Marlin is open daily from 8am to 1am. Beer is $1.75 to $2.50; schooner margaritas cost $4 to $6. Drinks are half-price during happy hour, from 2 to 6pm. On Cárdenas at Zaragoza, across from the marina. ☎1/143-0606. www.gigglingmarlin.com. No cover.

**Latitude 22+**    This raffish restaurant/bar never closes. License plates, signs, sports caps, and a 959-pound blue marlin are the backdrop for U.S. sports events that play on six TVs scattered among pool tables, dart boards, and assorted games. Dishes from hamburgers to chicken-fried steak are offered, or you can have breakfast any time. Latitude 22+ is 1 block north of the town's only traffic light. Blvd. Cárdenas.sin Numero ✆ 1/143-1516. Happy hour is 4 to 6pm.

**Sancho Panza Wine Bar and Bistro**    Finally, an alternative to beer bars. Sancho Panza combines a gourmet food market with a wine bar that features live jazz music plus an intriguing menu of Nuevo Latino cuisine. The place has a cozy neighborhood feeling, with tourists and locals taking advantage of the selection of more than 150 wines, plus espresso drinks. During high season, reservations are needed. Plaza las Glorias boardwalk, next to the Lighthouse. ✆ 1/143-3212. www.sanchopanza.com. Mon–Sat 3–midnight. No cover.

## DANCING

**Cabo Wabo Cantina**    Owned by Sammy Hagar (formerly of Van Halen) and his Mexican and American partners, this "cantina" packs in youthful crowds, especially when rumors fly that a surprise appearance by a vacationing musician is imminent. Live rock bands from the United States, Mexico, Europe, and Australia perform frequently on the well-equipped stage. When live music is absent, a disco-type sound system plays mostly rock but some alternative and techno as well. Overstuffed furniture frames the dance floor. For snacks, the Taco-Wabo, just outside the club's entrance, stays up late, too. The cantina is open from 11am to 4am. Vicente Guerrero at Cárdenas. ✆ 1/143-1188. No cover. Beer $3.00, margaritas $5. Live-music shows.

**Kokomo**    Lively and tropical in theme and spirit, Kokomo is gaining in popularity as a happening dance club. They serve lunch and dinner, but the drinks are better than the food. A happy hour features two-for-one drinks daily from 4 to 6pm. Grab a table along the oversized windows looking out over Blvd. Marina for people-watching. Open daily from 7am to 3am. Blvd. Marina s/n. Colonia Centro. ✆1/143-0600. kokomo@cabonet.net.mx. No cover. MC, V.

**MEN'S CLUBS**    Or should they be called "ladies' clubs," since that's who's doing the dancing? In any event, there's now a selection of places in Cabo that offer so-called exotic dancing. **Lord Black,** Blvd. Marina in the Plaza Náutica (✆ 1/143-5415), features not only showgirls, but sushi, too. **Showgirls 20,** corner of Lázaro Cárdenas and Francisco Villa (✆ 1/143-5380), calls itself a world-class cabaret. It also offers pool tables, satellite TVs, and private dancers. It's open from 8:30pm to 3am, has a cover charge of $6, and accepts major credit cards. It's located across the street from McDonald's.

## 4 North from Los Cabos

The coastline of the Sea of Cortez north of San José has long been a favored destination of die-hard anglers, who fly their private planes to airstrips at out-of-the-way lodges. The coastline has experienced considerable development in the past few years, and hotels have expanded their services to please even those who never plan to set foot on a boat. Housing developments are appearing along the main road, but there's still plenty of space for adventurous campers to find secluded beaches.

A rough dirt road, called the Coastal Road, runs along the east cape from San José to La Ribera; completing the 55-mile drive can take up to 4 hours. Along this route you pass by Cabo Pulmo, where Baja's only coral reef lies just offshore. There are no major hotels, restaurants, or dive shops here, and most divers reach the reefs via dive boats from Los Cabos. The more efficient approach to the east cape is to drive the paved Highway 1 from San José north to dirt roads leading off the highway to resorts and communities at Punta Colorado, Buena Vista, Los Barriles, and Punta Pescadero. Public buses from San José stop at major intersections, where you'll need to catch a cab to the hotels. Most guests who stay at the more secluded hotels take a cab from the airport and simply remain at the hotel.

### WHERE TO STAY & DINE

**Rancho Buena Vista**    A fishing resort with no pretensions, Rancho Buena Vista has several one-story bungalows spread about the grounds. The simple rooms have red-tiled floors, good showers, double beds, and small patios in front. Hammocks hang under palms and by the swimming pool, and the bar/restaurant is the center of the action. The hotel has an excellent deep-sea fishing fleet with its own dock, and a private airstrip.

Hwy. 1 at Buena Vista, 35 miles north of San José del Cabo. ©1/141-0177. Fax 1/141-0055. (Reservations: P.O. Box 1408, Santa Maria, CA 93456; ©800/258-8200 outside CA, or 805/928-1719; fax 805/925-2990.) 55 units. $170 double. Rates include 3 meals daily. MC, V. **Amenities:** Restaurant/bar; swimming pool; fishing charters; tour desk. *In room:* A/C.

## 5 Todos Santos: A Creative Oasis ★★★

42 miles N of Cabo San Lucas

A few years back, Todos Santos became known as "Bohemian Baja." It found its way on the travel agendas of those looking for the latest, the trendiest, and the hippest of artist outposts—or of those simply weary of the L.A.-ization of Cabo San Lucas. It didn't take long for it to unfold as a true gem of a place that seems to foster the creative spirit, while retaining the pervasive beauty and lovely heritage that held the original attraction.

The art and artistry created here now—from the culinary to the canvas—is of an evolved type that seems to care less about commercial appeal than quality, and in doing so, becomes more of a draw. Not to be overlooked are the attendant arts of agriculture, masonry, or weavings created by some of the town's original residents. From the superb meals at **Café Santa Fe** to an afternoon spent browsing at **El Tecolote Libros,** the best bookstore I've come across in Mexico, Todos Santos is intriguing to its core.

Not only is the town a cultural oasis in Baja, but an oasis in the true sense of the word—in this desert landscape Todos Santos enjoys an almost continuous water supply that stems from the peaks of the Sierra de la Laguna mountains. It's just over an hour's drive up the Pacific coast from Cabo San Lucas; you'll know you've arrived when the arid coastal scenery is suddenly interrupted by the verdant groves of palms, mangos, avocados, and papayas.

During the Mission Period of Baja, this oasis valley was deemed to be the only area south and west of La Paz worth settling, as it had the only reliable water supply. In 1723, an outpost mission was established, followed by the full-fledged Misión Santa Rosa de Las Palmas in 1733, endowed by one of Spain's leading families. The town, at the time, was known as Santa Rosa de Todos Santos, eventually shortened to its current name, which translates as "All Saints."

Over the next 200 years, the town alternated between prosperity and difficulty, reflecting the ebb and flow of Spanish conquest, mission conversion, Mexico's struggle for independence from Spain, the Mexican-American War of 1833, and Mexico's Revolution of 1910. Its most recent boom lasted from the mid-19th century until the 1950s, when the town prospered as a sugarcane production center and began to develop a strong cultural core. Many of the buildings now being restored and converted into galleries, studios, shops, and restaurants were built during this era. As the water table began to dry up, financial decline followed the cessation of sugarcane production. It wasn't until the 1980s that a paved road connected Todos Santos with La Paz, and tourism began to draw new attention to this tranquil town.

Demand for the town's older colonial-style structures by artists, entrepreneurs, and foreign residents has resulted in a real estate boom. New shops, galleries, and cafes are continuously cropping up. The coastal strip south of Todos Santos is in the process of being developed, with its first luxury hotel and spa slated to open in 2002. For the casual visitor, Todos Santos can easily be explored in a day, but a few tranquil inns welcome charmed guests who want to stay a little longer.

## WHAT TO DO IN TODOS SANTOS

During the **Festival Fundidor** (Oct 10 through 14), which celebrates the founding of the town in 1723, streets around the main plaza are filled with food, games, and wandering troubadours. Many of the shops and the Café Santa Fe are closed from the end of September through the festival. Todos Santos is a good stopover for those traveling between Cabo and La Paz; a day's visit can be arranged through tour companies in Los Cabos or done on your own with a rental car.

There are at least half a dozen galleries in town, including the noted **Galería de Todos Santos,** corner of Topete and Legaspi (© 1/145-0040), which features a changing collection of works by regional artists. The **Galería Santa Fe,** Centenario, across from the Plaza (© 1/145-0340) holds an eclectic collection of truly original and creative Mexican folk art and *artesanía* treasures that include Frida-adorned frames, and "shrines"—kid-sized chairs decorated in bottle caps, Virgin of Guadalupe images, *milagros,* and more. It's open Wednesday to Monday, from 10am to 5pm.

**El Tecolote Libros** 𝕽𝕽𝕽 (© 1/145-0295), though tiny, gets our vote for the best bookstore in Mexico, due to its exceptional selection of Latin American literature, poetry, children's books, and reference books centering on Mexico. Both English and Spanish editions, new and used, are offered up here along with maps,

---

*Fun Fact* **You Can Check Out Any Time You Like . . .**

In Todos Santos, the most renowned accommodation is the **Hotel California,** alleged namesake of the famous Eagles song. The hotel was originally constructed in 1928, in part from planks salvaged from a shipwrecked Norwegian vessel. Currently closed for a complete renovation, it's still worth a walk by—you'll find it on Calle Juárez Colonia Centro between Morelos and Marquez de León.

---

magazines, cards, and art supplies. Information on upcoming writing workshops and local reading groups is also posted here. The shop is located on the corner of Hidalgo and Juárez. It's open Monday to Saturday from 9am to 5pm, and Sunday from 10am to 3pm.

## WHERE TO STAY

Consider the **Todos Santos Inn** ⭐⭐⭐ (Calle Legaspi 33, between Topete and Obregón; ℂ1/145-0040). An impeccable place to stay, it is located in a historic house that has served, in turn, as a general store, cantina, school, and private residence, before becoming this elegant inn. Details include luxurious white bed linens, netting draped romantically over the beds, Talavera-tile bathrooms, antique furniture, and high, wood-beamed ceilings. Only two rooms and two suites border a courtyard terrace and garden, but owner Robert Whiting plans to add a few more. Rates run from $85 to $120 per night. The suites are air-conditioned, but expect neither television nor telephone to interrupt your relaxed stay. Currently no credit cards are accepted, but that could soon change. Seasonal discounts are available, but the inn closes for the month of September.

## WHERE TO DINE

For us—and we would suspect for many others—a meal at the **Café Santa Fe,** ⭐⭐⭐ Calle Centenario no. 4 (ℂ1/145-0340), is reason enough to visit Todos Santos. Much of the attention the town has received in recent years can be directly attributed to this outstanding cafe, and it continues to live up to its lofty reputation. Owners Ezio and Paula Colombo refurbished a large stucco house across from the plaza, creating an exhibition kitchen, several dining rooms, and a lovely courtyard adjacent to a garden of hibiscus, bougainvillea, papaya trees, and herbs.

Our favorite of the interior rooms is the one in homage to Frida Kahlo, with reproductions of her work on grand canvases that flatter her more than her originals. The excellent Northern Italian cuisine emphasizes local produce and seafood. Try the homemade ravioli stuffed with spinach and ricotta in a Gorgonzola sauce or the ravioli with lobster and shrimp, accompanied by one of their organic salads. Simply put, a meal here is likely to be one of the best you will have anywhere, at any price. In high season the wait for a table at lunch can last quite a while. Everything is prepared fresh when ordered, and reservations are recommended. Main courses run between $10 and $15. It's open Wednesday through Monday from noon to 9pm; closed September 29 to October 18.

A more casual option, and a magical place to start a day here, is the garden setting of the **Caffé Todos Santos,** Calle Centenario 33, located across from the Todos Santos Inn (© **1/145-0300**). Among the espresso drinks served is their bowl-sized café latte, to be accompanied by a freshly baked croissant or one of their signature cinnamon buns. Lunch or a light meal may include a frittata, or fish filet wrapped in banana leaves with coconut milk. Main courses average $3 to $6, and the cafe is open Tuesday through Sunday from 7am to 9pm, Monday from 7am to 2pm.

# La Paz: Peaceful Port Town

La Paz means "peace," and the feeling seems to float on the ocean breezes of this provincial Mexican town. Despite being an important port town of almost 200,000 inhabitants and the capital of the state of Baja California Sur, La Paz remains slow-paced and relaxed. It's an easygoing yet sophisticated city and the guardian of "old Baja" atmosphere, with beautiful deserted beaches just minutes away that complement the lively beach and palm-fringed *malecón* (sea wall) that fronts the town center.

The presence of the University of South Baja California has added a unique cultural element that includes museums, a theater, and an arts center. The surrounding tropical desert diversity and uncommon wildlife are also compelling reasons to visit, and lend themselves to countless options for adventurous travelers, including hiking, rock climbing, diving, fishing, and sea kayaking. Islands and islets sit just offshore; once the hiding place for looting pirates, they now are a place for kayakers and beachcombers. At Espírito Santo and Los Islotes, it's possible to swim with sea lions.

Despite its name, La Paz has been a historic place of conflict between explorers and indigenous populations, traders, and pirates. Beginning in 1535, Spanish conquistadors and Jesuit missionaries arrived, leaving their influence on the architecture and traditions of La Paz. From its founding—when conquistadors saw local Indians wearing pearl ornaments—through the late 1930s when an unknown disease killed off the oysters in the Bay of La Paz, this was the center of world pearl harvesting. Writer John Steinbeck immortalized a local legend of La Paz pearling in his novella *The Pearl*.

La Paz is ideal for anyone nostalgic for Los Cabos the way it used to be, before the development and burgeoning crowds. From accommodations to taxis, it's also one of Mexico's most outstanding beach-vacation values and a great place for family travelers.

# La Paz Area

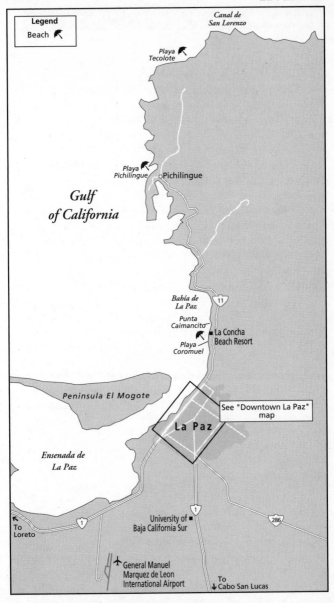

Legend
Beach

Canal de
San Lorenzo

Playa
Tecolote

Playa
Pichilingue

○ Pichilingue

Gulf
of California

Bahía de
La Paz

Punta
Caimancito

La Concha
Beach Resort

Playa
Coromuel

Peninsula El Mogote

See "Downtown La Paz"
map

La Paz

Ensenada de
La Paz

To
Loreto

11

1

286

University of
Baja California Sur

General Manuel
Marquez de Leon
International Airport

To
Cabo San Lucas

## 1 Essentials

110 miles N of Cabo San Lucas; 122 miles NW of San José del Cabo; 980 miles SE of Tijuana

## GETTING THERE & DEPARTING

**BY PLANE    AeroCalifornia** (© **800/237-6225** in the U.S., or 1/125-1023) has flights to La Paz from Los Angeles, Tijuana, and Mexico City. Aeromexico (© **800/237-6639** in the U.S., 1/122-0091, 1/122-0093, or 1/122-1636) connects through Tucson and Los Angeles in the United States, and also flies in from Mexico City, Guadalajara, Tijuana, and other points within Mexico.

**BY CAR**    From San José del Cabo, Highway 1 north is the longer, more scenic route; you can travel a flatter, faster route by taking Highway 1 east to Cabo San Lucas, then Highway 19 north through Todos Santos. A little before San Pedro, Highway 19 rejoins Highway 1 north into La Paz; the trip takes 2 to 3 hours. From the north, Highway 1 south is the only choice; the trip takes 4 to 5 hours.

**BY BUS**    The Central Camionera (main bus station) is at Jalisco and Héroes de la Independencia, about 25 blocks southwest of the center of town; it's open daily from 6am to 10pm. The bus lines serve La Paz with buses from the south (Los Cabos, 2½ to 3½ hr.) and north (as far as Tijuana). It's best to buy your ticket in person the day before, though reservations can be made over the phone. Taxis are available in front of the station.

All routes north and south, as well as buses to Pichilingue, the ferry pier, and close to outlying beaches, are available through the Aguila-line station, sometimes called the "beach bus terminal," located on the malecón at Alvaro Obregón and Cinco de Mayo (© **1/122-7898**). The station is open daily from 6am to 8pm. Buses to Pichilingue depart every hour.

**BY FERRY**    Two SEMATUR car ferries serve La Paz from Topolobampo (the port for Los Mochis) Monday through Saturday at 10pm (a 10-hr. trip), and from Mazatlán Sunday through Friday at 3pm (an 18-hr. crossing). In La Paz, tickets are sold at the SEMATUR office at Cinco de Mayo no. 502.

The SEMATUR car ferry departs for Topolobampo Monday and Wednesday through Saturday at 11am, and for Mazatlán Sunday through Friday at 3pm. The dock is at Pichilingue, 11 miles north of La Paz. Passengers pay one fee for themselves and another for their vehicles, with prices for cars varying, depending on the size of the car.

> ### *Tips*  Taking Your Car to the Mainland
>
> Those planning to take their cars on the ferry to the Mexican mainland will be required to meet all the requirements listed in chapter 1, "Planning a Trip to Baja California" (see "Getting There by Car," in that chapter), and all travelers going to the mainland need Tourist Cards.
>
> Tourism officials in La Paz say that Tourist Cards are available only in Mexicali, Tecate, Tijuana, Ensenada, and Guerrero Negro, and not in La Paz, although car permits to cross over into the mainland can be issued there. If you do happen to make it down Baja as far as La Paz, or anywhere outside the frontier zone, and are found not to have a Tourist Permit (FMT), you are subject to a fine of $40.

Least expensive is *salon* class with about 440 bus-type seats ($20 to Mazatlán) in one or more large rooms on the lower deck; these rooms can become very crowded. *Turista* class ($41 to Mazatlán) is next, providing a tiny room with four bunks, a chair, sink, and window, and individual bathrooms/showers down the hall. *Cabina* class ($62 to Mazatlán) is the best, with a small room with one bunk, chair, table, window, and private bathroom. *Note:* Not all these classes are available all the time, and ferry schedules change.

SEMATUR ferries are usually, but not always, equipped with a cafeteria and bar. Also, reserve as early as possible and confirm your reservation 24 hours before departure; you can pick up tickets at the port terminal ticket office as late as the morning of the day you are leaving. Ferry tickets are sold at the office of **Agencia de Viajes Aome,** Cinco de Mayo no. 502 at Guillermo Prieto in La Paz (℡ **1/125-2346,** ext. 104), the only agency in La Paz authorized to sell ferry tickets. The office is open daily from 8am to 6pm. For information only, call ℡ **1/125-6588.** Several tour agencies in town book reservations on the ferry, but it is best to buy your ticket in person at the ferry office. For information, you can also call ℡ **01/800/696-9600,** toll-free within Mexico.

Buses to Pichilingue depart from the beach bus terminal of **Transportes Aguila** (℡ **1/122-7898**) on the malecón at Independencia on the hour, from 7am to 6pm, and cost $1.50 each way.

## ORIENTATION
### ARRIVING

**BY PLANE**    The airport is 11 miles northwest of town along the highway to Ciudad Constitución and Tijuana. Airport *colectivos* (minivans) run only from the airport to town, not vice versa. Taxi service is available as well. Most major car-rental agencies have booths inside the airport. Two local numbers are **Budget** (℗ 1/124-6433 or 1/123-3622), and **Local Car Rental,** Alvaro Obregón 582 (℗ 1/123-3622).

**BY BUS**    Buses arrive at the Central Camionera, about 25 blocks southwest of downtown, or at the beach station along the malecón. Taxis line up in front of both.

**BY FERRY**    Buses line up in front of the ferry dock at Pichilingue to meet every arriving ferry. They stop at the beach bus station on the malecón at Independencia; it's within walking distance of many downtown hotels if you're not encumbered with luggage. Taxis meet each ferry as well and cost about $8 to downtown La Paz.

### VISITOR INFORMATION

The most accessible visitor information office is on Alvaro Obregón, across from the intersection with Calle 16 de Septiembre (℗ 1/122-5939; turismo@lapaz.cromwell.com.mx). It's open daily from 9am to 8pm. The extremely helpful staff speaks English and can supply information on La Paz, Los Cabos, and the rest of the region. This doubles as the office for the La Paz Tourist Police, who assist with directions or problems that visitors may encounter.

### CITY LAYOUT

Although La Paz sprawls well inland from the malecón (the seaside boulevard, Alvaro Obregón), you'll probably spend most of your

---

### *Moments*  Festivals & Events in La Paz

February features the biggest and best Carnaval/Mardi Gras in Baja, as well as a month-long Festival of the Gray Whale (starting in Feb or March). On May 3 a festival celebrates the city's founding by Cortés in 1535, and features *artesanía* exhibitions from throughout southern Baja. The annual marlin-fishing tournament is in August, with other fishing tournaments scheduled in September and November. And on November 1 and 2, the Days of the Dead, altars are on display at the Anthropology Museum.

time in the older, more congenial downtown section within a few blocks of the waterfront. The main plaza, Plaza Pública (or Jardín Velasco, as it's also called), is bounded by Madero, Independencia, Revolución, and Cinco de Mayo. The plaza centers on an iron kiosk where public concerts frequently are held in the evenings.

## GETTING AROUND

Because most of what you'll need in town is located on the malecón between the tourist information office and the Hotel Los Arcos, or a few blocks inland from the waterfront, it's easy to get around La Paz on foot. There are public buses that go to some of the beaches north of town (see "Beaches & Outdoor Activities," below), but to explore the many beaches within 50 miles of La Paz, your best bet is to rent a car or hire a taxi. There are several car-rental agencies on the malecón.

 **FAST FACTS: La Paz**

**Area Code** The telephone area code is **1**.

**Banks** Banks generally exchange currency during normal business hours: Monday through Friday from 9am to 6pm and Saturday from 10am to 2pm. ATMs are readily available, and offer bank exchange rates on withdrawals.

**Emergencies** Dial **060**.

**Hospitals** Hospital Especialidades Médicas, in the Fidepaz building (✆ **1/124-0400**), and Hospital Juan María de Salvatierra, Nicolas Bravo 1010, Col. Centro (✆ **1/122-1496**).

**Internet Access** BajaNet, Madero 430 (✆ **1/125-9380**) charges 1 peso per minute (10¢), with a $1 minimum (10-min.) charge; open 8am to 8pm Monday through Saturday, Sunday 9am to 7pm.

**Marinas** La Paz has two marinas: **Marina de La Paz,** at the west end of the malecón at Legaspi (✆ **1/125-2112**; marinalapaz@bajavillas.com), and **Marina Palmira,** south of town at Km 2.5 on the Pichilingue Highway Edificio la Plaza (✆ **1/121-6297**; mpalmira@prodigy.net.mx).

**Municipal Market** The public market is three blocks inland, at Degollado and Revolución, and sells mainly produce, meats, and utilitarian wares. Hours are Monday through Saturday 6am to 6pm and Sunday 6am to 1pm.

*Parking* In high season, street parking may be hard to find in the downtown area, but there are several guarded lots, and side streets are less crowded overall.

*Pharmacy* One of the largest pharmacies is **Farmacia Baja California,** Independencia and Madero (✆ **1/122-0240** or 1/123-4408).

*Post Office* The *correo* is 3 blocks inland, at Constitución and Revolución (✆ **1/122-0388**); open Monday through Fri 8am to 7pm, Saturday 9am to 1pm.

*Tourism Office* Located at Km 5.5 Carretera al Norte, Edificio Fidepaz (✆ **1/124-0199**).

## 2 Beaches & Outdoor Activities

La Paz combines the unself-conscious bustle of a small capital port city with beautiful isolated beaches, not far from town. Well on its way to becoming the undisputed adventure-tourism capital of Baja, it's the starting point for whale-watching, diving, sea kayaking, climbing, and hiking tours throughout the peninsula. For those interested in day adventures, everything mentioned above, plus beach tours, sunset cruises, and visits to the sea lion colony can usually be arranged through travel agencies in major hotels or along the malecón. These activities can also be arranged through agencies in the United States that specialize in Baja's natural history. (See "Active Vacations in Baja," in chapter 1.)

### BEACHES

Within a 10- to 45-minute drive from La Paz lie some of the loveliest beaches in Baja, many rivaling those of the Caribbean with their clear, turquoise water.

The beaches that line the **malecón** are the most convenient in town. Although the sand is soft and white, and the water appears crystal clear and gentle, locals don't generally swim there. As a result of the commercial port, the water is not considered to be as clean as that in the very accessible outlying beaches. With colorful children's playgrounds dotting the central beachfront, along with numerous open-air restaurants that front the water, the malecón is best for a casual afternoon of post-sight-seeing lunch and playtime.

The best beach in town is the beach immediately north of town at **La Concha Beach Resort;** nonguests may use the hotel restaurant/

bar and rent equipment for snorkeling, diving, skiing, and sailing. It's 6 miles north of town on the Pichilingue Highway, at Km 5.5. The other beaches are all farther north of town, but midweek you may have these far distant beaches to yourself.

At least 10 public buses from the beach bus station at Independencia on the malecón depart from 8am to 5:30pm for beaches to the north. The buses stop at the small **Playa Camancito** (3.1 miles), **Playa Coromuel** (5 miles), **Playa Tesoro** (8.9 miles), and **Pichilingue** (10.5 miles); from the ferry stop, walk north on the highway to the beach. Ask when the last bus will make the return trip. Pichilingue, Coromuel, and Tesoro beaches have palapa-shaded bars or restaurants, which may not be open midweek. You can pack a lunch and just rent a shade umbrella for $1 per group, with tables and chairs available for a minimum consumption charge.

The most beautiful of these outlying beaches is **Playa Tecolote** 🐾🐾, approximately 18 miles from La Paz at the end of a paved road. The water is a heavenly cerulean blue. There are several restaurants, including the **Club de Playa El Tecolote** (📞 1/122-8885), which also offers a round-trip transportation service for $6 from La Paz area hotels to their restaurant. The club has 30 sun *palapas,* a restaurant, water-sports-equipment rentals, and boat tours to Los Islotes or Espíritu Santo. To get to Playa Tecolote on your own, take a bus as far as Pichilingue; from there, take a taxi the remaining 8 miles. When the taxi drops you off, make arrangements for it to return. The road is paved as far as Playa Tecolote and Playa Balandra (18 miles), and turnoffs to these and other beaches are well marked.

For more information about beaches and maps, check at the tourist information office on the malecón. If you want to take a general tour of all the beaches before deciding where to spend your precious vacation days, **Vamonos Tours** (📞 1/121-6161, ext. 1494) offers a 4-hour beach tour for $18 per person, with stops at Balandra and El Tecolote beaches.

## CRUISES

A popular and very worthwhile cruise is to **Isla Espíritu Santo** and **Los Islotes** to visit the largest sea lion colony in Baja, stunning rock formations, and remote beaches, with stops for snorkeling, swimming, and lunch. If conditions permit, you may even be able to snorkel beside the sea lions. Both boat and bus tours are available to Puerto Balandra, where pristine coves of crystal-blue water and ivory sand are framed by bold rock formations rising up like hump-back whales. The **Jack Velez Travel Agency,** at Hotel Los Arcos (✆ 1/122-2744 or 1/122-2510; ask for the travel agency), **Viajes Palmira** (✆ 1/122-4030) on the malecón across from Hotel Los Arcos, and other travel agencies can arrange these all-day trips, weather permitting, for $65 per person.

## WATER SPORTS

**SCUBA DIVING**    Scuba-diving trips, best from June through September, can be arranged through Fernando Aguilar's **Baja Diving and Services,** at Obregón 1665-2, (✆ 1/122-1826; fax 1/122-8644; bajadiving@lapaz.cromwell.com.mx). Diving sites include the sea lion colony at Los Islotes, distant Cerralvo Island, the sunken ship *Salvatierra,* a 60-foot wall dive, several sea mounts (underwater mountains) and reefs, and a trip to see hammerhead sharks and manta rays. Rates start at $77 to $87 per person for an all-day outing and two-tank dive. They've recently added a sports lodge and beach resort, **Club Hotel Cantamar,** with 16 rooms and 2 suites. Rates run $65 per room for a double, and $100 per suite. **Baja Expeditions,** in La Paz at Sonora 586 (✆ 1/125-3828; fax 1/125-3829; bajaex@balandra.uabcs.mx; open daily 8am to 6pm; see chapter 1, "Planning a Trip to Baja California," for contact information in the U.S. and Canada), runs live-aboard and single-day dive trips to the above-mentioned locations and other areas in the Sea of Cortez. Cost is $110 for a three-tank dive.

**SEA KAYAKING**    Kayaking has become extremely popular in the many bays and coves near La Paz. Many enthusiasts bring their own equipment. Kayaking trips can be arranged in advance with several companies from the United States (see "Active Vacations in Baja," in chapter 1, for more information). Locally, **Mar y Aventuras,** Topete 564, between 5 de Febrero and Navarro (✆ 1/122-7039, or 1/125-4794; www.kayakbaja.com; maryaventuras@lapaz.comwell.com.mx), also arranges kayaking trips.

**SPORTFISHING**    La Paz, justly famous for its sportfishing, attracts anglers from all over the world. Its waters are home to more than 850 species of fish. The most economical approach is to rent a *panga* (skiff) with guide and equipment for $125 for 3 hours (but you don't go very far out). Super pangas, which have a shade cover and comfortable seats, start at around $180 for two people. Larger cruisers with bathrooms start at $240.

Sportfishing trips can be arranged locally through hotels and tour agencies. One of the best-known operations is **Jack Velez's Dorado Velez Fleet;** call him for reservations at the Hotel Los Arcos Fishing Desk (© **1/122-2744,** ask for the fishing trips extension), or write to him at Apdo. Postal 402, 23000 La Paz, B.C.S. Prices start at $140. David Jones of **The Fishermen's Fleet** (© **1/122-1313;** www.fishermensfleet.com; david@lapaz.cromwell.com.mx) uses the locally popular panga-style fishing boat. David is super-professional, speaks English, and truly understands area fishing. Average price is $225 for the boat, but double-check what the price includes, since you may need to bring your own food and drinks.

**WHALE-WATCHING** Between January and March (and sometimes as early as December), 3,000 to 5,000 gray whales migrate from the Bering Strait to the Pacific Coast of Baja. The main whale-watching spots are Laguna San Ignacio (on the Pacific, near San Ignacio), Bahía Magdalena (on the Pacific, near Puerto López Mateos—about a 2-hr. drive from La Paz), and Scammon's Lagoon (near Guerrero Negro).

Although it is located across the peninsula on the Sea of Cortez, La Paz has the only major international airport in the area and thus has become a center of Baja's whale-watching excursions. Most tours originating in La Paz go to Bahía Magdalena, where the whales give birth to their calves in calm waters. Several companies arrange whale-watching tours originating either in La Paz or other Baja towns or in the United States; 12-hour tours from La Paz start at around $100 per person, including breakfast, lunch, transportation, and an English-speaking guide. Make reservations at **Viajes López & Bustos,** 16 de Septiembre no. 408 between Revolución and Serdan streets (© **1/122-4680;** fax 1/125-9600; libs@bcsl.telmex. net.mx).

Most tours from the United States offer birding, sea kayaking, and other close-to-nature experiences during the same trip. (See "Active Vacations in Baja," in chapter 1, for details.)

You can go whale-watching without joining a tour by taking a bus from La Paz to Puerto López Mateos or Puerto San Carlos at Magdalena Bay (a 3-hr. ride) and hiring a boat there. It's a long trip to do in a day, but there are a few very modest hotels in San Carlos. Check at the La Paz tourist office for information.

For a more in-depth discussion, see "Whale-Watching in Baja: A Primer," in chapter 4.

## 3 A Break from the Beaches: Exploring La Paz

City tours of all the major sights are offered by most tour agencies. Tours last 2 to 3 hours, include time for shopping, and cost around $15 per person.

# HISTORIC LA PAZ

When Cortés landed here on May 3, 1535, he named it Bahía Santa Cruz. The name didn't stick. In April 1683, Eusebio Kino, a Spanish Jesuit priest, arrived and dubbed the place Nuestra Señora de la Paz (Our Lady of Peace). It wasn't until November 1, 1720, however, that a permanent mission was set up here by Jaime Bravo, another Jesuit priest. He used the same name as his immediate predecessor, calling it the Misión de Nuestra Señora de la Paz. The mission church stands on La Paz's main square on Revolución between Cinco de Mayo and Independencia, and today the city is called simply La Paz.

**The Anthropology Museum** *&* The museum features large, though faded, color photos of Baja's prehistoric cave paintings. There are also exhibits on various topics, including the geological history of the peninsula, fossils, missions, colonial history, and daily life. All information is in Spanish.

Altamirano and Cinco de Mayo. *Ⓒ* 1/122-0162. Free admission (donations encouraged). Mon–Fri 8am–6pm; Sat 9am–2pm.

**El Teatro de la Ciudad** The city theater is the city's cultural center, with performances by visiting and local artists. There's no extended calendar available, but performances include small ballet companies, experimental and popular theater, popular music, and an occasional classical concert or symphony.

Av. Navarro 700. *Ⓒ* 1/125-0486. Admission varies per performance; contact the box office.

**Biblioteca de las Californias** The small collection of historical documents and books at the Library of the Californias is the most comprehensive in Baja. Free international films are sometimes shown in the evenings.

In the Casa de Gobierno, across the plaza from the mission church on Madero, between Cinco de Mayo and Independencia. For information call the tourism office (*Ⓒ* 1/124-0199). Free admission. Mon–Fri 8am–8pm.

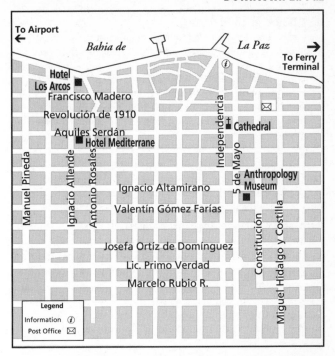

Map labels: To Airport, Bahia de, La Paz, To Ferry Terminal, Hotel Los Arcos, Francisco Madero, Revolución de 1910, Aquiles Serdán, Hotel Mediterrane, Manuel Pineda, Ignacio Allende, Antonio Rosales, Ignacio Altamirano, Valentín Gómez Farías, Independencia, 5 de Mayo, Cathedral, Anthropology Museum, Constitución, Miguel Hidalgo y Costilla, Josefa Ortíz de Domínguez, Lic. Primo Verdad, Marcelo Rubio R.

Legend
Information (i)
Post Office ✉

## 4 Shopping

La Paz has little in the way of folk art or other treasures from mainland Mexico. The dense cluster of streets behind the Hotel Perla between 16 de Septiembre and Degollado is full of small shops, some tacky, others quite upscale. In this area there is also a very small but authentic Chinatown, dating back to the time when Chinese laborers were brought to settle in Baja. Serdan from Degollado south offers dozens of sellers of dried spices, piñatas, and candy. Stores selling crafts, folk art, clothing, and handmade furniture and accessories lie mostly along the malecón (Alvaro Obregón), or a block or two in. The municipal market at Revolución and Degollado, however, has little of interest to visitors. Something you're sure to notice if you explore around the central plaza is the abundance of stores selling electronic equipment, including stereos,

## A Day Trip to El Arco

A day trip by car or guided tour to Los Cabos at the southern tip of Baja California, where the Pacific Ocean meets the Sea of Cortez, will take you past dramatic scenery and many photogenic isolated beaches. A guided tour that includes lunch and a glass-bottom-boat tour to El Arco in Cabo San Lucas costs $45 to $60 per person and can be booked through most travel agencies. Most tours last from 7am to 6pm, and some include breakfast.

cameras, and televisions. This is because La Paz is a principal port for electronic imports into Mexico from the Far East, and therefore offers some of the best prices in Baja and mainland Mexico.

**Artesanías Cuauhtémoc (The Weaver)**   If you like beautiful handwoven tablecloths, place mats, rugs, and other textiles, it's worth the long walk or taxi ride to this unique shop. Fortunato Silva, an elderly gentleman, weaves wonderfully textured cotton textiles from yarn he spins and dyes himself. He charges far less than what you'd pay for equivalent artistry in the United States. Open Monday through Saturday from 10am to 3pm and 5 to 7pm, and Sunday from 10am to 1pm. Abasolo 3315 between Jalisco and Nayarit. ℂ 1/122-4575.

**Dorian's**   If you've forgotten any essentials, or want to stock up on duty-free perfume or cosmetics, head for Dorian's, La Paz's major department store. La Paz is a duty-free port city, so prices here are excellent. They have a wide selection of stylish clothing, shoes, lingerie, jewelry, and accessories as well. Open daily from 9am to 9pm. 16 de Septiembre, between Esquerro and 21 de Agosto. No phone.

**Ibarra's Pottery**   Here, you not only shop for tableware, hand-painted tiles, and decorative pottery, you can watch it being made. Each piece is individually hand-painted or glazed, then fired. Open Monday to Friday from 8am to 3pm; Saturday from 8am to noon. Guillermo Prieto 625, between Torre Iglesias and República. ℂ 1/122-0404.

## 5 Where to Stay

### EXPENSIVE

**La Concha Beach Resort** 𝒜𝒜   Though 6 miles north of downtown La Paz, this resort's setting is perfect: on a curved beach ideal for swimming and water sports. All rooms face the water and have double beds, balconies or patios, and small tables and chairs. Condos with full kitchens and one or three bedrooms are also available on a nightly basis in the high-rise complex next door, and are worth the extra price, if available, for a perfect family vacation stay. The hotel offers scuba, fishing, and whale-watching packages.

Km 5 Carretera Pichilingue, 23000 La Paz, B.C.S. © 800/999-2252, 1/121-6161, or 1/121-6344. Fax 1/122-8644. ohpc@balandra.uabcs.mx. 107 units, 12 condos/suites. $95 double; $125 jr. suite; $112–$215 studio or 3-bedroom condo. AE, DC, MC, V. Free guarded parking. **Amenities:** Restaurant, 2 bars; beachside pool; complete aquatic-sports center with WaveRunners, kayaks, and paddleboats; beach club with scuba program available; tour desk; free twice-daily shuttle to town; room service; laundry service. *In room:* A/C, TV.

## MODERATE

**Hotel Los Arcos** 🅐🅐 *Value*    This three-story neocolonial-style hotel at the west end of the malecón, between Rosales and Allende, is the best place for downtown accommodations, with a touch of tranquility. Los Arcos is functional in its furnishings and amenities, and the hotel's rambling nooks and crannies are filled with fountains, plants, and even rocking chairs that lend lots of old-fashioned charm. Most of the recently remodeled rooms and suites come with two double beds and a balcony overlooking the pool in the inner courtyard or the waterfront, plus coffeemaker and Jacuzzi tub. I prefer the South Pacific–style bungalows with thatched roofs and fireplaces located in the back part of the property, nestled into an appealing jungle garden shaded by large trees. Satellite TVs carry U.S. channels.

Alvaro Obregón 498 (Apdo. Postal 112), 23000 La Paz, B.C.S. © 800/347-2252 or 714/450-9000 in the U.S., or 1/122-2744. Fax 1/125-4313. www.losarcos.com, www.bajahotels.com. 130 units; 9 suites; 52 bungalows. $75–$85 double; $85 suite; $60–$84 bungalows. AE, MC, V. Free guarded parking. **Amenities:** Cafeteria, restaurant, bar with live music; two pools (one heated); a sauna; Ping-Pong tables; travel agency; desk for fishing information; room service; laundry. *In room:* A/C, TV, minibar.

**Posada Santa Fe** 🅐🅐 *Finds*    La Paz's most romantic place to stay, this elegant B&B, which opened in 1999, has been a welcome addition to town. Each room is tastefully and uniquely decorated in high-quality rustic Mexican furniture and antiques, hand-loomed fabrics, and exquisite artisan details. Bathrooms are especially welcoming, with marble tubs and thick towels. Common areas include a cozy living room complete with piano; a self-serve honor bar; and a small pool. Full breakfast is served from 8 to 11am daily, and a free shuttle runs to the beaches and downtown. Telephone, fax, and Internet service are available through the office, run by the gracious owners Ed and Raquel Rose. Located on northern end of the malecón.

Alvaro Obregón 440, 23000 La Paz, B.C.S. ✆ 1/125-5871. www.quintasol.com/posadasantafe/. 5 units, including a house. $85 double; $105 suite; $185 house for 5 people, full breakfast included. No credit cards. **Amenities:** Small pool. *In room:* A/C, TV.

## INEXPENSIVE

**Hotel Mediterrane** 🐟🐟 Simple yet stylish, this unique inn mixes Mediterranean with Mexican for a cozy place for couples or friends to share. All rooms face an interior courtyard and are decorated with white tile floors and equipal furniture, with colorful Mexican sarapes draped over the beds. Some rooms have minifridges. All have VCRs. Its location is great—just a block from the malecón. Their adjacent La Pazta restaurant (see "Where to Dine," below) is one of La Paz's best, and there's an Internet cafe next door.

Allende 36, 23000 La Paz, B.C.S. ✆/fax: 1/125-1195. www.hotelmed.com. 9 units, including 1 junior suite and 1 suite. $65–70 double; $80 suite. Rates include use of kayaks, bicycles, and 1 hour of Internet service per day. Weekly discounts available. AE, MC, V. *In-room:* A/C, TV/VCR.

## 6 Where to Dine

Although La Paz is not known for culinary achievements, it has a growing assortment of small, pleasant restaurants that are good and reasonably priced. In addition to the usual seafood and Mexican dishes, you can find Italian, French, Spanish, Chinese, and even a growing selection of vegetarian offerings. Restaurants along the seaside malecón tend to be more expensive than those a few blocks inland. Generally, restaurant reservations are unnecessary in La Paz. It's a casual town, and except for perhaps Easter and Christmas weeks, crowds in restaurants should never be a problem.

## MODERATE

**Bismark II** 🐟 SEAFOOD/MEXICAN Bismark excels at seafood; you can order fish tacos, chiles rellenos stuffed with lobster salad, marlin "meatballs" and paella, breaded oysters, or a sundae glass filled with ceviche or shrimp. Extremely fresh dorado, halibut, snapper, or whatever else is in season is prepared in a number of ways. Chips and a creamy dip are served while you wait. It's a good place to linger over a late lunch. The decor of pine walls and dark wood chairs is reminiscent of a country cafe. Walk 7 blocks inland on Degollado to Altamirano. The owners will call a cab for you if you wish.

Degollado and Altamirano. ✆ 1/122-4854. Breakfast $2–$5; main courses $4–$17. MC, V. Daily 10am–10pm.

**Trattoria La Pazta** $\mathcal{R}\mathcal{R}$ ITALIAN/SWISS    The trendiest restaurant in town, La Pazta gleams with black lacquered tables and white tile; the aromas of garlic and espresso float in the air. The menu features local fresh seafood such as pasta with squid in wine and cream sauce, and crispy fried calamari. Lasagna is homemade, baked in a wood-fired oven. Choose from an extensive wine list to complement your meal. It's also appealing for breakfast, with full breakfasts running $2 to $4, or, you could simply opt for an espresso and croissant. The restaurant is in front of the Hotel Mediterrane, one block inland from the malecón.

Allende 36. ℂ 1/125-1195. Main courses $8–$11. AE, MC, V. Wed–Mon 7am–11pm; closed Tues.

## INEXPENSIVE

**El Quinto Sol** $\mathcal{R}$ *(Finds)* VEGETARIAN    Not only is this La Paz's principle health food market, it's a cheerful, excellent cafe for fresh-fruit *liquados* (shakes), tortas, and vegetarian dishes. Tables sit beside oversized wood-framed windows, with flowering planters in the sills. Sandwiches are served on whole-grain bread—also available for sale—and the potato tacos are an excellent way for vegetarians to indulge in a Mexican staple.

Ave. Independencia and B. Domínguez. ℂ 1/122-1692. Main courses $1.50–$6.50. No credit cards. Mon–Sat 7am–9:30pm.

**Caffé Gourmet** FRENCH/CAFÉ    You'll feel you've suddenly been transported across the Atlantic and onto the Continent in this incongruous but welcome addition to La Paz. Indulge in any number of espresso coffee drinks, plus French and Austrian pastries, while sitting at marble-topped bistro tables. Jazz music plays in the background.

Ave. Esquerro and 16 de Septiembre. No phone. Coffees and pastries, $1–$3. No credit cards. Mon–Sat 7am–8pm; Sun 9am–3pm.

## 7 La Paz After Dark

A night in La Paz logically begins in a cafe along the malecón as the sun sinks into the sea—have your camera ready.

A favorite ringside seat at dusk is a table at **La Terraza,** next to the Hotel Perla (ℂ 1/122-0777). La Terraza makes good schooner-sized margaritas. **Pelicanos Bar,** in the second story of the Hotel Los Arcos (ℂ 1/122-2744), has a good view of the waterfront and a clubby, cozy feel. **Carlos 'n' Charlie's La Paz-Lapa** (ℂ 1/122-9290) has live music on the weekends. **La Cabaña**

(© 1/122-0777) nightclub in the Hotel Perla features Latin rhythms. It opens at 9:30pm, and there's an $8 minimum consumption requirement.

For dancing, a few of the hottest clubs are: **Laser Disco** (no phone), at Alvaro Obregón and Degollado, playing dance music from the '70s to '90s; **Xtasis** (no phone), at Arreola and Zaragoza, spinning techno and alternative dance tunes; and the locally hip **Las Varitas** (© 1/125-2025), at Independencia and Dominguez, playing Latin rock, ranchero, and salsa. All three are open from 9pm to 3 or 4am, with cover charges around $3 (the charge could be waived or increased, depending on the quantity of the crowd).

The poolside bar overlooking the beach at **La Concha Beach Resort** (© 1/121-6161, or 1/121-6344), Km 5.5 Pichilingue Highway, is the setting for the ubiquitous Mexican fiesta at 7pm on Friday nights. Price is $18, including tax and tips.

# 4

# Mid-Baja: Loreto, Mulegé & Santa Rosalía

Halfway between the resort sophistication of Los Cabos and the frontier exuberance of Tijuana lies Baja's midsection, an area rich in history and culture. The indigenous cave paintings found here were named a World Heritage Site by UNESCO, and the area was home to numerous Jesuit missions in the 1700s. These days, travelers come to experience the quiet side of Baja and its remote, wild, natural beauty; the area is known for its excellent sea kayaking, sportfishing, and hiking.

Overlooked by many travelers—except avid, informed sportfishers—Loreto is a rare gem that sparkles under the desert sky. Here, the purple hues of the Sierra de la Giganta mountains meet the indigo waters of the Sea of Cortez, providing a spectacular backdrop of natural contrasts for the town's historical past. Mulegé is, quite literally, an oasis in the Baja desert. The only fresh water river (Río Mulegé) in the peninsula flows through town; it's a lush, green place, with towering date palms, olive groves, citrus trees, and flowering gardens. And the port town of Santa Rosalía, while slightly past its prime, makes a worthy detour, with its pastel clapboard houses and unusual steel-and-stained-glass church, designed by Gustave Eiffel (of Eiffel Tower fame).

The region is also a popular jumping-off point for many whale-watching tours; to find out when, where, and how to view these gentle giants, consult the whale-watching primer at the end of this chapter.

## 1 Loreto & the Offshore Islands ★★

243 miles NW of La Paz; 333 miles N of Cabo San Lucas; 703 miles SE of Tijuana

The unpretentious feel of the town of Loreto belies its historical importance to the area. Loreto was the center of the Spanish mission effort during colonial times, the first capital of the Californias, and the first European settlement in the peninsula. Founded on October

## *Tips* A Note on Phone Numbers

As with the rest of Mexico, the mid-Baja region has made the switch from five- to seven-digit local phone numbers (whereas before the local area code was 113, now the area code is 1, and 13 are the first two digits of the local phone number

25, 1697, it was selected by Father Juan María Salvatierra as the site of the first mission in the Californias. (California, at the time, extended from Cabo San Lucas in the south to the Oregon border in the north.) He held mass beneath a figure of the Virgin of Loreto, brought from a town in Italy bearing the same name. For 132 years Loreto served as the state capital, until an 1829 hurricane destroyed most of the town. The state capital was moved to La Paz the following year.

The Mexican government saw in Loreto the possibility for another megadevelopment along the lines of Cancún, Ixtapa, or Huatulco. It invested in a golf course and championship tennis facility, modernized the infrastructure, and built an international airport and full marina facilities at Puerto Loreto, several miles south of town. The economics, however, didn't make sense, and few hotel investors and even fewer tourists came, to the disappointment of developers. Loreto remains today the wonderfully funky fishing village and well-kept secret it's been for decades, although this could soon change—the government in 2001 once again announced it is focusing development attention on this area. The recent celebration of the town's 300th anniversary had the added benefit of updating the streets, plaza, and mission in Loreto. Old Town Loreto is now a quaint showplace.

The main reasons to come to Loreto are centered around the Sea of Cortez and the five islands that float just offshore: kayaking, sailing, diving, and fishing are all exceptional. Isla del Carmen and Isla Danzante are wonderful overnight sailing destinations. And kayakers launch here for trips to the offshore islands or down the remote coast of the Sierra de la Giganta to La Paz. An abandoned salt-mining town lies on the northwestern tip of Isla del Carmen, and recent rumors peg it as the site of a new eco-oriented hotel, complete with landing strip. For the present, though, simply enjoy the island as it is—a remote sanctuary of desert wildlife.

# The Lower Baja Peninsula

Bahía de Sebastián Viscaíno
Playa San Rafael
B. San Rafael
Bahía Tortugas
Guerrero Negro
18
Pto. Nuevo
Scammon's Lagoon
B. San Carlos
La Trinidad
Bahía Asuncion
B. La Asunción
Guadalupe
B. Sta. Ana
Gulf of California
Bahía San Hipólito
DESIERTO DE
San Ignacio
VIZVAINO
1
Santa Rosalía
Laguna de San Ignacio
Mulegé
Bahía Concepción
S.E. COYOTE
La Purisima
B. San Basílio
San Isidro
Pacific Ocean
Loreto
Isla Del Carmen
Boca La Soledad
Va. Ignacio Zaragoza
Pto. Adolfo Lopez Mateos
Ciudad Insurgentes
Sea of Cortéz
Puerto San Carlos
B. Sta. María
Ciudad Constitución
1
Bahía Magdalena
El Ciruelo
Isla San José
San Ignacio
B. Coyote
Isla La Partida
Isla Espíritu Santo
Pichilingue
Isla Cerralvo
La Paz
Las Crúces
San Pedro
La Ventana
B. de los Muertos
Buena Vista
B. de Palmas
19
Los Barriles
SIERRA DE LA LAGUNA
La Rivera
Todos Santos
1
Santiago
Miraflores
Cabo Pulmo

Cabo San Lucas
San José del Cabo

Legend
Airport ✈
Beach ↗

0        50 Mi
0        50 Km

## ESSENTIALS
### GETTING THERE & DEPARTING

**BY PLANE**   The **Loreto International Airport** (LTO)
(© 1/135-0565) is located 4 miles southwest of Loreto. It is serv-
iced by **AeroCalifornia** (© **800/237-6225** in the U.S.,
1/135-0500, or 1/135-0555; fax 1/135-0566), which has direct
flights from Los Angeles; **Aerolitoral** (© **1/135-0999**) has flights
from Ciudad Obregón with connections to Tucson and to other
cities in Mexico.

**BY CAR**   From La Paz, take Highway 1 northwest to Ciudad
Constitución; from there continue northeast on Highway 1 to
Loreto. This route takes you twice over the mountain range that
stretches down the Baja Peninsula, through mountain and desert
landscapes, and into the heart of the old mission country. From
Tijuana travel south down Highway 1. The drive takes 17 to 20
hours straight into Loreto.

**BY BUS**   The bus station (Terminal de Autobuses)
(© 1/135-0767) is located on Salvatierra and Paseo Tamaral, a
10-minute walk from downtown. It's open from 7am until midnight. Buses stop in Loreto en route to Santa Rosalía, Tijuana,
Mexicali, Guerrero Negro, and La Paz. The trip to La Paz takes 5
hours. You can usually get a ticket in any bus, except during Easter,
summer, and Christmas holidays when buses tend to be more
crowded. The bus terminal is a simple building and the personnel
are very friendly and helpful.

### ORIENTATION

**ARRIVING**   At the airport, taxis are lined up on the street to
receive incoming passengers. They charge about $7 to Loreto, and
the ride takes approximately 10 minutes.

If you plan to rent a car, Thrifty and Budget counters at the
airport are open during flight arrivals, and branch offices are in
town. Local Car Rental is on Hidalgo 113 and Pino Suárez
(© **1/135-0048;** fax 1/135-0816; open daily 8am to 6pm); Budget
is on Hidalgo between Pípila and López Mateos (© **1/135-1090;**
open daily 8am to 1pm and 3 to 6pm). Advance reservations are not
always necessary.

If you arrive at the bus station, it's about a 10-minute walk to the
downtown area and a little farther to the hotels by the water. A taxi
from the bus station to the different hotels costs $2 to $5.

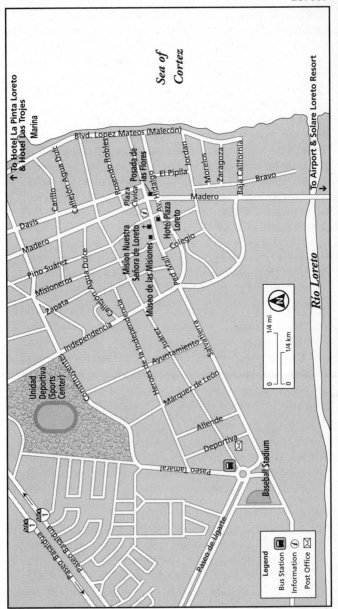

# Loreto

Sea of Cortez

To Hotel La Pinta Loreto & Hotel Las Trojes

Marina

Blvd. Lopez Mateos (Malecón)

To Airport & Solare Loreto Resort

Río Loreto

Carillo
Callejón Agua Dulc
Rosendo Robles
Davis
Madero
Pino Suárez
Misioneros
Zapata
Callejón Agua Dulce
Independencia
Hidalgo
El Pipila
Jordan
Morelos
Zaragoza
Baja California
Bravo
Madero
Plaza
Cívica
Posada de
las Flores
Misión Nuestra
Señora de Loreto
Museo de las Misiones
Pedi Mall
Colegio
Hotel Plaza
Loreto
Ayuntamiento
Salvatierra
Héroes de la Independencia
Juárez
Márquez de León
Allende
Deportiva
Paseo Tamaral
Constituyentes
Unidad
Deportiva
(Sports
Center)
Paseo de Ugaste
Baseball Stadium
MEX 1
empleas Basajal
Paseo Basajal

1/4 mi
1/4 km
0
0

Legend
Bus Station
Information ⓘ
Post Office

107

**VISITOR INFORMATION**   The city tourist-information office (☏ 1/135-0411) is located in the southeast corner of the Palacio de Gobierno building, across from the town square. It offers maps, local free publications, and other basic information about the area. It's open Monday through Friday from 9am to 5pm.

**CITY LAYOUT**   Salvatierra is the main street that runs northeast, merging into Paseo Hidalgo, toward the beach. Calle Playa runs parallel to the water, and it is along this road where you'll find many of the hotels, seafood restaurants, fishing charters, and the marina. There's an old section of town along Salvatierra, between Madera and Playa, with mahogany and teak homes that date back to the 1800s. Most of the town's social life revolves around the central square and the old mission.

**GETTING AROUND**   Most addresses don't have a street number and the references are usually the perpendicular streets, or the main square and the mission. There is no local bus service around town. Taxis or walking are the way to go. The town itself is quite small and manageable for walking around. Taxis are inexpensive, with average fares in town ranging from $1.50 to $2.50. The main taxi stand is on Salvatierra, in front of the El Pescador supermarket.

 **FAST FACTS: Loreto**

*Area Code*   The telephone area code is **1**, and local phone numbers are given with seven digits. *Banks*   There is only one bank in Loreto, where you can exchange currency. Bancomer is located on Francisco I. Madero, across the street from the Palacio Municipal (City Hall). Bank hours are Monday through Friday from 9am to 3pm. There is also a *Casa de Cambio* (money-exchange house) on Salvatierra, close to the main square.

*Beach Safety*   The beaches are generally safe for swimming, with the main beach located along the *malecón* (sea wall).

*General Store*   Super El Pescador, on Salvatierra and Independencia (☏ **1/135-0060**), is the best place to get toiletries, film, bottled water, and other basic staples, as well as newspapers and telephone calling cards.

*Internet Access*   Cafe Internet, on Francisco I. Madero between Hidalgo and Salvatierra (☏ **1/135-0084**), offers

Internet access. It is open Monday to Friday from 9am to 2pm and 4 to 7pm, Saturday from 10am to 2pm.

*Marinas*  Loreto's marina for *pangas* (small fishing boats) is located along the malecón. Cruise ships and other large boats will anchor at Puerto Loreto, also known as Puerto Escondido, located 16 miles south of Loreto. For details about the marina and docking fees, contact the Capitanía de Puerto in Loreto (② **1/135-0465**).

*Medical Care*  Medical services are offered at the **Centro de Salud** (② **1/135-0039**) on Salvatierra 68, near the corner with Allende.

*Parking*  Street parking is generally easy to find in the downtown area.

*Pharmacy*  The **Farmacia del Rosario** (② **1/135-0670**) is located on Juárez, between Independencia and Zapata, and is open daily from 8am to 10pm.

*Post Office*  The *correo* (② **1/135-0647**) is at Deportiva between Salvatierra and Benito Juárez, and is open Monday through Friday from 8am to 3pm.

## BEACHES & CRUISES

**BEACHES**    Beautiful beaches front Loreto and the hotels that surround it. The beaches are safe for swimming, with the main beach located along the malecón, near Chili Willi's restaurant. It's a popular place for locals, especially on Sundays. Most visitors go to Loreto for the excellent sportfishing and other outdoor activities, so relaxing at the beach is one of the optional pleasures offered by this naturalist's paradise. For those seeking more pristine, secluded beaches, the options are unlimited in the several islands that lie just offshore Loreto. Isla del Carmen offers several beaches that are particularly attractive, with the best anchorage on the western shores of the island. You can either take one of the cruises mentioned below, or hire a *lancha* (small wooden fishing boats available along the malecón) to take you there; the price depends on what you want and how sharp your bargaining skills are (the *lancheros,* or captains, take cash only).

**CRUISES**    More than cruises, Loreto offers island exploration tours that take in one, or a combination, of the five islands located just offshore. They usually offer the opportunity to visit sea lion

---

### *Moments*  Festivals in Loreto

The feast of the patron saint of Loreto is celebrated September 5 to September 8, with a fair, music, dancing, and other cultural events, closing with the procession of the miraculous figure of the Virgin of Loreto. During October, Loreto celebrates the anniversary of its founding with a series of cultural events that include music and dance. There is also a reenactment of the landing of the Spanish missionaries that is part of a popular festival held from October 19 to October 25.

---

colonies and do some snorkeling and beachcombing, for around $35. Arrange cruises through a travel agency, your hotel, or call **Las. Parras Tours** (© 1/135-1010). Las Parras offers the widest selection of outdoor activities and tours. Each island is unique and offers a spectrum of eco-activities that include sea kayaking, snorkeling, diving, hiking, or simply exploring the local desert flora and fauna (see "A Visit to Isla del Carmen," below).

## LAND SPORTS

**GOLF**  The 18-hole **Campo de Golf Loreto,** Blvd. Misión San Ignacio, Fraccionamiento Nopoló (© **1/133-0554,** or 1/133-0788), is quite spectacular, and is probably the least crowded coastal golf course in the area. The back nine holes are more challenging than the front nine, and the 14th hole is reputed to be particularly tough. Reservations are recommended. Prices are $40 for 18 holes, with an additional $35 for cart, $20 for caddy, and $20 for gear.

**HIKING**  There are virtually no formal trails in the Sierra de la Giganta, but the locals know their way to many magical spots in these towering mountains. Ask at **Deportes Blazer,** Hidalgo 18 (© **113/5-0911**), or call **Las Parras Tours** (© 1/135-1010) for help finding a guide or for current trail information.

**HORSEBACK RIDING**  More practical for this terrain are the mule-riding excursions that visit the San Javier mission. These can be arranged through **Las Parras Tours** (© 1/135-1010). Other horseback riding tours are also available through this company, which offers the most options and the friendliest service. They also offer mule-trail tours where you camp and sleep in different ranches in the surrounding area. These tours can be arranged to last between 3 and 5 nights, with prices varying on length, location, and amenities.

**SPORTING TOURS**   Trekking, hiking, mountain biking, and mule- and horseback riding tours are available through **Las Parras Tours** (✆ 1/135-1010), where José Salas will be happy to explain the many options in detail. The **Loreto Learning Center,** Hidalgo and Pino Suárez (✆ **800/848-4333** in the U.S. or 1/135-0798; www.loretocenter.com; e-ail: info@loretocenter.com), offers tours and personal-growth workshops combined with the tours, making a very special experience of the exploration of the area. Make sure you call the U.S. number or visit the website to make reservations, because at the local number they can service clients, but are not able to book tours or take reservations. Local travel agencies also offer the tours, but most likely will hire them from Las Parras Tours, since they are the best-organized tour operator in Loreto.

**TENNIS**   You can play tennis at the Centro Tenístico Loreto, adjacent to the Eden Resort (also known as the John McEnroe Tennis Center, since the tennis pro designed these facilities). The nine courts are lighted for night play, and there is also a pool, a sundeck, stadium, and pro shop. Court fees are $7 per hour ($17 per hour at night). The fee also gives you access to the pool. If you want to use the pool only, the access fee is $5 for the day.

## WATER SPORTS & ACTIVITIES

**SEA KAYAKING**   Kayaking season is from October through April. Fully guided, personal-growth-oriented, half-day kayaking adventures are offered from January through March by **The Loreto Learning Center,** Hidalgo and Pino Suárez (✆ **800/848-4333** in the U.S. or 1/135-0798; www.loretocenter.com; e-mail: info@ loretocenter.com). **Las Parras Tours** (✆ 1/135-1010) offers sit-on-top kayak tours for beginners from $25 to $100. The more expensive tour visits three islands and the guide does all the hard work, while you learn how to paddle close to shore and get to enjoy all the sights. They also offer kayaking expeditions of 6 to 8 days, with camping on small islands and kayaking between them. They are fully guided with all gear provided, but it is recommended that you take your own sleeping bag. The kayaking expeditions are approximately $100 per day per person. Puerto Escondido is also an ideal starting point for experienced kayakers who want to reach Isla Monserrate; call Las Parras Tours for details.

**SNORKELING/DIVING**   Several companies offer snorkeling; most island exploration trips include snorkeling, and trips to Isla del Carmen, Islas Coronados, Isla Monserrate, and Isla Catalina all include snorkeling opportunities. The **Loreto Learning Center**

## *Finds* A Visit to Isla del Carmen

The largest of Loreto's offshore islands is Isla del Carmen. It is mostly inaccessible and privately owned, so you'll need permission to go ashore. Access to Isla del Carmen is available through one of a number of tour companies in Loreto. Chose your company based on your preferred activity and mode of exploration.

The island was once the site of an impressive salt-mining operation, but increased competition—not to mention the opportunity to earn a dollar from granting landing permissions to tourism purveyors—encouraged the company to shut down and refocus its economic endeavors. You can see the remains of the salt-mining town, completely abandoned in 1983, at the northeastern tip of the island.

Volcanic in origin, Isla del Carmen also has deposits of *coquina,* a limestone-like rock of cemented shell material that was quarried by the Jesuit missionaries for use in constructing the church and other buildings in Loreto. One of the favored coves of Isla del Carmen is Puerto Balandra, where crystal-blue water and ivory sand are framed by bold rock formations rising up like humpback whales.

The craggy desert terrain offers up a cornucopia of plant life ranging from elephant trees with their fragrant leaves and berries, desert asparagus (pickleweed), mesquite trees, jojoba, agave, cardón cacti, and passion flower vines. Be careful of the choya cacti, as its spines enter your skin in a crisscross pattern. To remove them, cut the spines from the plant, then remove them one at a time. The topography alternates between salt-crusted ground, spongy surfaces—a sure sign that snakes, iguanas, and burrowing animals are nearby—and the rocky remains of former riverbeds. There is a variety of fauna as well, including a population of goats that were introduced to the island in order to provide a meat supply to its inhabitants. Feral cats, black-tailed hares, and birds that include osprey and heila woodpeckers are among the wildlife you'll regularly spot.

(© **800/848-4333** in the U.S. or 1/135-0798; www.loretocenter. com) turns snorkeling into a personal-growth experience in which you really come in contact with the submarine environment.

Snorkeling trips start at $35. Some fishing trips carry snorkeling gear on board to give anglers a chance to check out the underwater world. For scuba diving, contact **Las Parras Tours** (℗ 1/135-1010); they offer several diving sites where you can admire the underwater bounty of the Sea of Cortez. Trips cost $70 to $80 per diver and all tours are guided by an SSI Certified Dive Con instructor. Snacks, tanks, and weights are included. The tour company recommends wearing a wet suit from November to May and a skin for the rest of the year. Las Parras also offers a resort course in diving, at a cost of $300, taking 4 days to complete.

**SPORTFISHING**    The fishing near Loreto is exceptional, with a different sportfish for every season. Winter months are great for yellowtail, while spring is the time for roosterfish. During the summer, tie into big marlin, sailfish, tuna, dorado, and grouper, and for something unusual, take advantage of the run of large Humboldt squid that pass inshore to spawn between Isla del Carmen and Isla Danzante during the fall. These 10-pound, ink-squirting sea creatures are hard fighting but good eating. The best fishing is said to be in the waters east of Isla del Carmen.

There are several different sportfishing operations in town. The least expensive way to enjoy deep-sea fishing is to pair up with another angler and charter a panga from the Loreto Sportfishing Cooperative at the main pier in Loreto, known as Barcena del Malecón. Prices range from $125 to $250 per boat, depending on the size and availability of shade. You can also arrange your trip in advance through most tour operators or contact the fleets directly. At **Arturo's Fleet,** Calle Juárez (℗ 1/135-0766, 1/135-0132, or 1/135-0165), trips are priced from $165 to $280, with rod rentals at $7 each, and an extra charge for drinks and snacks. MasterCard and Visa are accepted, with a 5% surcharge. People with their own boats can launch at the ramp just north of the malecón in town or at Puerto Loreto, several miles south of town. If you plan on running out to Isla del Carmen, it's better to launch from Puerto Loreto, which cuts 10km off the crossing. For tackle, head to Deportes Blazer, the catchall sporting goods store in town.

**WHALE-WATCHING** ᗰᗰᗰ    Loreto is the nearest major airport and city to Bahía Magdalena (Magdalena Bay), the southernmost of the major gray-whale-calving lagoons on the Pacific coast of Baja. For more information on popular whale-watching spots and tour operators, see "Whale-Watching in Baja: A Primer," later in this chapter. **Las Parras Tours** (℗ 1/135-1010) conducts whale-watching trips for blue, fin, and humpback whales in the waters between Loreto, Concepción, and Magdalena islands, as well as traveling to San Carlos on the Pacific Coast to see gray whales.

## HISTORICAL LORETO & OTHER INTERESTING SITES

**Misión Nuestra Señora de Loreto** was the first mission in the Californias, started in 1699. The catechization of California by Jesuit missionaries was based from this mission, and lasted through the 18th century. The inscription above the entrance reads CABEZA Y MADRE DE LAS MISIONES DE BAJA Y ALTA CALIFORNIA (Head and Mother of the Missions of Lower and Upper California). The current church in the shape of a Greek cross was finished in 1752 and, even though it has great historical importance, the building, which was restored in 1976, is quite simple. The original Virgen de Loreto, brought to shore by Padre Kino in 1867, is displayed in the church's 18th-century gilded altar. The mission is on Salvatierra, across from the central square of town.

Adjacent to the mission church is the **Museo de las Misiones,** Salvatierra 16 (© 1/135-0441), of equal or even greater interest. It has a small but complete collection of historical and anthropological exhibits. On display are interesting facts about the indigenous Guaycura, Pericúe, and Cochimí populations, along with accomplishments of the Jesuit missionaries—including their zoological studies, scientific writings, architectural sketches, and details on the role they played in the demise of indigenous cultures. Also on display are several religious paintings and sculptures dating back to the 18th century. The museum has a small shop where the INAH (Instituto Nacional de Antropología e Historia) sells books about the history of Mexico and Baja California. The museum is open Tuesday through Sunday from 9am to 1pm and 1:45 to 6pm. Admission is $2.

Located about 2 hours from Loreto, in a section of the old Camino Real used by Spanish missionaries and explorers, is **Misión San Francisco Javier** (⚑), one of the best preserved, most spectacularly set missions in Baja—located high in a mountain valley beneath volcanic walls. Founded in 1699 by the Jesuit priest Francisco María Píccolo, it was the second mission to be established in California, and completed in 1758. The church was built with blocks of volcanic stone from the Sierra de la Giganta mountains. It is very well preserved with its original walls, floors, gilded altar, and religious artifacts. Day tours from Loreto, organized by several local

> ### *Finds*  Cave Paintings: A Trip for the Physically Fit
>
> One fascinating excursion that demands good physical condition is a visit to the aboriginal cave paintings of Baja. The tour lasts approximately 12 hours and takes you to the foothills of the Guadalupe mountains, between Loreto and Bahía de los Angeles. The paintings date back an estimated 1,500 years and have been designated a part of the historical patrimony of mankind by UNESCO. The murals and petroglyphs are larger and more numerous than those found in Altamira, Spain. The tour takes you on a hike through the desert, where you have to swim in a couple of canyons before you reach the site. Authorized guides must accompany all visitors. Contact Las Parras Tours (© 1/135-1010) for more details.

tour operators, visit the mission, with stops to view aboriginal cave paintings and an oasis settlement with a small chapel. The trips run between $35 and $50, and some offer mule riding and hiking options. If you are driving a high-clearance four-wheel-drive vehicle and are an experienced off-road driver, you can get there yourself by traveling south on Highway 1 and taking the detour on Km 118. The 25-mile drive takes about 2 hours on this rocky, graded road.

**Primer Agua,** a palm oasis in a fenced-off section of the Arroyo de San Javier, serves as a prime picnic spot, complete with natural spring and swimming pool. You have to stop by the Nopoló FONATUR offices (© 1/133-0245) to make sure the oasis will be open to visitors on the day you plan your visit and to pay the entrance fee. It is recommended to do this 2 days prior to your visit to make sure that the gate is open. Access is $5 per person, and it's open from 9am until 6pm. The oasis is closed on Tuesdays, when they clean the pool. The road to Primer Agua is unpaved and graded, of fairly easy access during the dry season. The entrance is 4 miles off Highway 1 on the Km 114 detour.

## SHOPPING
Quite frankly, you won't be coming to Loreto to shop, and if you do, you're going to be disappointed. Loreto has little in the way of shopping, either for basics or for folk art and other collectibles from mainland Mexico. There are a handful of the requisite shops selling souvenirs and some *artesanía*, all clustered within a block from the

tourist magnet, the mission. Some, such as the following, are better than others:

**El Alacrán** This shop carries a fine selection of arts and crafts from throughout Mexico, interesting books about Baja, fine silver jewelry, and handmade and cotton clothing. Open Monday through Saturday from 10am to 5pm, closed Sunday. Salvatierra and Misioneros. No phone.

**La Casa de la Abuela** "Grandma's House" offers better-than-average knickknacks, with an emphasis on indigenous crafts. Located in the oldest house in Loreto, it also serves coffees, pastries, and light meals. Open Wednesday through Monday from 7am to 10pm. Calle Misionero, across from the Mission. No phone.

## WHERE TO STAY

In general, accommodations in Loreto are the kind travelers to Mexico used to find regularly: inexpensive and unique, with genuinely friendly owner-operators. You can choose between a secluded resort, more casual beachfront inns, or even greater values in town.

### EXPENSIVE

**Solare Loreto Resort** 𝒜 The Solare is the only hotel in the so-called hotel zone, located south of the town of Loreto, on the way to Puerto Loreto and the airport. This megadevelopment operates as an all-inclusive, adults-only resort. A claim to fame is their hot tub—allegedly the largest in Baja—where clothing is optional. The same dress code applies for the beach. Rates include unlimited golf and tennis at the Club de Golf Loreto and the Centro Tenístico Loreto. When you stay here you will be spotted as a tourist in town, thanks to the colorful wristbands that all guests must wear.

The air-conditioned rooms are functional and clean, with tile floors and two double beds, as well as either a covered patio or balcony—choose an upper floor if you can, as they have significantly more privacy. The all-inclusive nature of this resort makes it a good choice for those who want to just stay put at one place and enjoy it.

Blvd. Misión de Loreto s/n, Fraccionamiento Nopoló, 23880, Loreto, B.C.S. 𝄞 **888/282-EDEN** in the U.S., or 1/133-0700. Fax 1/133-0377. solare@loretodesertsun.com.mx. 236 units. High season $260 garden-view room, $300 oceanfront room. Low-season rates go down by approximately 20%. Prices are per room for 2 persons, and include all meals, drinks, and activities. AE, MC, V. **Amenities:** 4 restaurants ; 2 pools; hot tub; golf; tennis; gym; kayaks, windsurfing boards, sailboats; bicycles; tour desk; shopping arcade; room service for continental breakfast; laundry service; safe-deposit boxes are available at the front desk. *In room:* A/C, TV.

**Posada de las Flores** 𝆑𝆑𝆑 *(Finds)*  The newest, most luxurious and exclusive hotel in Loreto conveniently sits adjacent to the main square, in the heart of historic Loreto. Every room is beautifully decorated with fine Mexican arts and crafts, including heavy wood doors, Talavera pottery, painted tiles, candles, and Mexican scenic paintings. The colors and decor of the hotel are nouveau-colonial Mexico, with rustic wood and tin accents. Large bathrooms have thick white towels and bamboo doors. Every detail has been carefully selected, including the numerous antiques tucked into corners. This hotel exudes class and refinement, from the general ambience to the wake-up service of coffee and pastries. Italian-owned and operated, the sophisticated service has a European style to it. Only children 12 and older are welcome.

Salvatierra and Francisco I. Madero, Centro, 23880, Loreto, B.C.S. ⓒ 877/ 245-2860 in the U.S., or 1/135-1162. 15 units. $140 standard; $199 jr. suite. Breakfast is included. A service charge in lieu of tipping is added to your room, board, and bar bill; no further gratuities are necessary. MC, V. **Amenities:** 2 restaurants, 1 bar; roof-top pool with glass bottom—quite an experience; free shuttle to the golf course; exclusive tours for guests only; car-rental desk. *In room:* A/C, TV, hair dryer.

## MODERATE
**Villas de Loreto** 𝆑  One of the best aspects of this comfortable hotel is the friendly staff that makes you feel right at home. The basic, clean rooms have refrigerators and old-style Baja charm, with stone walls and rustic decor accents. Complimentary coffee, juice, fruit, and pastries are served each morning. There's also a swimming pool, with views to the five offshore islands. While the hotel welcomes families, it is more a quiet getaway for nature lovers. Located on the beach, past the *arroyo* (small riverbed).

Antonio Mijares y Playa. Col. Zaragoza, 23880, Loreto, B.C.S. ⓒ 1/135-0586. www.villasdeloreto.com. E- 13 units. High season $79 double. Continental breakfast included. MC, V. **Amenities:** Restaurant/bar; swimming pool; bicycles; tour desk. *In room:* A/C.

**Hotel La Pinta Loreto** 𝆑𝆑  On the beach and close to downtown, La Pinta offers spacious rooms with stone accents, heavy wood furnishings, and oceanviews of the offshore islands from individual terraces and private balconies. Accommodations are in two-story buildings that border a central pool and grassy courtyard.

Francisco I. Madero s/n, Playas de Loreto, 23880, Loreto, B.C.S. ⓒ 1/135-0026. 48 units, 20 w/fireplace. $100 double w/fireplace; $79 double hacienda style; $89 villa w/fireplace. Extra person $15. AE, MC, V. **Amenities:** Restaurant, 2 bars; swimming pool; private fishing fleet; tour desk. *In room:* A/C, TV.

## INEXPENSIVE

**Hotel Las Trojes**   This unusual bed-and-breakfast is built from authentic wooden granaries (*trojes*) brought over from the state of Michoacán. The rooms have all-wood interiors and floors, and oceanviews. A path leads through a yard to the hotel's small, pebbly beach and beach bar. It's rustic and a little run-down, but the service is friendly and the experience quite nice for the price. Located 400 yards north of the La Pinta hotel.

Calle Davis Norte s/n, 23880, Loreto, B.C.S. © 1/135-0277. 8 units. $50 double. Rates vary depending on the season. Continental breakfast included. No credit cards. **Amenities:** Bar; tour services. *In room:* A/C.

**Plaza Loreto**   The location of the long-standing Plaza Loreto, just one block from the mission church, makes it easy to find and a perennial favorite. Recently remodeled and well maintained, this two-story motel frames a courtyard with shady seating areas. Each of the basic, clean rooms has one or two double beds, a table and two chairs, and a bathroom with shower. Here, you're a short walk from the mission, the museum, several favorite restaurants, and all the notable nightlife.

Paseo Hidalgo 2. Centro. 23880, Loreto, B.C.S. © 1/135-0280. Fax 1/135-0555. 24 units. $51 single; $62 double; $73 triple. AE, MC, V. **Amenities:** Restaurant/bar. *In room:* A/C, TV.

## WHERE TO DINE

Dining in Loreto has a surprising variety of options, given the small size and simple nature of the town. The dominant menu features some combination of seafood and Mexican cuisine, with the ambience and price being the key variables. Among the exceptions is the exquisite Vecchia Roma (© 1/135-1162) restaurant, in the Posada de las Flores hotel, which serves authentic southern Italian cuisine prepared by chef Alessandro Bargelletti. It's open for dinner only, Tuesday through Sunday from 6 to 11pm, and reservations are recommended.

### MODERATE

**Carmen's Restaurant**   HAMBURGERS/SEAFOOD /MEXI-CAN   It's a popular meeting place for the gringo community, with TV sports, barbecue, oceanviews, and a friendly proprietor. Along with Carmen's Snorkelburger, other popular choices are the paella and the barbecued tri-tips. Breakfast is served American style, and in ample portions. There's usually blues or jazz playing to accompany your meal. Located across from the malecón.

Blvd. Costero López Mateos s/n. No phone. Main courses $2.50–$8. No credit cards. Daily 7am–11pm.

**El Chile Willie** ★★ SEAFOOD/MEXICAN   Chile Willie serves an eclectic menu that specializes in seafood in an appropriate setting—an attractive restaurant right at the water's edge. The extensive menu features choco clams (a local type of clam, not as bizarre as it sounds), clams Rockefeller, lobster served many different ways, and a succulent fish filet baked in foil with a tamarind herb sauce. They also have chicken breast stuffed with nopal cactus, beef burger in barbecue sauce, and (what they claim to be) the world's largest Mexican combo for two. During winter months, an all-glass semicircle oceanfront window keeps the cool air out while retaining the view; it opens up when the weather warms. The place is lively and its location on the main beach in town makes it great for people-watching, especially during weekend breakfast or lunch. From 4 to 6pm, El Chile Willie features a two-for-one happy hour with free appetizers.

Blvd. Costero López Mateos s/n. ℂ 1/135-0677. Main courses $3–$10. MC, V. Daily 10am–11pm.

**El Nido Steakhouse** ★ STEAK/SEAFOOD   The main link in a chain of steak restaurants found in Baja, El Nido's specialty is a thick cut of prime, tender beef, served with obligatory salad and baked potato. Hearty appetites are satisfied here, with seafood options also available. Located on the main boulevard as you enter Loreto from Highway 1.

Salvatierra 154. ℂ 1/135-0284. Main courses $6–$20. No credit cards. Daily 2–10:30pm.

**La Casa de Adobe** ★ MEXICAN/SEAFOOD   Elegant yet casual, this adobe-walled, thatched-roof restaurant offers great food in a comfortable ambience, surrounded by the works of modern Mexican artists. Although the construction is new, the restaurant was built using traditional methods and all local, natural materials. Even the tables are made from cardón cacti. The menu features fairly standard Mexican dishes and seafood; the Camarones Casa de Adobe, a plate of grilled shrimp stuffed with cheese and wrapped in bacon, is delicious.

Paseo Hidalgo y Colegio. No phone. Main courses $3–$14. No credit cards. Daily 11am–9:30pm.

## INEXPENSIVE
**Café Ole** ★ LIGHT FARE   Along with specialty coffees, this breezy cafe is a good option for breakfast; try the eggs with nopal cactus, the hotcakes, or a not-so-light lunch of a burger and fries.

Tacos and some Mexican standards are also on the menu, as are the fresh-fruit shakes, *liquados.*

Francisco I. Madero 14. ℰ 1/135-0495. Breakfast $2–$5. Sandwiches $2–$3.50. No credit cards. Mon–Sat 7am–10pm; Sun 7am–2pm.

## LORETO AFTER DARK

Although selection is limited, Loreto seems to offer a place for almost every preference in terms of nightlife—from rowdy beach pubs to an elegant billiard bar. Generally, though, closing time is around midnight.

The most elegant finish to an evening is at **Jarros y Tarros,** on Salvatierra, next to Deportes Blazer (just before crossing Francisco I. Madero; no phone). It has a few elegant pool tables, as well as high round tables where you can sit and sip one of their many fine tequilas. Beers run about $2, with mixed drinks priced at $3. They're open daily from 11am to 3am, and play exceptional contemporary Latin music and Mexican rock.

If you're staying at the **Solare resort,** you've got the latest nightlife and the only dance club in town on premises. Guests from outside are occasionally permitted to enter for a fee, but it's best to call first to check the policy (ℰ 1/133-0700).

**Mike's Bar** (no phone) is an intimate, friendly place with "gringo bar" written all over it—it's very popular with North American visitors. Located two blocks from the beach on Paseo Hidalgo, it's great for sports and people-watching, and has live music most nights from 9:30 until closing. It's open from 2pm to 2am daily. TV sports and beers are also a regularly featured specialty at **Carmen's,** on the malecón (see "Where to Dine," above).

And, as is the tradition in Mexico, Loreto's central plaza offers a free concert in the bandstand every Sunday evening.

## 2 Mulegé: Oasis in the Desert ★★

618 miles SE of Tijuana; 85 miles N of Loreto; 308 miles NW of La Paz; 441 miles NW of Cabo San Lucas

Verdant Mulegé offers a shady coolness in an otherwise scorching part of the world. Founded in 1705, it is also home to one of the most well-preserved and beautifully situated Jesuit missions in Baja—a visit there is a worthwhile side trip, if only to take in the view.

Besides the respite of the landscape, Mulegé, located at the mouth of beautiful Bahía Concepción, has great diving, kayaking, and fishing. There are also several well-preserved Indian caves with stunning paintings, which can be reached by guided hikes into the mountains. Accommodations are limited and of the basic variety. Good beach camping is also available just south of town along the Bahía Concepción.

## ESSENTIALS
### GETTING THERE & DEPARTING

**BY PLANE**  If you're planning to fly to Mulegé, the closest international airport is in Loreto, 85 miles south. From Loreto, you'll need to rent a car or hire a taxi to take you there; taxis average $75 each way, for the 1½-hour trip. Two airlines fly into Loreto: **AeroCalifornia** (© **800/237-6225** in the U.S., 1/135-0500, or 1/135-0555; fax 1/135-0566) has direct flights from Los Angeles; **Aerolitoral** (© **1/135-0999**) has flights from Ciudad Obregón, with connections to Tucson and other cities inside Mexico.

Mulegé has a well-maintained, graded, 4,000-foot airstrip (**El Gallito**) adjoining the Hotel Serenidad (Transpeninsular Hwy., Km 30; no phone, use radio frequency UNICOM 122.8), so small regional or private charter planes could get you all the way to town, if desired. *Note:* Fuel is generally not available. For additional information, contact the Comandancia del Aeropuerto in Loreto (© **1/135-0565**), from 7am to 7pm daily.

**BY CAR**  From Tijuana, take Highway 1 direct to the Mulegé turnoff, 620 miles south (a drive of approximately 16 hours). From La Paz, take Highway 1 north, a scenic route that winds through foothills and then skirts the eastern coastline.

**BY BUS**  There is no formal bus station in Mulegé, but buses will pick up and drop passengers on the main highway at the La Cabaña restaurant, where the "Y" entrance to town is. Buses running south to Bahía Concepción, Loreto, and La Paz generally pass by about three times a day; while buses traveling north to Santa Rosalía, Ensenada, and Tijuana have twice-daily service. Schedules are highly variable, but buses stay for about 20 minutes while dropping off and picking up passengers. Tickets to Tijuana average $30, while trips to La Paz cost about $12 each way.

### ORIENTATION

**ARRIVING**  If you arrive by bus, you will be dropped off at the restaurant at the entrance to town. From there, you can walk the few blocks downhill and east into town, or take a taxi. Taxis also line up around the plaza, and will usually charge around $2 to $4 for a trip anywhere in town.

**VISITOR INFORMATION** There is no official tourist information office, but tourist information is available at the office of the centrally located Hotel Las Casitas, Calle Fco. Madero 50 (© 1/153-0019). The local laundry, **Efficient Lavamática Claudia,** at the corner of Zaragoza and Moctezuma (© 1/153-0057; open Monday to Saturday 8am to 6pm), is also known as a prime source for local information, with a well-used community bulletin board. Use the bulletin board for gathering info rather than calling the phone number listed above, as the staff can't answer questions—the board is just a community service. Several maps that list key attractions, as well as a local biweekly English-language newspaper, the *Mulegé Post,* are available in locations throughout town. Also of interest to serious travelers to Mulegé is Kerry Otterstrom's self-published book *Mulegé: The Complete Tourism, Souvenir, and Historical Guide,* available at various shops and hotels in town.

The **State Tourism Office of Baja California Sur** can be reached by calling © **1/124-0199,** or you may contact the City of Mulegé (© **1/152-2345,** 1/152-2238, or 1/153-0049).

**CITY LAYOUT** Mulegé has an essentially east-west orientation, running from the Transpeninsular Highway in the west to the Sea of Cortez. The Mulegé River (also known as Río Santa Rosalía) borders the town to the south, with a few hotels and RV parks located along its southern shore. It's easy to find the principal sights downtown, as two main streets will take you either east or west, and both border the town's central plaza. The main church is several blocks east of the plaza, breaking with the traditional layout of most Mexican towns. The Bahía Concepción is located just a few miles south of town.

**GETTING AROUND** There is no local bus service in town or to the beach, but you can easily walk or take a taxi. Taxis line up around the central plaza, or you can call the taxi dispatch at © 1/153-0420.

Bicycles are available for rent from Cortez Explorers, Moctezuma 75-A (© **1/153-0500**). Prices start at $15 for the first day, then drop to $10 per day for the first week, and $8 per day after that. They also rent ATVs by the hour, and have full dive- and snorkel-equipment rentals. They are open Monday through Saturday from 10am to 1pm and 4 to 7pm.

*FAST FACTS:* Mulegé

*Area Code* The telephone area code is **1,** and local phone numbers are given with seven digits that begin with 15. However, as mentioned in "A Note on Phone Numbers" earlier in this chapter, as this book went to press, you could still make a local phone call in mid-Baja by dialing only the last five digits of a phone number (minus 1, the area code, and, in Mulege, the first 15). If dialing the seven-digit number does not work, you could always try dropping the first 15 and dialing the last five digits.

*Banks* *Important note:* there are no banks in Mulegé.

*Beach Safety* Beaches in the area are generally tranquil and safe for swimming. The more protected waters of Bahía Concepción are especially calm. Avoid swimming at the mouth of the Mulegé River, which is said to be polluted.

*Internet Access* At press time, there were no Internet cafes open in Mulegé, nor local Internet access service providers.

*Medical Care* Emergency medical services are offered by the Mexican Red Cross (✆ **1/153-0280,** or 1/153-0110), or by the Health Center ISSSTE (✆ **1/153-0298**).

*Parking* Street parking is generally easy to find in the downtown area. Note, however, that Mulegé's streets are very narrow, and difficult for RVs or other large vehicles to navigate.

*Pharmacy* Farmacia Ruben is a small drugstore with a sampling of basic necessities and medicines, located on the northwestern corner of the central plaza (Calle Fco. Madero s/n, no phone). The owner speaks some English. Across the plaza, a Supermercado Alba has a somewhat wider selection of other goods and toiletries. Both are open Monday through Saturday from 9am to 7pm.

*Post Office* The *correo* is located at the intersection of calles Fco. Madero and Gral. Martínez, on the north side of the street, opposite the downtown Pemex station (✆ **1/153-0205**). It is open Monday through Friday from 8am to 3pm, and Saturday from 8 to 11am.

## BEACHES & OUTDOOR ACTIVITIES

Mulegé has long been a favorite destination for adventurous travelers looking for a place to relax and enjoy the diversity of nature. Divers, sportfishermen, kayakers, history buffs, and simple admirers of beautiful beaches all find reasons to stay just a little longer in this true oasis.

**BEACHES**   To the north and east of Mulegé lies the Sea of Cortez, known for its abundance and variety of species of fish, marine birds, and sea mammals. To the north are the mostly secluded beaches of **Bahía Santa Inez** and **Punta Chivato,** both known for their beauty and tranquility. Santa Inez is reachable by way of a long dirt road that turns off from Highway 1 at Km 151. A few miles south is the majestic **Bahía Concepción,** a 30-mile-long body of water protected on three sides by more than 50 miles of beaches, and dotted with islands. Its waters, crystal clear and turquoise in color, are bordered by the mountainous peninsula to the east. Along with fantastic landscapes, the bay has numerous soft, white-sand beaches such as **Santispác, Concepción, Los Cocos, El Burro, El Coyote, Buenaventura, El Requesón,** and **Armenta.** Swimming, diving, windsurfing, kayaking, and other water sports are easily enjoyed, with equipment rentals locally available. Here's a rundown on some of the area beaches with restaurant service:

**Punta Arena** is accessed off of Highway 1, at Km 119. A very good *palapa* restaurant is found there, along with camping facilities and primitive beach palapas.

**Playa Santispác,** at Km 114, has a nice beachfront, lots of RVs parked there in the winter, and two good restaurants, with Ana's being the most popular.

**Playa El Coyote** is the most popular (meaning most crowded) of the Bahía Concepción beaches. The restaurant El Coyote is located on the west side of Highway 1 at the entrance to this beach, one-half mile from the water, while Restaurant Bertha's serves simple meals on the beachfront.

**Playa Buenaventura,** located at Km 94, is the most developed of the beaches, with a large RV park, motel, convenience store, boat ramp, and public restrooms, along with George's Olé restaurant and bar.

**FISHING**   All of the hotels in town can arrange guided fishing trips to Punta Chivato, Isla San Marcos, or Punta de Concepción, the outermost tip of Bahía Concepción.

The best fishing in the area is for yellowtail, which run in the winter, and summer catches of dorado, tuna, and billfish like marlin and sailfish. Prices run $120 per day for up to three people in a panga, $180 for four in a small cruiser, or $200 and up for larger boats. El Candil restaurant has a fleet of five pangas it rents out to sportfishing groups (© 1/153-0185).

**HIKING & PAINTED CAVE EXPLORATIONS** 𝕉𝕉𝕉    One of the big attractions to this region is the proliferation of large cave paintings in the Sierra de Guadalupe. UNESCO declared the cave paintings a World Heritage Site, and the locals take great pride in protecting them. Unlike many typical cave paintings, these are huge and complex murals. You are legally only allowed to visit the caves with a licensed guide.

The most popular series of caves is in **La Trinidad,** a remote rancho 29km (18 miles) west of Mulegé. You'll be driven there by your guide, and then the hiking begins. Count on hiking about 4 miles and getting wet. To reach the caves, several river crossings are necessary in spots deep enough to swim. Rock walls fringe a tight canyon, and there is no way through except by swimming. Allegedly, this river in Cañon La Trinidad is the source of the river that flows through Mulegé, although it disappears underground for many miles in between.

Among the representations of the cave murals are large deer silhouettes, and a human figure called the "cardón man" because of his resemblance to a cardón cactus.

Another favorite cave-art site is **San Borjitas.** To get there, you travel down a bad four-wheel-drive road to Rancho Las Tinajas, where your guide will either take you hiking or by mule to the caves.

For about $35 per person (6 hours, minimum 5 people, lunch included), you can arrange for a guide in Mulegé to take you to La Trinidad; San Borjitas will cost around $50 per person (7 hours, 2 meals included). The best known is **Ramón Monroy** (© 1/153-0223), who also leads other guided excursions to regional cave-painting sites. If Ramón is booked, check at Hotel Las Casitas or on the board of the local laundromat for recommendations of other guides.

**SCUBA DIVING & SNORKELING**    Although diving here is very popular, be aware that visibility right in Mulegé is marred by the fresh water and the not-so-fresh water that seems to flow into the sea from the numerous septic tanks in this area. But as you head south into Bahía Concepción, there is excellent snorkeling at the numerous shallow coves and tiny offshore islands. Work the middle of the sandy coves looking for oysters and scallops. For bigger fish and colorful sea life, you'll have to swim out to deeper waters along the edges of each cove.

Boat diving in Mulegé tends to head over to Punta de Concepción or north of town to Punta Chivato and the small offshore islands of Santa Inez and San Marcos. Numerous sites are perfect for both snorkeling and scuba. The marine life here is colorful—you're likely to see green moray eels, angelfish, parrot fish, and a variety of lobster—and dolphins and other sea mammals are common sights. The best diving is between August and November, when the visibility averages 100 feet and water temperatures are warmer (mid-80s° F).

Cortez Explorers bought out and took over the operations of the long-known Mulegé Divers, and continues its reputation as one of the best-run dive operations in the state, now with personalized service from owners Bea and Andy Sidler. They are located at Moctezuma 75-A (©/fax **1/153-0500;** www.cortez-explorer.com). If Mulegé has become known as a prime dive site in Baja, credit goes to both of these shops for their excellent prices and exceptional services. Their rates are extremely affordable and they have a great environmental consciousness, too. Cortez Explorers runs their trips from a large, custom dive boat, and uses only well-maintained, current equipment.

Two-tank dive trips generally involve a 45-minute boat ride offshore, and range in price from $40 to $65 per person, depending on the equipment needed. Snorkeling trips are priced at $25 to $35 (again, based on the need to rent equipment). Wet suits, jackets, and/or farmer johns are available, and they're necessary during winter months. Resort courses are also available.

**SEA KAYAKING**    Bahía Concepción is a kayaker's dream—clear, calm waters, fascinating shorelines, and lots of tempting coves to pull into, with white sandy beaches. Rent your own kayak at **El Candil** restaurant (© **1/153-0185**) for $29 per day, and explore on your own.

**Baja Tropicales,** Mulegé's undisputed kayak experts, also rent kayaks to experienced paddlers for $25 to $35 per day, depending on the type of kayak—open deck, closed deck, single, or tandem. Longer-term rentals are also available, as is full gear, including car racks and VHF radios. In addition, they offer fully guided, ecologically oriented kayak tours in Bahía Concepción, and full-day Paddle, Snorkel, Dive, & Dine excursions that combine a day of sporting fun with a seafood fiesta at their own palapa restaurant—The Kayak Kafe—on the beach. The trip, meal, and beverages cost $39, with a four-person minimum. Reserve at © **1/153-0409;** fax 1/153-0190; or in person at the Las Casitas Hotel office, Calle Fco. Madero 50. The trip departs from the EcoMundo kayaking and natural history center, an extension of Baja Tropicales located at Km 111, just south of Playa Santispác. No previous experience is necessary, as complete instruction is given at the start of the tour. Kayaks are the most popular and practical way to explore the pristine coves that dot this shoreline. They also offer 4- and 5-day trips around Bahía Concepción, down the coast, and even over in Scammon's Lagoon on Baja's west coast.

**WINDSURFING**   Bahía Concepción, south of Mulegé, gets quite windy in the afternoons and has numerous coves for beginners to practice in. It has never developed the kind of cachet with the hard-core sailboarding crowd of places like Buenavista or La Ventana, but it's a worthy place to stop and rig up.

## EXPLORING MULEGÉ

**Misión Santa Rosalía de Mulegé,** originally founded in 1706 by father Juan de Ugarte and Juan María Basaldúa, is located just upstream from the bridge where Highway 1 crosses the Mulegé River. The original mission building was completed in 1766, to serve a local Indian population of about 2,000. In 1770, a flood destroyed nearly all the common buildings, and the mission was rebuilt on the site it occupies today, on a bluff overlooking the river. Although not the most architecturally interesting of Baja's missions, it remains in excellent condition and still functions as a Catholic church, despite the fact that mission operations were halted in 1828.

It's also a popular tour site, as a lookout point 100 feet behind the mission provides a spectacular vantage point for taking in the view of a grove of palm trees backed by the Sea of Cortez. To reach the mission from town, take Calle Zaragoza (the longest north-south street in Mulegé) south, then cross the river by using the small footbridge beneath the elevated highway bridge. Turn back sharply to the right and follow the dirt road through palm groves and up a graded path to the mission. The towers of the church will be visible.

In 1907, a **state penitentiary** was built on a hill overlooking the town of Mulegé. It became known as the "prison without doors" because it operated on an honor system—inmates were allowed to leave every morning to work in town, on the condition that they return when the afternoon horn sounded. Escape attempts were rare, and when someone did escape, the other prisoners pursued the escapees to bring them back to jail. It functioned as such until the mid-1970s.

About 10 years ago, a local historian and citizen's group established the small **Museo Regional de Historía** (Regional Museum of History) inside, which details the prison's operations. It also houses an eclectic collection of local historical artifacts. Admission is by donation, and hours are supposed to be Monday through Friday from 9am to 1pm, but have been known to vary. The museum is located at the end of Calle Cananea.

## SHOPPING

The town has a very limited selection of shops, unless you're looking for basic groceries or auto parts. There are a few exceptions:

**Artesanías Cochimi**   This shop sells the highest-quality selection of Mexican arts and decorative items in town, including pottery, silver jewelry, and hand-crafted iron furniture. Shipping is available. Hours are Monday through Saturday from 9am to 6pm and Sunday from 10am to 2pm. If you call in advance, the owner will open at special hours. No credit cards. Calle Zaragoza and Moctezuma. ℂ 1/153-0378 or 1/153-0452.

**Plantas Medicinales Sarah**   If you're either curious about or committed to natural health, this small but complete shop offers mineral salts, teas, powders, spirit waters, and herbs to care for your every ailment. Open Monday through Saturday from 9am to 1pm; no credit cards. Fco. Madero, across from the church. No phone.

## WHERE TO STAY

Accommodations in Mulegé are basic, but generally clean and comfortable. The biggest hotel in town, the Hotel Serenidad, has a recent history of closings due to ownership disputes with the local *ejido* (indigenous) community. It is open now, and claims to have resolved all questions of proprietorship.

### MODERATE

**Hotel Serenidad** 𝕬𝕬   Serenity, seclusion, and casual comfort are the hallmarks of the Serenidad, located just south of town between the local airstrip and a long stretch of beach. Low-rise,

Mediterranean-style buildings border either Mulegé's largest pool with palapa bar, or a courtyard. Most rooms have working fireplaces, and all have ceiling fans, plus a large bathroom with a skylight. Decor is stylish for the area, and all rooms have a king-size bed, tile floors, and a small seating area with a glass-topped table and chairs. The larger bungalows have two bedrooms and two baths, a small living area, and outside terrace, making them ideal for families or friends traveling together.

The locally popular restaurant/bar has satellite TV, and on Saturdays the place fills up for the weekly pig roast and fiesta with mariachis, a regional specialty. The Serenidad has an adjacent RV park with 10 available spaces. It's located on the south side of the mouth of the river, 2½ miles south of the town center, off Highway 1. The Serenidad traditionally closes for the month of September.

Km 30 Transpeninsular Hwy S., P.O. Box 9, CP 23900 Mulegé, B.C.S. ℂ 1/153-0540. Fax 1/153-0311. www.serenidad.com. 48 units. $65 double; $75 1-bedroom suite; $120 2-bedroom casitas. MC, V. Free parking; private airstrip available. **Amenities:** Restaurant/bar; swimming pool with bar; sand volleyball court; telephone and fax service available through the front desk. *In room:* A/C.

## INEXPENSIVE

**Hotel Hacienda Mulegé** ℜ   A former 18th-century hacienda with double courtyards and a small, shaded swimming pool makes for a comfortable and value-priced place to stay. You couldn't be more centrally located in Mulegé, and the Hacienda is known for its locally popular bar, which also has satellite TV featuring sporting events. The bar closes for the night anywhere between 10 and 11pm, so it shouldn't keep you awake. The cozy restaurant with stone walls and a fireplace also has a pleasant patio. Rooms surround the courtyard, and have beds with foam mattresses and brightly colored Mexican accents. Bathrooms are simple but large, with showers.

Calle Fco. Madero 3, Mulegé, B.C.S., one half-block east of the central plaza. ℂ 1/153-0021. Fax 1/153-0481. 24 units. $33 per room. No credit cards. Free parking. **Amenities:** Restaurant/bar; small swimming pool; tourist guide services; currency exchange; book exchange; fax available at front desk; room service; laundry service. *In room:* A/C, TV.

**Hotel Las Casitas** ℜ *Value*   This long-standing favorite in Mulegé welcomes many repeat visitors, along with the local literati—it is the birthplace of Mexican poet Alan Gorosave. Rooms are set in a courtyard just behind (and adjacent to) the Las Casitas Restaurant, one of Mulegé's most popular. The clean, basic accommodations all have high ceilings, tile bathrooms, and recently have been remodeled in a rustic decor. Plants fill a small central patio that is limited for guest

**Camping Bahía Concepción**

For many people who travel down the Baja in RVs, Mulegé is the chosen destination, along with Bahía Concepción. This big bay just south of town is scalloped with powdery white beaches, perfectly clear water, and framed by plunging cliffs. It is a coastline you might invent in a dream. You can still just pull out onto some of the many beaches and camp, but an increasing number have been developed into more formal camping arrangements, and several have turned into motor home colonies. Regardless, it's a stunning place. Camping is much less structured in Mexico than it is in the U.S., Canada, or the U.K.; you can't reserve in advance—sites are available on a first-come, first-served basis.

The first beach camping is at **Playa Punta Arena,** 10 miles south of Mulegé. The beach isn't visible from the road, but it, like all the beaches here, is nice. It's an RV spot, but the rough dirt road keeps it from being overrun. You can rent a palapa right on the sand for around $5 per night. Camping is $3 per night.

A few more miles into the bay will bring you to **Playa Santispác.** There is a restaurant/bar here, and many snowbirds pull their trailers onto the beach in the fall and stay here through spring. Much better for tent campers is **Playa Los Cocos,** 15 miles south of Mulegé. The name means Palm Beach, and indeed there are some nice palms here. Although it's motor home–accessible, it's also very good for tents. Camping is $4 per night and there are pit toilets and garbage receptacles. **Playa El Coyote** is another nice one for tent camping, 17 miles south of Mulegé. Sites are $4 per night.

usage, but the more socially inclined gravitate to the popular restaurant and bar, which is open from 7am to 10pm. The place is especially lively on weekends—Fridays evenings they feature a Mexican fiesta. The inn and restaurant are located on the main east-west street in Mulegé, one block from the central plaza.

Calle Fco. Madero 50, Col. Centro 23900 Mulegé, B.C.S. ℰ **1/153-0019.** Fax 1/153-0190. 8 units. $21 double. MC, V. Limited street parking available. **Amenities:** Restaurant/bar; tour desk. *In room:* A/C.

## WHERE TO DINE

By now you may have figured out that the must-have meal in Mulegé is the traditional pig roast. It's an event—with the pig roasted Polynesian-style in a palm-lined open pit for hours, generally while guests enjoy a few beers or other beverages. When done, the succulent pork is accompanied by homemade tortillas, salsas, an assortment of toppings, and the ubiquitous rice and beans. Remember—it's more than a pig, it's a party. The perennially popular pig roasts happen each Saturday night at both the Las Casitas Restaurant and the Hotel Serenidad, and cost about $10 for the meal.

Another Mulegé—and Mexican—dining staple is the taco. The best are reportedly found either at Las Casitas' adjoining taco stand, or at the popular Taqueria Doney, located at Madero and Romero Rubio, just as you enter town, past the *depósito* (warehouse) on the right.

### MODERATE

**Las Casitas** 🍴🍴 SEAFOOD/MEXICAN    La Casitas remains a popular mainstay with both locals and visitors to Mulegé. The bar has a steady clientele day and night and often features special sporting events on satellite TV. Choose to dine either in the interior stone-walled dining area or on its adjoining, plant-filled patio. Sometimes, live music plays from 6pm on, and Fridays feature a Mexican fiesta and buffet. If you're just dining off the menu, how can you resist fresh lobster priced at $10? The menu offerings are standard fare with an emphasis on fresh seafood, but the quality is good, added to the comfort of seeing the extra-clean exhibition kitchen as you enter.

Calle Fco. Madero 50. 📞 1/153-0019. Breakfast $1.50–$4; main courses $3–$11. MC, V. Daily 7am–10pm.

**Los Equipales** 🍴 MEXICAN/SEAFOOD    First off, you won't find any here—*equipales,* that is. (Equipales are those rustic palm-and-leather bucket chairs.) In their place, this restaurant has white, faux-wicker chairs that are comfy but hardly authentic. This is one of Mulegé's ever-popular hangouts, with homestyle cooking matched by family-friendly service. Its second-story location offers diners the only lofty view in town, and this is the only place in Mulegé that serves complimentary chips and salsa with your meal. Traditional Mexican fare and Sonoran beef are the specialties, especially the barbecued ribs. Tropical drinks, like mango margaritas, are also popular.

Calle Moctezuma, 2nd floor. 📞 1/153-0330. Main courses $3–$10. No credit cards. Daily 8am–10pm.

## INEXPENSIVE

**Eduardo's** MEAT/CHINESE   Most of the time, Eduardo's is known for its grilled meats—tender ribs, traditional carne asada, and thick steaks. However, on Sunday the menu changes, and Eduardo serves up an extensive buffet of Chinese food. The attractiveness of the stone-walled dining area is somewhat diminished by the white plastic chairs, but the graciously friendly service compensates. Full bar service is also available. Located across the street from the downtown Pemex station.

Gnl. Martinez. (£) 1/153-0258. Main courses $3–$10. No credit cards. Friday–Wednesday 4–10pm; Sun 1–8pm.

**El Candil** MEXICAN   Filling platters of traditional Mexican fare at reasonable prices are the specialty of this casual restaurant, which has been run by the same family for more than three decades. Tacos are always popular, but the best of the house is their heaping Mexican combination plate.

Zaragoza 8, near the central plaza. (£) 1/153-0185. Main courses $2–$8. No credit cards. Mon–Sat 11am–11pm; Sun 1–8pm.

## MULEGÉ AFTER DARK

Beyond the pig-roast fiestas, which have been known to last through the wee hours of a Saturday night, Mulegé's nightlife pretty much centers around the bars of the Hacienda Hotel and Las Casitas in town. In addition, try these other two options:

**La Jungla Bambú**   The name—Bamboo Jungle—is an accurate description of the decor of this otherwise American-style sports bar. Sports posters and plants line the bamboo walls, giving the impression that an adrenaline-inspired George of the Jungle may pop in for a cold *cerveza* (beer) at any moment. They also serve hamburgers for hungry drinkers. Corner of Gnl. Martinez and Zaragoza. No phone.

**Super Disco**   Well, no need to travel far to arrive at the other nightlife alternative in town—just climb the stairs. Playing—you guessed it—predominantly dance music, this place packs in the town, but is open on Friday, Saturday, and Sunday nights only, from 9pm. Late night is when the biggest crowds arrive, post-pig party, of course. Occasionally, they'll have a live band, but there's rarely a cover. Note that the music is not generally disco, but more often Mexican *norteño* or *banda ranchera* music. Corner of Gnl. Martinez and Zaragoza, 2nd floor. No phone.

## 3 Sidetrips from Mulegé: Santa Rosalía

38 miles N of Mulegé

Located in an arroyo north of Mulegé is Santa Rosalía, a unique mining town dating back to 1855. Founded by the French, the town has a decidedly European architectural ambience, though it's now inhabited by a distinctly Mexican culture. Pastel clapboard houses surrounded by picket fences line the streets, giving the town its nickname, *ciudad de madera* (city of wood). Its large harbor and the rusted ghost of its copper-smelting facility dominate the central part of town bordering the waterfront.

The town served at the center for copper mining in Mexico for years; a French company, Compañía de Boleo (part of the Rothschild family), obtained a 99-year lease back in the 1800s. Operations began in 1885 and continued until 1954, when the Mexicans regained the use of the land. During the French operation, more than 400 miles of tunnels were built underground and in the surrounding hills, primarily by Indian and Chinese laborers. Mexican President Porfirio Díaz originally granted the lease to the German shipping company, Casa Moeller, which sold the mining operation rights to the Rothschild family but retained exclusive rights to transport ore from the mine. Following the reversion of the mining operations to the Mexican government, the facility was plagued with problems, including the alleged leakage of arsenic into the local water supply, so the plant was permanently closed down in 1985.

The French influence is apparent everywhere in Santa Rosalía—especially in the town's wooden, colonial-style houses. The French also brought over thousands of Asian workers, who have integrated into the local population (Chinese cuisine is still particularly popular here), along with the German and French residents. The French administrators built their homes on the northern Mesa Francia, the part of town with the museum and historic buildings, while the Mexican residents settled on the southern Mesa Mexico. The town still has a noticeably segregated feel to it.

Today Santa Rosalía, with a population of 14,000, is notable for its man-made harbor—the recently constructed Marina Santa Rosalía, complete with concrete piers, floating docks, and full docking accommodations for a capacity of a dozen ocean cruisers. Santa Rosalía is the main seaport of northern Baja, located directly across from Guaymas. A ferry link established during the mining days still operates between the two ports. Because this is the prime entry point of manufactured goods into Baja, the town is filled with auto-parts and electronic appliance stores, along with shops selling Nikes and sunglasses.

The town has no real beach to speak of, and fewer recreational attractions. The rusted, dilapidated smelting foundry, railroad, and pier all border the docks and give the town an abandoned, neglected atmosphere.

## EXPLORING SANTA ROSALÍA

The principal attraction in Santa Rosalía is the Iglesia de Santa Barbara, a structure of galvanized steel designed by Gustave Eiffel (of Eiffel Tower fame) in 1884. It was originally created for the 1889 Paris World Expo, where it was displayed as a prototype for what Eiffel envisioned as a sort of a "prefab mission." The concept never took off, and the structure was left in a warehouse in Brussels, where it was later discovered and deemed destined for Baja by officials of the mining company. Section by section the church was transported, then reassembled in Santa Rosalía in 1897. The somber gray exterior belies the beauty of the intricate stained-glass windows viewed from inside.

Along with the church, the other obligatory site to see is the **ex-Fundación del Pacífico,** or **Museo Histórico Minero de Santa Rosalía.** Located in another landmark wooden building, it houses a permanent display of artifacts from the days of Santa Rosalía's mining operations. There are miniature models of the town and its buildings, old accounting ledgers and office equipment, and samples of the minerals extracted from local mines. It's open Monday through Saturday from 8:30am to 2pm and from 5 to 7pm. Admission is $1.50.

Bordering the museum are the most attractive of the clapboard houses, painted in a rainbow of delicious colors—mango, lemon, blueberry, and cherry. The wood used to construct these houses was the return cargo on ships that transported copper up to refineries in Oregon and British Columbia during the 1800s.

Other sites of note are the Plaza Benito Juárez, or central *zócalo* that fronts the Palacio Municipal (City Hall), an intriguing structure of French Colonial architecture. The square is bordered by the streets of Constitución, Carranza, Plaza, and Altamirano. Just down Constitución is the Biblioteca Mahatma Gandhi, more notable for the uniqueness of its name in Mexico than for the library itself, which is the only one in operation between Ensenada and La Paz. The library has a permanent exhibition of historic photos on display.

## WHERE TO STAY & DINE

Santa Rosalía claims to have the best bakery in all of Baja—**El Boleo** (© 1/152-0310)—which has been baking crusty French baguettes since the late 1800s. It's located on Ave. Obregón at Calle 3, 3 blocks west of the church, and is open from 8am to 6pm.

**Hotel Francés** 🏵🏵    Founded in 1886, the Hotel Francés once set the standard of hospitality in Baja Sur, welcoming European dignitaries and hosting the French administrators and businessmen of the mining operations. Today, it has a worn air of elegance, but retains its position as the most welcoming accommodations in Santa Rosalía. The lobby and restaurant/bar make up the front part of the building, along with its colonial-style, wrap-around veranda. Rooms are in the back, with wooden porches and balconies that overlook a small courtyard pool and wooden lounge chairs between the two sections. Each room has individually controlled air-conditioning, plus windows that open for ventilation. Floors are wood-planked, and the bathrooms are beautifully tiled, although small. You have a choice of two double beds or one king-size bed. Security boxes and telephone service are available in the lobby. The popular restaurant is open from 6am to 1pm, and currently serves breakfast only, although it begins serving other meals at a later date.

Calle Jean Michel Cousteau s/n, Santa Rosalía B.C.S. ©/fax **1/152-2052**. 17 units. $44 single or double. No credit cards. Free parking. **Amenities:** Restaurant/bar; small pool. *In room:* A/C, TV.

## 4  Whale-Watching in Baja: A Primer

There are few sights that inspire as much reverence as close contact with a whale in its natural habitat. The thrill of seeing one of these giant inhabitants of the sea up close is a life-changing event for many people. Few places in the world can offer as complete an experience as Mexico's Baja peninsula. The various protected bays and lagoons on the Pacific coast of Baja are the preferred winter waters for migrating gray whales as they journey south to mate and give birth to their calves.

While the entire Pacific coast of the Baja peninsula offers opportunities for whale sightings, the experience is particularly rewarding in the protected areas of the El Vizcaíno Biosphere Reserve, due to the large number of whales that can be seen easily. This area encompasses the famous Laguna Ojo de Liebre—also known as Scammon's Lagoon—close to Guerrero Negro, Laguna San Ignacio, and Bahía Magdalena.

> ## (Tips) Should I Take a Tour or Hire a Boat?
>
> You'll often get a better deal if you hire the services of a local panga operator; head down to the local pier to price it out. Expect to pay anywhere from $30 to $45 per person for a day trip with a local guide (plus a tip for good service); an organized tour can run almost double that price. It's always a good idea to check for licensed, experienced operators who know how to approach the whales with calm, caution, and respect for the environment. The most important thing about whale-watching is to enjoy it while practicing guidelines that ensure both your safety and the safety of the whales. (We've recommended several tour operators and organizations below.)

Because these protected waters offer ideal conditions for gray whales during the winter, the neighboring towns have developed the necessary infrastructure and services to accommodate whale-watchers. Avid eco- and adventure-lovers seem to follow their own migratory patterns and arrive at these shores between January and March to gaze in awe at the gentle cetaceans.

## WHAT YOU'LL SEE

Gray whales are the favorite species for whale-watchers because they tend to swim and feed mostly in coastal shallows, occasionally resting with their abdomen on the bottom, while their close relatives prefer to frequent the deeper realms of the ocean. Whale-watching in one of Baja's lagoons can be truly exciting, as there are times when gray whales appear to be on all sides, displaying the full spectrum of typical whale behavior.

Watchers might be showered with a cloud of water from a whale spouting—clearing its blowhole—or might witness an enormous male spyhopping—lifting its head vertically out of the water, just above eye level, to pivot around before slipping back in the water. Perhaps the most breathtaking spectacle of all is a breach, when a whale propels itself out of the water and arches through the air to land on its back with a splash. These gray whales are known to be so friendly and curious that they frequently come up to the whale-watching boats and stay close by, sometimes allowing people to pet them.

To be close to these magnificent creatures is a privilege. Above all, respect their environment and their integrity as inhabitants of the marine world.

## The Bloody History of a Whale-Watching Haven

Located 25 miles southwest of Guerrero Negro is Laguna Ojo de Liebre, also known as Scammon's Lagoon. It takes its name from an infamous whaler, Charles Melville Scammon, who followed a pod of gray whales into Laguna Ojo de Liebre. Taking advantage of geography—the lagoon has a very narrow mouth—he managed to slaughter the entire lot by using explosive harpoons. Before Scammon's "accomplishment," gray whales had remained safe from whalers because of their aggressive nature when under attack. But after Scammon's massacre, scores of whalers hopped on the bloody bandwagon, killing an estimated 10,000 gray whales in less than 20 years, and bringing the population close to extinction. (In an ironic turn of events, Scammon became a naturalist of some note later in life and wrote an important book about whales and the whaling industry.) The gray whales have made a remarkable comeback in the last 20 years—so much so that they are now off the endangered-species list.

## WHICH TOWN? WHICH TOUR?

Regardless of where you decide to stay in Baja, you most likely will easily find tours to the whale-watching areas of Bahía Magdalena and the lagoons of Ojo de Liebre and San Ignacio. (For whale-watching tours that depart from La Paz, see chapter 3.) However, if you want to center your visit on whale-watching, the best places to visit are Guerrero Negro, San Ignacio, Ciudad Constitución, Puerto San Carlos, and Puerto López Mateos.

While the above-mentioned towns have basic facilities, Loreto may actually be the wisest base to choose; it has a well-developed tourist infrastructure and a number of lovely resort hotels. From here, whale-watching cruises along the Pacific coast are easily accessible. The trips take you by road to Bahía Magdalena, where you board a skiff to get up close to the gentle giants. En route you get a chance to view the spectacular desert landscape; guides offer a wealth of natural and historical information. Locally based **Loreto Learning Center** (© 800/848-4333 in the U.S., or 1/135-0798; www.loretocenter.com) and **Las Parras Tours** (© 1/135-1010) offer excellent tours, although there are many groups that run expeditions to see the whales. Included among them is the U.S.-based **Baja Expeditions,** 2625 Garnet Ave., San Diego, CA 92109 (© **800/843-6967**, or 1/125-3828 in La Paz). Prices for package trips from Loreto run around between $90 and $100 per person for a day-long trip.

**Guerrero Negro** sits on the dividing line between southern and northern Baja. It has a modest but well-developed tourism infrastructure in an otherwise industrial town; it's the site of the world's largest evaporative saltworks. Despite the industrial nature of the town, the lagoon where gray whales calve and spend the winter has remained safe, and has witnessed a remarkable comeback of this almost-extinct species. This is partly because the salt produced in Guerrero Negro is shipped from an offshore artificial island, built away from the whale area, and also because of the designation of the area as part of the El Vizcaíno Biosphere Reserve in 1988.

**San Ignacio** is a small town built by the Spaniards in the middle of a palm oasis, and is full of Jesuit history. It is the ideal point of departure for **Laguna San Ignacio** ＲＲ, located 46 miles southwest of the town. The San Ignacio lagoon is an excellent spot for whale-watching because it is common for whales in this area to approach the small whale-watching boats, occasionally coming so close to allow you to touch them.

**Bahía Magdalena** is another spot preferred by wintering gray whales. Two towns located on the bay's shore offer whale-watching tours. **Puerto López Mateos,** on the northern shore, is the closest town to the whales' calving areas. Accommodations are limited to a few modest hotels and restaurants, but several boat operators do offer tours. For recommendations, contact the Unión de Lancheros y Servicios Turísticos del Puerto (© **1/131-5171**), an association of fishing-boat operators located on Adolfo López Mateos, or the Sociedad Cooperativa de Servicios Turísticos (© **1/131-5112** or 1/131-5198).

**Puerto San Carlos** offers a more developed tourism infrastructure with well-appointed hotels and restaurants, trailer parks, travel agencies, a bus station, and other services. To arrange a tour try Viajes Mar y Arena, Puerto La Paz s/n (© **1/136-0076;** fax 1/136-0232).

**Ciudad Constitución,** the largest of the three towns, is located 38 miles inland. It has a well-developed tourism infrastructure, with tour organizers that offer daily whale-watching tours during the season.

**GETTING THERE**   To get to Puerto López Mateos, take the only road going west from Loreto for about 75 miles. When you arrive in the town of Insurgentes, turn right and continue 1½ miles to the PUERTO LÓPEZ MATEOS exit. Turn left and continue 21 miles to Puerto López Mateos. To get to Puerto San Carlos, take the same road west to Insurgentes, then drive south about 15 miles until you reach Ciudad Constitución. From Ciudad Constitución take the exit to PUERTO SAN CARLOS, and continue the remaining 39 miles to town. Both routes are well paved and maintained.

# 5

# Northern Baja: Tijuana, Rosarito Beach & Ensenada

Northern Baja California is not only Mexico's most infamous border crossing, it's also the land that claims to be the birthplace of the original Caesar salad and the margarita. Who could resist that? As you travel south along the Pacific coastline, the three towns of Tijuana, Rosarito Beach, and Ensenada together make one of the most important introductions to Mexico; it's a trip that combines the boisterous, the beachy, and the beautiful of Baja.

Long notorious as a party-hard, 10-block border town, Tijuana has cleaned up its act a bit on its way to becoming a full-scale city. A growing number of sports and cultural attractions now augment the legendary shopping experience and wild nightlife. Rosarito Beach remains a more tranquil resort town, despite recently spending time in Hollywood's spotlight; the decidedly laid-back atmosphere makes it easy to enjoy miles of beachfront. Continue south past stellar surf breaks, golf courses, and fish-taco stands, and Ensenada emerges, a favored port of call and a lovely town with plenty of appeal for active travelers.

## EXPLORING NORTHERN BAJA

If you have a car, it's easy to venture into Baja Norte from Southern California for a few days' getaway. Since 1991, American car-rental companies have allowed their cars to be driven into Baja. Avis (© **800/331-1212** or 619/688-5000) and many other car-rental companies let their cars go as far south as the 28th parallel, the dividing line between the states of Baja North and Baja South. San Diego's Bob Baker Ford (© **619/297-5001,** ext. 9) allows its cars to be driven the entire 1,000-mile stretch of the Baja peninsula. Whether you drive your own car or a rented one, you'll need Mexican auto insurance in addition to your own; it's available at the border in San Ysidro or through the car-rental companies (see "Getting Around/By Car" in chapter 1).

## A Suggested Itinerary

Begin your trip in Tijuana with an afternoon, or maybe an overnight stay that includes watching some fast-paced jai alai (see "Outdoor Activities & Spectator Sports," in section 1, "Tijuana: Bawdy Border Town," for in-depth information), then head down the coast to the seaside town of Rosarito Beach, and then on to Puerto Nuevo and Ensenada.

It takes relatively little time to cross the international border in Tijuana, but be prepared for a delay of an hour or more on your return to the United States through San Diego. If you take local buses down the Baja coast (which is possible), the delays come en route rather than at the border.

## 1 Tijuana: Bawdy Border Town

16 miles S of San Diego

In northern Baja California, the first point of entry from the West Coast of the U.S. is infamous Tijuana, a town which continues to delude travelers into thinking that a visit there means they've been to Mexico. An important border town, Tijuana is renowned for its hustling, carnival-like atmosphere and easily accessible decadence.

But Tijuana is increasingly an important city in Mexico; the population has swelled to nearly two million, making it the second largest city on the Pacific coast of North America (after Los Angeles). Despite obvious signs of widespread poverty, the town claims one of the lowest unemployment rates in the country, thanks to the rise in *maquiladoras,* the foreign-owned manufacturing operations that continue to proliferate under NAFTA (North American Free Trade Agreement). High-rise office buildings testify to increased prosperity, as does the rise of a white-collar middle class that shops at modern shopping centers away from the tourist zone. And there's tourism from elsewhere in northern Mexico; visitors are drawn by the availability of imported goods and the lure of a "big city" experience.

Tijuana's "sin city" image is gradually morphing into that of a shopper's mecca and a nocturnal playground. A growing wine industry and its associated vineyards are nearby, and an increasing number of cultural offerings are being added to the traditional sporting attractions of greyhound racing, jai alai, and bullfights.

Tijuana first received notoriety during the U.S. Prohibition, when scores of visitors found the time and the inclination to come here, to the site of the world's largest saloon bar, The Whale. Around the same time, the Hotel Casino de Aguacaliente—the first resort of its kind in Mexico—attracted Hollywood stars and other celebrities with its casino, greyhound racing, and hot-springs spa.

Like many large cities in developing nations, Tijuana is a mixture of new and old, rich and poor, modern and traditional. You are less likely to find the Mexico you may be expecting—charming town squares and churches, women in colorful embroidered skirts and blouses, and bougainvillea spilling out of every orifice—and more likely to find an urban culture, a profusion of U.S.-inspired goods and services, and relentless hawkers playing to the thousands of tourists who come for a taste of Mexico.

## ESSENTIALS
### GETTING THERE & DEPARTING

A visit to Tijuana requires little in the way of formalities—no passport or tourist card is required of people who stay less than 72 hours in the border zone. If you plan to stay longer, a tourist card is required, available free of charge from the border crossing station, or from any immigration office.

**BY PLANE**   **AeroCalifornia** (℃ **800/237-6225** in the U.S., or 6/684-2100) has nonstop or direct flights from Los Angeles; **Aeromexico** (℃ **800/237-6639** in the U.S., or 6/683-2700 or 6/638-8444; www.aeromexico.com) has connecting flights from Houston, New York, Guadalajara, La Paz, and Mexico City. **Mexicana** (℃ **800/531-7921** in the U.S., 6/634-6566, www.mexicana.com) has direct or connecting flights from Guadalajara, Los Angeles, Mexico City, and Cancún.

**BY CAR**   If you plan to visit only Tijuana and are arriving from Southern California, you should consider leaving your car behind, as the traffic can be challenging. One alternative is to walk across the border; you can either park your car in one of the safe, long-term parking lots on the San Diego side for about $8 a day, or take the San Diego Trolley to the border. Once you're in Tijuana, it's easier to get around by taxi than to take on the local drivers. Cab fares from the border to downtown Tijuana run about $5. You can also charter a taxi to Rosarito for about $20 (one-way) or to Ensenada for $100 (one-way).

# Tijuana

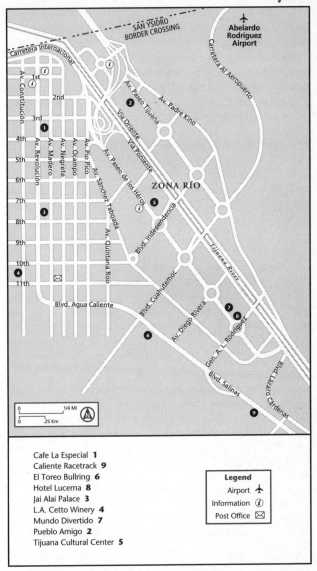

Cafe La Especial **1**
Caliente Racetrack **9**
El Toreo Bullring **6**
Hotel Lucerna **8**
Jai Alai Palace **3**
L.A. Cetto Winery **4**
Mundo Divertido **7**
Pueblo Amigo **2**
Tijuana Cultural Center **5**

| Legend | |
|---|---|
| Airport | ✈ |
| Information | ⓘ |
| Post Office | ⊠ |

To reach Tijuana from the U.S., take I-5 south to the Mexican border at San Ysidro. The drive from downtown San Diego takes about half an hour.

Many car-rental companies in San Diego now allow their cars to be driven into Baja California, at least as far as Ensenada. Cars from **Avis** (© 800/331-1212 or 619/688-5000) and **Southwest** (© 619/497-4800) may be driven as far as the 28th parallel and Guerrero Negro, the dividing line that separates Baja into two states, North and South. **Bob Baker Ford** (© 619/297-5001, ext. 9) allows their cars to be driven the entire 1,000-mile stretch of the Baja Peninsula.

Keep in mind that if you drive in, you'll need Mexican auto insurance in addition to your own. You can get it in San Ysidro, just north of the border at the San Ysidro exit; from your car-rental agency in San Diego; or from an AAA office if you're a member.

From the south, take Highway 1 (Carretera Transpeninsular) north to Tijuana. It's a long and sometimes difficult drive.

**BY TROLLEY**  From downtown San Diego, you also have the option of taking the bright-red trolley headed for San Ysidro and getting off at the last stop (it's nicknamed the Tijuana Trolley for good reason). From here, just follow the signs to walk across the border. It's simple, quick, and inexpensive; the one-way trolley fare is $2. The last trolley leaving for San Ysidro departs downtown around midnight; the last returning trolley from San Ysidro is at 1am. On Saturdays, the trolley runs 24 hours.

**BY BUS**  **Mexicoach/Five Star Tours,** in San Diego at the intersection of Broadway and Kettner (© 619/232-5049; fax 619/575-3075), offers specialized trips across the border. For approximately $25 per person, they will take you across the border, recommend shops and restaurants, then pick you up to return to San Diego at a pre-established time. The Mexicoach stop is at the Tijuana Tourist Terminal at 1025 Av. Revolución (between calles 6 and 7).

Also from San Diego, **Gray Line** (© 619/491-0011) offers a tour to Tijuana for $26 ($36 with lunch), with a drop-off in the middle of town; you can spend a few hours or all day. **Contact Tours** (© 619/477-8687) also offers a tour to Tijuana for $26.

## ORIENTATION

**ARRIVING**  Upon arrival at the airport, buy a ticket inside the building for a taxi, which can be shared by up to five passengers, and costs about $9 to and from anywhere in the city. Public buses to downtown Tijuana, marked CENTRO, are also available and cost 45¢

per passenger. The airport is located about 5 miles (8km) east of the city.

The major car-rental agencies all have counters at the airport, open during flight arrivals: **Avis** (© **800/331-1212** from the U.S., or 6/683-2310); **Budget** (© **800/527-0700** from the U.S., or 6/683-2905); **Hertz** (© **800/654-3131** from the U.S., or 6/683-2080); and **National** (© **800/328-4567** from the U.S). Advance reservations are not always necessary, but they are recommended.

If you've come to Tijuana on the San Diego Trolley or if you leave a car on the U.S. side of the border, you will walk through the border crossing. The first structure you'll see on your left is a Visitor Information Center, open daily from 9am to 7pm; ask for a copy of the *Baja Visitor* magazine and the *Baja Times*. From here, you can easily walk into the center of town or take a taxi.

Tijuana taxicabs are easy to find, available at most of the visitor hot spots. It's customary to agree upon the rate before stepping into the cab, whether you're just going a few blocks or hiring a cab for the afternoon. One-way rides within the city cost between $4 and $8, and tipping is optional. Some cabs are "local" taxis, frequently stopping to take on or let off other passengers during your ride; they are less expensive than private cabs.

**VISITOR INFORMATION**    Prior to your visit, you can write for information, brochures, and maps from the Tijuana Convention & Visitors Bureau, P.O. Box 434523, San Diego, CA 92143-4523. Once in Tijuana, pick up visitor information at the **Tijuana Tourism Board,** Paseo de los Héroes 9365, Zona Río (© **888/775-2417** toll-free in the U.S., or 6/684-2854 or 6/634-0223; www.seetijuana.com; e-mail: info@seetijuana.com). You can also try the **Mexican Tourism Office** (© **6/688-0555;** open Monday to Friday from 8am until 5pm, Saturday and Sunday from 10am until 2pm), or the **National Chamber of Commerce** (© **6/685-8472;** open Monday through Friday only, 9am to 2pm and 4 to 7pm). Both have offices at the corner of Avenida Revolución and Calle 1, and are extremely helpful with maps and orientation, local events of interest, and accommodations; in addition, the tourism office provides legal assistance for visitors who encounter problems while in Tijuana.

The following countries have **consulate offices** in Tijuana: the **United States** (© **6/681-7400**), **Canada** (© **6/684-0461**), and the **United Kingdom** (© **6/681-7323** or 6/686-5320).

You can also get a preview of events, restaurants, and more online at www.seetijuana.com.

**Fast Facts: Tijuana**

*Area Code* The local telephone area code is **6**.

*Banks* Banks exchange currency during business hours, generally Monday through Friday from 8:30am to 6pm and Saturday from 9am to 2pm. Major banks with ATMs and *Casas de Cambio* (money-exchange houses) are easily found in all the heavily trafficked areas discussed in this book. The currency of Mexico is the peso, but you can easily visit Tijuana (or Rosarito and Ensenada, for that matter) without changing money because dollars are accepted virtually everywhere.

*Climate & Weather* Tijuana's climate is similar to Southern California's. Don't expect sweltering heat just because you're south of the border, and remember that the Pacific waters won't be much warmer than off San Diego. The first beaches you'll find are about 15 miles south of Tijuana.

*Pharmacy* Sanborn's (✆ 6/688-1462), the 24-hour megastore with a pharmacy, has several locations in Tijuana; corner of Avenida Revolución and Calle 8 is one. There are also numerous discount pharmacies located along Avenida Constitución and Avenida Revolución; one to try is **Le Drug Store** (✆ 6/685-8075).

*Post Office* The main *correo* is located at Calle 11 at Ave. Negrete (✆ 6/627-2699), open Monday through Friday from 8am to 7pm, and Saturdays from 9am to 1pm.

*Taxes & Tipping* An added value tax of 10%, called **IVA** (*Impuesto al Valor Agregado*), is added to most bills, including those in restaurants; however, legislation reform was being reviewed at press time that would extend the 15% tax rate to all businesses here. This does not represent the tip; the bill will read "IVA incluído," but you should add about 15% for the tip if the service warrants.

## EXPLORING TIJUANA

One of the first major tourist attractions below the border is also one of the strangest—the **Museo de Cera** (Wax Museum), Calle 1 between avenidas Revolución and Madero (✆ 6/688-2478). Featured statues include the eclectic mix of Whoopi Goldberg,

Laurel and Hardy, and Bill Clinton, arranged in an exhibit otherwise dominated by figures from Mexican history. If you aren't spooked by the not-so-lifelike figures of Aztec warriors, brown-robed friars, Spanish princes, and 20th-century military leaders (all posed in period dioramas), step into the Chamber of Horrors, where wax werewolves and sinister sadists lurk in the shadows. When the museum is mostly empty, which is most of the time, the dramatically lit Chamber of Horrors can be a little creepy. This side-street freak show is open daily from 10am to 8pm, and admission is $1.

For many visitors, Tijuana's "main event" is the bustling **Avenida Revolución,** the street whose reputation precedes it. Beginning in the 1920s, American college students, servicemen, and hedonistic tourists discovered this street as a bawdy center for illicit fun. Some of the original attraction has fallen by the wayside: Gambling was outlawed in the 1930s, back-alley cockfights are also illegal, and the same civic improvements that repaved Revolución to provide trees, benches, and wider sidewalks also vanquished the girlie shows whose barkers once accosted passersby. Drinking and shopping are the main order of business these days; while revelers from across the border knock back tequila shooters and dangle precariously at the upstairs railings of glaring bars, bargain hunters peruse the never-ending array of goods (and not-so-goods) for sale. You'll find the action between calles 1 and 9; the information centers (mentioned earlier) are at the north end, and the landmark jai alai palace anchors the southern portion. To help make sense of all those tchotchkes, see "Shopping," below.

Visitors can be easily seduced—then quickly repulsed—by tourist-trap areas like Avenida Revolución, but it's important to remember there's more to Tijuana than American tourism. If you're looking to see a different side of Tijuana, the best place to start is the **Centro Cultural Tijuana,** Paseo de los Héroes at Mina (© 6/687-9600). You'll easily spot the ultramodern Tijuana Cultural Center complex, designed by irrepressible modern architect Pedro Ramírez Vásquez. Its centerpiece is that gigantic sand-colored dome housing an OMNIMAX theater, which screens two different 45-minute films (subjects range from science to space travel), each of which has one English-language show per day. Inside, the center houses the museum's permanent collection of Mexican artifacts from pre-Hispanic times through the modern political era, plus a gallery for visiting exhibits that have included everything from the works of artist Diego Rivera to a well-curated yet disturbing exhibit chronicling torture and human rights

violations throughout the ages. Music, theater, and dance performances are held in the center's concert hall and courtyard, and there's
also a cafe and an excellent museum bookshop. Wednesdays and
Sundays a free jazz concert is offered. The center is open daily from
9am to 8:30pm. Admission to the museum's permanent exhibits is
free; there's a $2 charge for the special-event gallery, and tickets for
OMNIMAX films are $4 for adults and $2.50 for children.

Don't be discouraged if the Cultural Center sounds like a field
trip for schoolchildren; it's a must-see, if only to drag you away from
tourist kitsch and into the more sophisticated Zona Río (river area).
While there, stop to admire the wide, European-style Paseo de los
Héroes. The boulevard's intersections are marked by gigantic traffic
circles (*glorietas*), at the center of which stand statuesque monuments to leaders ranging from Aztec Emperor Cuauhtémoc to
Abraham Lincoln. Navigating the congested glorietas will require
your undivided attention, however, so it's best to pull over to admire
the monuments.

In the Zona Río you'll find some classier shopping and a colorful
local marketplace, plus the ultimate kid destination, **Mundo
Divertido,** Paseo de los Héroes at Calle José María Velasco
(℗ **6/634-3213**). Literally translated, it means "world of amusement," and one parent described it as the Mexican equivalent of "a
Chuck E. Cheese's restaurant built inside a Malibu Grand Prix." You
get the idea—noisy and frenetic, it's the kind of place kids dream
about. Let them choose from miniature golf, batting cages, a roller
coaster, a kid-sized train, a video game parlor, and go-carts. There's
a food court with tacos and hamburgers; if you're in luck, the picnic
area will be festooned with streamers and piñatas for some lucky
child's birthday party. The park is open daily, from noon to 8pm,
Saturday and Sunday from 10am until 8:30pm. Admission is free,
and several booths inside sell tickets for the various rides.

The fertile valleys of Northern Baja produce most of Mexico's
finest wines and export many high-quality vintages to Europe;
they're mostly unavailable in the U.S. For an introduction to
Mexican wines, stop into **Cava de Vinos L.A. Cetto** (L.A. Cetto
Winery), Av. Cañón Johnson 2108, at Av. Constitución Sur
(℗ **6/685-3031**). Shaped like a wine barrel, this building's striking
facade is made from old oak aging barrels in an inspired bit of recy-
cling. In the entrance stand a couple of wine presses (ca. 1928) that
Don Angel Cetto used back in the early days of production. His
family still runs the winery, which opened this impressive visitor
center in 1993. L.A. Cetto bottles both red and white wines, some

*Moments*  **First Crush: The Annual Harvest Festival**

If you enjoyed a visit to L.A. Cetto, Tijuana's winery (or Ensenada's Bodegas de Santo Tomás, discussed later in this chapter), then you might want to come back for the festive Harvest Festival, held each year in late August or early September. Set amongst the endless vineyards of the fertile Guadalupe Valley, the day's events include the traditional blessing of the grapes, wine tastings, live music and dancing, riding exhibitions, and a country-style Mexican meal. L.A. Cetto offers a group excursion from Tijuana (about an hour's drive); San Diego's Baja California Tours (© 619/454-7166) also organizes a day-long trip from San Diego.

of them award winners, including petite sirah, nebbiolo, and cabernet sauvignon. Most bottles cost about $5; the special reserves are a little more than $10. The company also produces tequila, brandy, and olive oil, all for sale here. Admission is $2 for a tour and generous tasting (for those 18 and older only; those 17 or younger are admitted free with an adult but cannot taste the wines), $3 with souvenir wine glass. Open Monday through Friday from 9:30am to 6:30pm and Saturday from 9:30am to 5:30pm. Tours Monday to Friday 10am to 2pm and 4 to 5:30pm, and Saturday 10am to 2pm.

## OUTDOOR ACTIVITIES & SPECTATOR SPORTS
Tijuana is a spectator's (and bettor's) paradise.

**BULLFIGHTING**   While some insist this spectacle promotes a cruel disregard for animal rights, others esteem it as a richly symbolic drama involving the courage Ernest Hemingway called "grace under pressure." Whatever your opinion, bullfighting has a prominent place in Mexican heritage, and is even considered an essential element of the culture. The skill and bravery of matadors is closely linked with cultural ideals regarding machismo, and some of the world's best perform at Tijuana's two stadiums. The season runs from May through September, with events held Sundays at 4:30pm. Ticket prices range from $17 to $40 (the premium seats are on the shaded side of the arena), and can be purchased at the bullring or in advance from San Diego's **Five Star Tours** (© 619/232-5049). El

**Toreo** (📞 **6/686-1510**) is 2 miles east of downtown on Blvd. Agua Caliente at Avenida Diego Rivera. **Plaza de Toros Monumental** (Bullring-by-the-Sea) (📞 **6/680-1808**) is 6 miles west of downtown via Highway 1-D (before the first toll station); it's perched at the edge of both the ocean and the California border. You can take a taxi easily to El Toreo—while fares are negotiable, around $10 one way should be fair. You can also negotiate a fare to Bullring-by-the-Sea, but fares are unpredictable.

**DOG RACING**    There's satellite wagering on U.S. horse races at the majestic **Caliente Racetrack** (off Blvd. Agua Caliente, 3 miles east of downtown), but these days only greyhounds actually kick up dust at the track. Races are held daily at 7:45pm, with Saturday and Sunday matinees at 2pm. General admission is free, but bettors in the know congregate in the comfortable Turf Club; admission there is $10, refundable with a wagering voucher. For more information, call 📞 **6/685-7833**, or 619/231-1910 in San Diego. For other racing information, call 📞 **800-PICK-BAJA.**

**GOLF**    Once the favorite of golfing celebrities and socialites (and a very young Arnold Palmer) who stayed at the now-defunct Agua Caliente Resort, the **Tijuana Country Club** (Blvd. Agua Caliente at Av. Gustavo Salinas; 📞 **6/681-7855**) is near the Caliente Racetrack and behind the Grand Hotel Tijuana; it's about a 10-minute drive from downtown. The course is well maintained and frequented mostly by business travelers staying at nearby hotels, many of which offer golf packages (see Grand Hotel Tijuana in "Where to Stay," below). Weekend greens fees are $40 a person, and optional cart rental is $20 per cart; club rental is available at $20, with caddies an additional $20 plus tip. Ask for seasonal specials. Stop by the pro shop for balls, tees, and a limited number of other accessories; the clubhouse also has two restaurants, complete with cocktail lounges.

**JAI ALAI**    A lightning-paced ballgame played on a slick indoor court, jai alai (pronounced *high*-ah-lye) is an ancient Basque tradition incorporating elements of tennis, hockey, and basketball. You can't miss the Frontón Palacio, Avenida Revolución at Calle 7; it's a huge, box-like arena in the center of town, painted with giant red letters spelling JAI ALAI. Games are held Monday through Saturday at 8pm, with matinee events Monday and Friday at noon. General admission is $2, and there are betting windows inside the arena. For more information, call 📞 **6/634308,** or 619/231-1910 in San Diego.

## SHOPPING

Tijuana's biggest attraction is shopping—ask any of the 44 million people who cross the border each year to do it. They come to take advantage of the reasonable prices on a variety of merchandise: terra-cotta and colorfully glazed pottery, woven blankets and serapes, embroidered dresses and sequined sombreros, onyx chess sets, beaded necklaces and bracelets, silver jewelry, leather bags and huarache sandals, rain sticks (bamboo branches filled with pebbles that simulate the patter of raindrops), hammered tin picture frames, thick drinking glasses, novelty swizzle sticks, Cuban cigars, and Mexican liquors like Kalúha and tequila. You're permitted to bring $400 worth of purchases back across the border (sorry, no Cuban cigars allowed), including 1 liter of alcohol per person.

When most people think of Tijuana, they picture **Avenida Revolución,** which appears to exist solely for the extraction of dollars from American visitors. Dedicated shoppers quickly discover that most of the curios spilling out onto the sidewalk look alike, despite the determined seller's assurances that their wares are the best in town. Browse for comparison's sake, but for the best souvenir shopping, duck into one of the many *pasajes,* or passageway arcades, where you'll find items of a slightly better quality and merchants willing to bargain. Some of the most enjoyable pasajes are on the east side of the street between calles 2 and 5; they also provide a pleasant respite from the quickly irritating tumult of Avenida Revolución.

An alternative is to visit **Sanborn's,** Av. Revolución between calles 8 and 9 (© **6/688-1462**), a branch of the Mexico City department store long favored by American travelers. They sell an array of regional folk art and souvenirs, books about Mexico in both Spanish and English, and candies and fresh sweet treats from the bakery— and you can have breakfast in their sunny cafe.

One of the few places in Tijuana to find better-quality crafts from a variety of Mexican states is **Tolán,** Av. Revolución between calles 7 and 8 (© **6/688-3637**). In addition to the obligatory selection of standard Avenida Revolución souvenirs, you'll find blue glassware from Guadalajara, glazed pottery from Tlaquepaque, crafts from the Oaxaca countryside, or distinctive tilework from Puebla. Prices at Tolán are fixed, so you shouldn't try to bargain the way you can in some of the smaller shops and informal vendor stands. If a marketplace atmosphere and spirited bargaining are what you're looking for, head instead to **Mercado de Artesanías** (crafts market), Calle 2

---

*Tips* **Where to Park in Tijuana**

Plaza Río Tijuana has ample free parking and is just across the street from the Cultural Center, where private lots charge $5 to $8 to park.

---

and Ave. Negrete, where an entire city block is filled with vendors of pottery, clayware, clothing, and other crafts.

Shopping malls are as common in Tijuana as in any big American city; you shouldn't expect to find typical souvenirs there, but shopping alongside residents and other intrepid visitors is often more fun than feeling like a sitting-duck tourist. One of the biggest, and most convenient, is **Plaza Río Tijuana** (on Paseo de los Héroes at Av. Independencia; © 6/684-0402), an outdoor plaza anchored by several department stores and featuring dozens of specialty shops and casual restaurants.

On the other side of Paseo de los Héroes from Plaza Río Tijuana is **Plaza del Zapato,** a two-story indoor mall filled with only shoe (*zapato*) stores. Though most are made with quality leather rather than synthetics, inferior workmanship ensures they'll likely last only a season or two. But with prices as low as $30, why not indulge? For a taste of everyday Mexico, visit **Mercado Hidalgo,** one block west at Av. Sánchez Taboada and Av. Independencia, a busy indoor/outdoor marketplace where vendors display fresh flowers and produce, sacks of dried beans and chilies by the kilo, and a few souvenir crafts (including some excellent piñatas). Morning is the best time to visit the market, and you'll be more comfortable paying with pesos, since most sellers are accustomed to a local crowd.

## WHERE TO STAY

When calculating room rates, always remember that hotel rates in Tijuana are subject to a 12% tax, though this tax possibly may have increased to 15% by the time this book comes out.

**Grand Hotel Tijuana** *<sub></sub>* Popular with business travelers and visiting celebrities, and for society events, the hotel has the best-maintained public and guest rooms in Tijuana, which helps make up for what it lacks in regional warmth. You can see the unusually high mirrored twin towers of this hotel from all of the surrounding city. Modern and sleek in design, it was opened in 1982—the height of Tijuana's prosperity—under the name Fiesta Americana, a name locals (and many cab drivers) still use. Rooms have spectacular views of the city from the top floors (the tower is 32 stories high). The lobby, whose dark carpeting and '80s mirrors and neon accents feel like a Vegas hotel/casino, gives way to several ballrooms and an airy atrium that serves elegant international cuisine at dinner and weekend brunch. Next to the atrium is a casual Mexican restaurant, beyond which the Vegas resemblance resumes with an indoor shopping arcade. The hotel offers a golf package for $82 per person—it includes one night's lodging with a welcome cocktail and a round of 18 holes (including cart) at the adjacent Tijuana Country Club.

Agua Caliente 4500, Tijuana (P.O. Box BC, Chula Vista, CA 92012). © **800/ GRANDTJ** in the U.S., or 6/681-7000 in Tijuana. Fax 6/681-7016. www.grand-hoteltijuana.com. 422 units. $130 double; from $190 suite. AE, MC, V. Free underground parking. **Amenities:** 2 restaurants, lobby bar; heated pool; sauna, concierge, tour desk, business center, shopping arcade, 24-hour room service; laundry and dry cleaning service. *In room:* A/C, dataport, minibar, iron, safe-deposit boxes.

**Hotel Lucerna** ⊛   Once the most chic hotel in Tijuana, Lucerna now feels slightly worn, but the place still has personality. The flavor is very Mexican colonial—wrought-iron railings and chandeliers, rough-hewn heavy wood furniture, brocade wallpaper, and traditional tiles. The hotel is in the Zona Río, away from the noise and congestion of downtown, so a quiet night's sleep is easily attainable here. All the rooms in this five-story hotel have balconies or patios, but are otherwise unremarkable. Sunday brunch is served outdoors by the swimming pool; there's also a coffee shop that provides room service. The Lucerna's staff is friendly and attentive.

Av. Paseo de los Héroes 10902, Zona Río, Tijuana. © 800/582-3762 U.S., or 6/634-2000. 179 units. $85 double; $88 suite. AE, DC, MC, V. **Amenities:** 1 restaurant; swimming pool; tour desk; room service; laundry service. *In room:* TV.

## WHERE TO DINE
### EXPENSIVE

**Cien Años** ⊛⊛⊛ MEXICAN   An elegant and gracious Zona Río restaurant offering artfully blended Mexican flavors (tamarind, poblano chile, mango) in stylish presentations. If you're interested in true haute cuisine, the buzz around Tijuana is all about this place.

Calle José María Velasco 1407. © **6/634-3039** or 6/634-7262. Main courses $12–$30. AE, DC, MC, V. Daily 1pm–midnight.

**La Costa** ⊛ MEXICAN-STYLE SEAFOOD   Fish gets top billing here, starting with the hearty seafood soup. There are combination platters of half a grilled lobster, stuffed shrimp, and baked

shrimp; fish filetstuffed with seafood and cheese; and several
abalone dishes.

Calle 7, no. 8131 (just off Avenida Revolución), Zona Centro. ✆ 6/685-8494. Main
courses $8–$20. AE, DC, MC, V. Daily 10am–midnight.

**Tour de France** ✿✿ FRENCH    Martín San Román, the chef and
co-owner of Tour de France, was sous-chef at San Diego's famous
Westgate hotel and then went on to open the top-class Marius
restaurant in the former Le Meridian resort in Coronado. His loyal
clientele has followed him from San Diego, and he has acquired new
devotees in Tijuana. It's worth a trip to Tijuana just to sample
Martín's patés or his escargots; and the vegetables, prepared and presented with the flair of an artist, all come fresh from local Ensenada
farms. The wine list is extensive and international, and the atmosphere is as fine as the food.

Gobernador Ibarra 252, a.k.a. Av. 16 de Septiembre (on the old road to Ensenada
between the Palacio Azteca Hotel and the La Sierra Motel). ✆ 6/681-7542.
www.sdro.com/tourfrance. Reservations recommended. Main courses (including
soup and salad) $18–$21. AE, MC, V. Mon–Thurs 8am–10:30pm; Fri–Sat
8am–11:30pm.

## MODERATE
**Hard Rock Cafe** AMERICAN/MEXICAN    Had an overload of
Mexican culture? Looking for a place with all the familiar comforts
of home? Then head for the Tijuana branch of this ubiquitous
watering hole, which promises nothing exotic; the standard Hard
Rock chain menu, which admittedly features an outstanding ham-
burger, is served in the regulation Hard Rock setting (dark, clubby,
walls filled with rock 'n' roll memorabilia). While the restaurant's
street presence is more subdued than most Hard Rock locations,
you'll still be able to spot the trademark Caddie emerging from
above the door. But while the cafe and all its trimmings may have
migrated south of the border, prices are more in line with what you'd
see in the U.S.—and therefore no bargain in competitive Tijuana.

520 Av. Revolución (near Calle 1), Zona Centro. ✆ 6/685-0206. Menu items
$5–$10. AE, MC, V. Daily 11am–2am.

## INEXPENSIVE
**Cafe La Especial** MEXICAN    Tucked away in a shopping pasaje
at the bottom of some stairs (turn in at the taco stand of the same
name), this restaurant is a well-known shopper's refuge and pur-
veyor of home-style Mexican cooking at reasonable (though not
dirt-cheap) prices. The gruff, efficient waitstaff carry out platter
after platter of carne asada, grilled marinated beef served with fresh

tortillas, beans, and rice—it's La Especial's most popular item. Traditional dishes like tacos, enchiladas, and burritos round out the menu, augmented by frosty cold Mexican beers. Open daily for breakfast, lunch, and dinner.

Av. Revolución 718 (midway between calles 3 and 4), Zona Centro. ℂ 6/685-6654. Menu items $4–$12. MC, V. Daily 9am–10pm.

**Carnitas Uruapán** 🌟🌟 MEXICAN   *Carnitas*—marinated pork that's roasted on a spit till falling-apart tender, then served in chunks with tortillas, salsa, cilantro, guacamole, and onions—are a beloved dish in Mexico and the main attraction at Carnitas Uruapán. Here the meat is served by the kilo (or portion thereof) at long, communal wooden tables to a crowd of mostly locals. The original is a little hard to find, but now there's a branch in the fashionable Zona Río—they're both open from early morning until the wee hours. A half-kilo of carnitas is plenty for two people and costs around $12, including beans as well as that impressive array of condiments. It's a casual feast without compare, but vegetarians need not apply. Another location, which specializes in seafood options as well, is on Paseo de los Héroes at Av. Rodríguez (no phone).

Blvd. Díaz Ordáz 12650 (across from Plaza Patria), La Mesa. ℂ 6/681-6181. Menu items $2.50–$8. No credit cards. Daily 8am–5am.

**La Fonda de Roberto** 🌟🌟 MEXICAN   Although its location may seem out-of-the-way on the map, this modest restaurant's regular appearances on San Diego "Best Of" lists attest to its continued appeal. A short drive (or taxi ride) from downtown Tijuana, La Fonda's colorful dining room opens onto the courtyard of a kitschy 1960s motel, complete with retro kidney-shaped swimming pool. The light-filled and festive atmosphere is perfect for enjoying a variety of regional Mexican dishes, including a decent chicken mole and generous portions of *milanesa* (meat—beef, chicken, or pork—pounded paper thin, then breaded and fried). A house specialty is *queso fundido,* deep-fried cheese with chilies and mushrooms, served with a basket of freshly made corn tortillas.

In the La Sierra Motel, 2800 Blvd. Cuauhtémoc Sur Oeste (a.k.a. Av. 16 de Septiembre, on the old road to Ensenada). ℂ 6/686-4687. Most dishes $5–$11. MC, V. Tues–Thurs 10am–10pm.

## TIJUANA AFTER DARK

Avenida Revolución is ground zero for the city's nightlife; many compare it with Bourbon Street in New Orleans during Mardi Gras—except here it's a regular occurrence, not a once-a-year blowout. Tijuana has several lively discos, and perhaps the most popular is **Baby Rock,** 1482 Diego Rivera, Zona Río (© 6/634-2404), an obvious cousin to Acapulco's lively Baby O, which features everything from Latin rock to rap. It's located close to the Guadalajara Grill restaurant.

Also popular in Tijuana are the proliferation of sports bars, featuring satellite wagering from all over the United States as well as from Tijuana's Caliente track. The most popular of these bars cluster in **Pueblo Amigo, Vía Oriente,** and **Paseo Tijuana** in the Zona Río, a new center designed to resemble a colonial Mexican village. Even if you don't bet on the horses, you can soak up the atmosphere. Two of the town's hottest discos, **Rodeo de Media Noche** (© 6/682-4967) and **Señor Frogs** (© 6/682-4962), are in Pueblo Amigo, as well as **La Tablita de Tony** (© 6/682-8111), an Argentinean restaurant. Pueblo Amigo is conveniently located less than 2 miles from the border: a short taxi ride or—during daylight hours—a pleasant walk.

## 2 Rosarito Beach & Beyond: Baja's First Beach Resorts

34 miles S of San Diego; 18 miles S of Tijuana

Just a 20-minute drive south of Tijuana and a complete departure in ambience, Rosarito Beach is a tranquil, friendly beach town. It also gained early renown during the U.S. Prohibition, when the elegant Rosarito Beach Hotel catered to Hollywood stars. This classic structure still welcomes numerous guests, despite the fact that its opulence has lost some luster. Hollywood has likewise played a major part in Rosarito's recent renaissance—it was the location for the soundstage and filming of the Academy Award–winning *Titanic.* The Titanic Museum here continues to draw fans of the film.

Two roads run between Tijuana and Ensenada (the largest and third-largest cities in Baja)—the scenic, coast-hugging toll road (marked CUOTA, or 1-D), and the free but slower-going public road (marked LIBRE, or 1). We strongly recommend starting out on the toll road, but use the free road along Rosarito Beach if you'd like to easily pull on and off the road to shop or look at the view. The beaches between Tijuana and Rosarito are also known for excellent surf breaks.

**VISITOR INFORMATION**    The best source of information is **Baja California Tourism Information** (© 800/522-1516 in California, Arizona, or Nevada; 800/225-2786 in the rest of the

U.S. and Canada; or 619/298-4105 in San Diego). This office provides advice and makes hotel reservations throughout Baja California. You can also contact the local **Secretaría de Turísmo,** in the Villa Floresta shopping center, on Blvd. Benito Juárez (© **6/612-0200**). The office is open Monday to Friday from 8am to 5pm, and Saturday and Sunday from 10am to 3pm.

## EXPLORING ROSARITO BEACH

Once a tiny resort town that remained a "best-kept secret" despite its proximity to Tijuana, Rosarito Beach saw an explosion of development in the prosperous '80s; now it's settled down into it's own spirited personality. Why does its popularity persist? Location is one reason—it's the first beach resort town south of the border, and party-minded tourists aren't always too discriminating. This should give you an idea of the crowd to expect on holiday weekends and school breaks.

Reputation is another draw: For years the **Rosarito Beach Hotel** (see "Where to Stay," below), built around 1927, was the preferred hideaway of celebrities and other fashionable Angelenos. Movie star Rita Hayworth and her royal husband Prince Ali Khan would vacation here; Paulette Goddard and Burgess Meredith were married at the resort. Although the hotel's entry still features the gallant inscription POR ESTA PUERTA PASAN LAS MUJERES MÁS HERMOSAS DEL MUNDO ("Through this doorway pass the most beautiful women in the world"), today's vacationing starlets are more often found at resorts on Baja's southern tip. While the glimmer (as well as the glamour) has worn off, the Rosarito Beach Hotel is still the most interesting place in town, and nostalgia buffs will want to stop in for a look at some expert tile- and woodwork, as well as the panoramic murals throughout the lobby. Check out the colorful Aztec images in the main dining room, the magnificently tiled rest rooms, and the glassed-in bar overlooking the sparkling pool and beach, or peek into the original owner's mansion on the property (now home to a health spa and gourmet restaurant).

Rosarito Beach has caught the attention of Hollywood for years; most recently, the megahit *Titanic* was filmed here in a state-of-the-art production facility. *Titanic*'s allure is fading fast, however, and the former set was just reopened as a theme park with broader appeal.

If it's not too crowded, Rosarito is a good place to while away a few hours. Have a swim or horseback ride at the beach, then dine on fish tacos or tamales from any one of a number of family-run stands along Blvd. Benito Juárez, the town's main (and only) drag. You can have a drink at the local branch of Ensenada's enormously popular Papas & Beer (see "Rosarito Beach After Dark" below), or shop for souvenirs along the Old Ensenada Highway just south of town.

## SHOPPING

The dozen or so blocks of Rosarito north of the Rosarito Beach Hotel are packed with the stores typical in Mexican border towns; curio shops, cigar and *licores* (liquor) stores, and *farmacias* (where drugs like Viagra, Retin-A, Prozac, Rogaine, and many more are available at low cost and without a prescription). Rosarito has also become a center for carved furnishings—plentiful downtown along Blvd. Benito Juárez—and pottery, best purchased at stands along the old highway, south of town. A reliable, but more expensive, furniture shop is **Casa la Carreta**, at Km 29.5 on the old road south of Rosarito (© **6/612-0502**), where you can see plentiful examples of the best workmanship—chests, tables, chairs, headboards, cabinets, and cradles.

## WHERE TO STAY

**Rosarito Beach Hotel & Spa** *(Value)*   Although this once-glamorous resort has been holding steady since its heyday, the vestiges of vacationing movie stars, a well-heeled gambling casino, and 1930s elegance have been all but eclipsed by the glaring night-time neon and party-mania that currently defines the former retreat of Rosarito. Despite the resort's changed personality, unique features of artistic construction and lavish decoration remain, setting it apart from the rest. Located along a wide stretch of a family-friendly beach, the hotel draws a mixed crowd. The stately on-site home of the original owners has been transformed into the full-service Casa Playa Spa, where massages and other treatments are only slightly less costly than in the U.S.

The mansion's dining room (now Chabert's Steakhouse), complete with crystal chandeliers, antiques, and dinnertime harpists, charges top dollar for Continental cuisine; there's also Azteca, a casual Mexican restaurant in the main building. You'll pay more for an oceanview, and more for the newer, air-conditioned rooms in the tower; the older rooms in the poolside building may have only ceiling fans, but they prevail in the character department, with hand-painted trim and original tile.

# The Upper Baja Peninsula

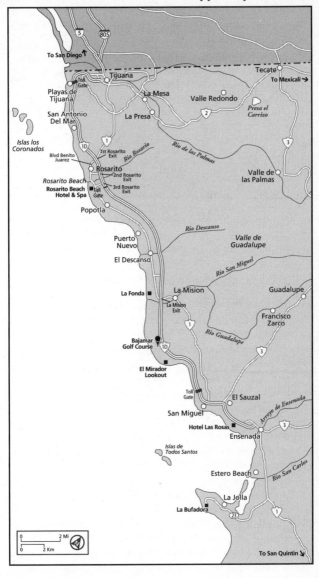

To San Diego↑

La Toll Gate
Tijuana
Tecate
To Mexicali →

Playas de Tijuana

La Mesa
Valle Redondo

San Antonio Del Mar

La Presa

Presa el Carrizo

Islas los Coronados

1st Rosarito Exit

Blvd Benito Juarez

Rio Rosario
Rio de las Palmas

Rosarito

Valle de las Palmas

2nd Rosarito Exit

3rd Rosarito Exit

Rosarito Beach
Rosarito Beach Hotel & Spa
Toll Gate

Popotla

Rio Descanso
Valle de Guadalupe

Puerto Nuevo

El Descanso

Rio San Miguel

La Fonda
La Mision
Guadalupe

La Mision Exit

Francisco Zarco

Bajamar Golf Course
1D

Rio Guadalupe

El Mirador Lookout

Toll Gate

El Sauzal

Arroyo de Ensenada

San Miguel

Hotel Las Rosas
Ensenada

Islas de Todos Santos

Estero Beach
Rio San Carlos

La Jolla

La Bufadora
23

1

0 — 2 Mi
0 — 2 Km

To San Quintin ↘

Blvd. Benito Juárez, Zona Centro, Rosarito, B.C. Mexico (P.O. Box 430145, San Diego, CA 92143). (C) **800/343-8582** U.S., or 6/612-0144. Fax 6/612-1125. www.rosaritohtl.com. 280 units. $59–$129 Sept–June; $89–$139 July–Aug and U.S. holidays. 2 children under 12 stay free in parents' room. Packages available. MC, V. Free parking. **Amenities:** 2 restaurants; bar; 2 swimming pools; racquetball and tennis courts; kids' playground; room service. *In room:* TV.

## WHERE TO DINE

While in Rosarito, you may want to try Chabert's (elegant, French) or the more casual Azteca Restaurant, both in the Rosarito Beach Hotel. Outside the hotel, a branch of **Puerto Nuevo's Ortega's** ((C) **6/612-0022**) on the main drag is the place for lobster; early risers out for a stroll can enjoy fresh, steaming-hot tamales, a traditional Mexican breakfast treat sold from sidewalk carts for around 50¢ each.

**El Nido** 𝓡𝓡 MEXICAN/STEAKS   One of the earliest eateries in Rosarito, El Nido remains popular with visitors unimpressed by the flashier, neon-lit joints that pop up to please the college-age set. The setting is Western frontier, complete with rustic candles and rusting wagon wheels; sit outside in the enclosed patio, or opt for the dark, cozy interior warmed by a large fireplace/open grill. The mesquite fire is constantly stoked to prepare the grilled steaks and seafood that are El Nido's specialty; the menu also includes free-range (and super-fresh) quail and venison from the owner's ranch in the nearby wine country. Meals are reasonably priced and generous, including hearty bean soup, American-style green salad, baked potatoes, and all the fresh tortillas and zesty salsa you can eat.

Blvd. Juárez 67. (C) **6/612-1430.** Main courses $5.50–$20. No credit cards. Daily 8am–midnight.

## ROSARITO BEACH AFTER DARK

Because the legal drinking age in Baja is 18, the under-21 crowd from Southern California tends to flock across the border on Friday and Saturday nights. The most popular spot in town is **Papas & Beer** ((C) **6/612-0444**), part of the Rosarito Beach Hotel. It's a relaxed come-as-you-are–type club on the beach, just a block north of the hotel. Even for those young in spirit only, it's great fun, with open-air tables and a bar surrounding a sand volleyball court. Or choose from several other adjacent clubs, each offering booming music, spirited dancing, and all-night-long energy. Cover charges vary depending on the season, the crowd, and the mood of the staff. The **Salon Méxican** ((C) **6/612-0144**), in the Rosarito Beach Hotel, attracts a slightly more mature crowd, with live music on Friday, Saturday, and Sunday nights.

## EN ROUTE FROM ROSARITO TO ENSENADA

A few miles south of Rosarito proper lies the seaside production site of 1997's megablockbuster film, *Titanic*. An 800-foot-long *Titanic* replica was constructed for filming, and many local citizens served as extras in the movie. Although the gargantuan ship was sunk and destroyed during filming, soundstages still contain partial sets (like a first-class hallway) and numerous props, including lifeboats, furnishings, and "Titanic"-labeled crates from dockside scenes. A combination museum and Hollywood-theamed amusement part has evolved here, popular for an afternoon attraction. Admission is a hefty $6 per person. The Titanic Museum (℗ **6/614-0110**) is open Friday, Saturday, and Sunday from 10am to 4pm.

Leaving Rosarito, drive south on the toll highway or the local-access old road that parallels it. In addition to the curious juxtaposition of ramshackle villages and luxurious vacation homes, you'll pass a variety of restaurants and resorts—this stretch of coastline has now surpassed Rosarito in drawing the discriminating visitor. Many places are so Americanized you feel as though you never left home, so our favorites are the funkier, more colorfully Mexican places, like Calafia restaurant, Puerto Nuevo lobster village, and La Fonda resort (all detailed below in "Where to Stay" and "Where to Dine"). After La Fonda, be sure to get back on the toll road, because the old road veers inland and you don't want to miss what's coming next.

Development falls off somewhat for the next 15 miles, but the coastline's natural beauty picks up the pace. You'll see green meadows running down to meet white-sand beaches and wild sand dunes, as you skirt rocky cliffs reminiscent of the coast at Big Sur. The ideal place to take it all in is El Mirador lookout, about 11 miles south of La Fonda. Feel the drama build as you climb up the stairs and gasp at the breathtaking view, which sweeps from the deep-blue open sea past steep cliffs and down the curved coastline to Salsipuedes Point, around which lies Ensenada. If vertigo doesn't trouble you, look straight down from El Mirador's railing and you'll see piles of automobiles lying akimbo where they were driven off before El Mirador was built. Whether the promontory was a popular suicide spot or merely a junkyard with an enticing twist is best left to urban legend-makers; it nevertheless reinforces your sense of a different culture (nowhere in image-conscious California would that twisted pile of metal be left on the rocks).

A few miles farther south on the toll road, you'll come to a sign for SALSIPUEDES BAY (the name means "leave if you can"). The dramatic scenery along the drive ends here, so you can take the exit if you want to turn around and head north again; or if you plan to do some camping, head down the near mile-long, rutted road to Salsipuedes Campground, set under olive trees on a cliff. Each campsite has a fire ring and costs $5 a day (day use is also $5). There's a natural rock tub with hot-spring water at the campground, and some basic cottages that rent for $30 a day. There is no easy access to the beach, known for its good surfing, from the campground.

Ensenada, with its shops, restaurants, and winery, is another 15 miles away.

## NEARBY GOLFING

Located 20 miles north of Ensenada, **Bajamar** (© 800/225-2418 in the U.S., or 6/155-0152) is a self-contained resort with 27 truly spectacular holes of golf, and the place to go if you want to feel just like you're in the United States. Originally conceived as a vacation home/planned community/country club, the bottom dropped out of '80s speculation, leaving a lot of unbuilt house pads on cul-de-sacs behind Bajamar's grandiose guardhouse. The main attraction is now the golf club and sister hotel, which play host to high-level retreats, conventions, and Asian tourists attracted by great golf deals. Featuring oceanfront, Scottish-style links reminiscent of the courses on the Monterey Peninsula, Bajamar lets you combine any two of their three nine-hole courses. Public greens fees for 18 holes (including mandatory cart) are $50 Sunday through Thursday, and $60 Friday or Saturday. Hotel guests pay $5 less, but the lavish **Hacienda las Glorias** offers a bevy of different golf packages (see "Where to Stay," below). Services include pro shop, putting and chipping greens, driving range, and an elegant bar and restaurant.

## WHERE TO STAY

**Hacienda las Glorias (at Bajamar golf resort)** 🏨🏨   Situated 20 miles north of Ensenada, Hacienda las Glorias is tucked away in the Bajamar golf resort/community. Popular with business conventions and family gatherings, Bajamar is as Americanized as it gets, and so is this luxury hotel, near the clubhouse. Architecture buffs will note the hotel is built like an early Spanish mission, with an interior outdoor plaza and garden surrounded by long arcades shading guest-room doorways. The 27 holes of golf are the main draw to

> ## ⌒ Fun Fact   The Bartender Who Launched a Thousand Hangovers
>
> The hotel and restaurant Rancho La Gloria claims to be the original birthplace of the margarita. Here's the deal: Carlos "Danny" Herrera says he invented the drink in 1948 for movie starlet Marjorie King, who allegedly fared badly if she drank any type of alcohol other than tequila. But she didn't want to appear unladylike by downing straight tequila—so Danny added fresh lime juice and Cointreau to soften the taste for Margarita, as she was known south of the border. The libation quickly gained popularity with fellow hotel guests and Hollywood friends Phil Harris and Alice Faye. Soon the concoction was being mixed up at La Plaza, a hotel in La Jolla, California, before making its way to Los Angeles and eventual beverage superstardom.

this hotel, since the long road from the highway is lined with signs for phases of the surrounding vacation-home development that never really got off the ground. Rooms and suites are very spacious and comfortable, with vaguely colonial furnishings and luxurious bathrooms. A variety of golf packages are available, including pricing for couples with only one golfer. For greens fees, see "Nearby Golf," above.

Highway 1-D, Km 77.5 (mail: 416 W. San Ysidro Blvd., Suite #L-732, San Ysidro, CA 92173). ⓒ **800/225-2418** U.S., or 6/155-0152. 80 units. $84–$112 double; $184–$208 suite. Children under 12 stay free in parents' room. Golf packages available. AE, MC, V. **Amenities:** Restaurant; heated swimming pool; tennis courts; spa; concierge; tour desk; business center; room service; laundry and dry cleaning services. *In room:* A/C, TV.

**Hotel Las Rocas** 𝔊𝔊   This polished hotel is run by an American, for Americans, and it shows. English is spoken fluently everywhere, and there are only as many signs in Spanish as you'd expect to see in Los Angeles. Built in a Mediterranean style, with gleaming white stucco, cobalt-blue accents, and brightly painted tiles everywhere, Las Rocas has a lovely setting perched above the sea. There's no beach below the rocky edge, but the hotel's oceanfront swimming pool and secluded whirlpool lagoons more than make up for it. Tropical drinks and snacks are dispensed from the thatched-roof *palapa* in the poolside garden, and swaying palms rustle throughout the property. Like most Baja resorts, Las Rocas is oriented toward

## *Tips* Surfing, Northern Baja Style

From California and beyond, surfers come to the northern Baja coastline for perpetual right-breaking waves, cheap digs and eats, and an *Endless Summer*–type of camaraderie.

Undoubtedly, the most famous surf spot in all of Mexico is Killers, at Todos Santos Island. This was the location of the winning wave in the 1997–98 K2 Challenge (a world-wide contest to ride the largest wave each winter—and be photographed doing it). Killers is a very makeable wave for confident, competent surfers. To get there you need a boat. You can get a lift from the local *panga* (skiff) fleet, for about $100 for the day. That's pretty much the going rate, and you won't find the tightly knit Ensenada *pangueros* anxious to undercut each other. It's about 10 miles out to the island; there you'll anchor and paddle into the lineup. It goes without saying that you must bring everything you'll need—food, drink, sunscreen, and so on.

Other less radical and easier-to-reach spots include Popotla, just south of Rosarito, where you'll walk to the beach through the Popotla trailer park. Calafia, also just a mile or two south of Rosarito, has a reeling right point that can get extremely heavy. San Miguel is the point break just south of the final tollbooth on the highway into Ensenada. It's an excellent wave but generally crowded.

If you're a surfer looking to get your bearings, or a spectator wanting to get your feet wet, stop by Inner Reef (Km 34½; no phone). Opened in 1998 by a friendly Southern California ex-pat named Roger, this tiny shack offers all the essentials; wax, leashes, patch kits, surfboard sales and rentals, even expert repairs at bargain prices. Roger is there from noon until sunset every day in summer, and from Wednesday to Sunday in winter.

the sea, so all rooms have an oceanfront private terrace. The rooms and suites are very nicely furnished in a Mexican colonial style, and bathrooms are well equipped and beautifully tiled. The hotel's restaurant, Cafe Carnaval, attempts to offer both Mexican cuisine and Continental fare; neither really succeeds, but they do make outstanding guacamole, which you can order by the bowl for chip-dipping at either the indoor or poolside bar. *Tip:* Try to stay in the main building, and don't rule out a suite—even the $115 junior suite is spacious and includes a romantic fireplace and minikitchen.

Km 38.5 Free Road (P.O. Box 189003 HLR, Coronado, CA 92178-9003) Take the second Rosarito exit off the toll road, then drive 6 miles south, or follow the free road south from Rosarito; Las Rocas will be on the right. © 888/LAS-ROCAS in the U.S., or 6/612-2140. www.lasrocas.com. 74 units. $75–$95 double; $115–$250 suite; midweek rates available Oct–Apr only. Senior discounts and packages available. AE, MC, V. **Amenities:** Restaurant; pool with Jacuzzi; tour desk. *In room:* A/C, TV.

**La Fonda** 𝒜 *Value*  Just as American-style Las Rocas has its staunch devotees, plenty of folks are loyal to La Fonda's rustic rooms, none of which comes with minibar, state-of-the-art TV, or phone. What they do have is an adventuresome appeal unlike any other northern Baja coast resort, a place for people who truly want to get away from it all. Relaxation and romance are the key words at this small hotel and restaurant, which was opened in the '50s and hasn't changed a whole lot since then. Perched cliffside above a wide, sandy beach, all of La Fonda's rooms have wide-open views of the breaking surf below. By day, surfers and porpoises frolic in the waves, and at night the beach glows with moonlight reflected off white froth. Although there are some newer motel-style rooms, there's more charm to the older apartments with fireplaces (some with kitchenettes), which are reached via narrow winding staircases, much like the pathway down to the sand. The best rooms are numbers 18 to 22, closest to the sand and isolated from the main building; ask for one of these when you reserve. During particularly cold winter months, unheated La Fonda can get chilly—an important consideration. At the very least, be sure you're in a room with a fireplace.

Bamboo and palm fronds decorate the genial bar next to La Fonda's acclaimed casual restaurant (see "Where to Dine," below). Ensenada is a scenic 45-minute drive south, and Puerto Nuevo a mere 8 miles up the road—if you decide you need to leave this hideaway at all, that is.

Highway 1-D, Km 59, La Misión exit. Mail: P.O. Box 430268, San Ysidro, CA 92143. No phone. 22 units. $55 standard; $75 deluxe (with fireplace and/or full kitchen). No credit cards. Write for reservations; allow 2 weeks for response. **Amenities:** Restaurant/bar. *In room:* TV.

## WHERE TO DINE

Three miles south of Rosarito Beach, elaborate stucco portals beckon drivers to pull over for **Calafia** (© **6/612-1581**), because this restaurant and trailer park isn't visible from the highway. We don't recommend the dismal accommodations, but Calafia's restaurant is worth a stop, if only to admire the impressive setting above the crashing surf. Your meal is served at tables on terraces, balconies, and ledges wedged into the rocks all the way down to the bottom, where an outdoor dance floor and wrecked Spanish galleon sit on the beach. At night, when the outdoor landings are softly lit, and the mariachis' gentle strumming complements the sound of crashing waves, romance is definitely in the air. The menu is standard Mexican fare with the addition of some Americanized dishes like fajitas, but it's all prepared well and served with fresh, warm tortillas and good, strong margaritas. Calafia serves breakfast, lunch, and dinner daily. Another excellent choice for sunset cocktails is the Moroccan-style **Hotel Cafe Americana,** Carretera Libre a Ensenada, Km 51 (*©* **6/614-0070**), whose whimsical white minarets beckon travelers to this once-private home turned inn and restaurant. The bar offers a superb selection of premium tequilas, for sipping by the fire or on a dramatic oceanfront terrace.

A trip down the coast just wouldn't be complete without stopping at **Puerto Nuevo,** a tiny fishing town with nearly 30 different restaurants—and they all serve exactly the same thing! Some 40 years ago the fishermen's wives here started serving local lobsters from the kitchens of their simple shacks; many eventually built small dining rooms onto their homes or built proper restaurants. The result is a lobster lover's paradise, where a feast of lobster, beans, rice, salsa, limes, and fresh tortillas costs around $10. Puerto Nuevo is 12 miles south of Rosarito on the Old Ensenada Highway (parallel to the toll Highway 1)—just drive through the arched entryway, park, and stroll the town's three or four blocks for a restaurant that suits your fancy. Some have names, and some don't; **Ortega's** is one of the originals, and has expanded to five separate locations within the village. There's also **La Casa de la Langosta** ("House of Lobster"), which even opened a branch in Rosarito Beach. But regulars prefer the smaller, family-run spots, where mismatched dinette sets and chipped plates underscore the earnest service and personally prepared dinners.

About 10 miles farther south, roughly halfway between Rosarito and Ensenada, is the **La Fonda** hotel and restaurant (no phone; see also "Where to Stay," above). Plenty of San Diegans make the drive Sunday mornings for La Fonda's outstanding buffet brunch, an orgy of meats, traditional Mexican stews, *chilaquiles* (a saucy egg-and-tortilla scramble), fresh fruits, and pastries. Breakfast, lunch, and dinner are always accompanied by a basket of Baja's best flour tortillas (try rolling them with some butter and jam at breakfast). The best seating is under thatched umbrellas on La Fonda's tiled terrace overlooking the breaking surf; an adjacent bar means margaritas and Bloody Marys are yours for the asking, and live music keeps the joint jumping on Friday and Saturday nights (strolling mariachis entertain the rest of the time). House specialties include banana pancakes, pork chops with salsa verde, succulent glazed ribs, and a variety of seafood; plan to walk off your heavy meal along the sandy beach below, accessible by a stone stairway. Relaxing ambience coupled with exceptionally good food and service make La Fonda a must-see along the coast. Sunday brunch is around $12 a person; main courses otherwise are $4 to $15. They're open daily from around 9am to 10pm; Sunday's buffet brunch is from 10am to 3:30pm.

## 3  Ensenada: Port of Call ⍟

84 miles S of San Diego; 68 miles S of Tijuana

Ensenada is an attractive, classic town on a lovely bay, surrounded by sheltering mountains. It's about 40 minutes from Rosarito, and is the kind of place that loves a celebration. Most any time you choose to visit, the city is festive—be it for a bicycle race or a seafood festival.

One of Mexico's principal ports of call, Ensenada welcomes half a million visitors a year, attracted to its beaches, excellent sportfishing, nearby wineries, and surrounding natural attractions.

**GETTING THERE**    After passing through the final tollbooth , Highway 1-D curves sharply toward downtown Ensenada. Watch out for brutal metal speed bumps slowing traffic into town—they're far less forgiving on the average chassis than those in the U.S.!

**VISITOR INFORMATION**    There are a couple of tourist information offices in Ensenada. The **Tourist and Convention Bureau booth** (© 6/178-2411) is located at the western entrance to town, where the waterfront-hugging Boulevard Lázaro Cárdenas—also known as Boulevard Costero—curves away to the right. The booth is open daily from 9am till dusk and can provide a downtown map, directions to major nearby sites, and information on special events throughout the city. As with most of the commonly visited areas of Baja, English is spoken fluently by one or more employees. Eight blocks south you'll find the State Secretary of Tourism at Boulevard Lázaro Cárdenas no. 1477, Government Building (© 6/172-3022;

fax 6/172-3081), which is open Monday through Friday from 9am to 7pm, Saturday from 10am to 3pm, and Sunday from 10am to 2pm. Both offices have extended hours on U.S. holidays. Taxis park along López Mateos.

## EXPLORING ENSENADA

While technically a "border town," one of Ensenada's appeals is its multilayered vitality, borne out of being concerned with much more than tourism. The bustling port consumes the entire waterfront—beach access can be found only north or south of town—and the economy is dominated by the Pacific fishing trade and agriculture in the fertile valleys surrounding the city. Try not to leave Ensenada without getting a taste of its true personality; for example, stop by the indoor/outdoor fish market at the northernmost corner of the harbor. Each day, from early morning to midday, merchants and housewives gather to assess the day's catch—tuna, marlin, snapper, plus many other varieties of fish and piles of shrimp from the morning's haul.

Outside the market is the perfect place to sample the culinary craze of Baja California, the Baja fish taco. Several stands prepare this local treat; strips of freshly caught fish are battered and deep fried, then wrapped in corn tortillas and topped with shredded cabbage, cilantro, salsa, and various other condiments. They're delicious, cheap, and filling, and it's easy to see why surf bums and collegiate vacationers consider them a Baja staple.

Elsewhere in town, visit the Bodegas de Santo Tomás Winery, Avenida Miramar 666 (at Calle 7), (© 6/178-2509; www.santo-tomas.com.mx). While most visitors to Mexico are quite content quaffing endless quantities of cheap *cerveza* (beer), even part-time oenophiles should pay a visit to this historic winery—the oldest in Mexico, and the largest in all of Baja—where they use old-fashioned methods of processing grapes grown in the lush Santo Tomás Valley, first cultivated by Dominican monks in 1791. A 45-minute tour introduces you to low-tech processing machinery, hand-hammered wood casks, and cool, damp, stone aging rooms; it culminates in an invitation to sample several Santo Tomás vintages, including an international medal-winning cabernet and delightfully crisp sparkling blanc de blanc. The wood-paneled, church-like tasting room is adorned with paintings of mischievous altar boys being scolded by stern friars for pilfering wine or ruining precious grapes. Anyone used to the pretentious, assembly-line ambience of more trendy wine regions will relish the friendly welcome and informative tour presented here. Tours in English are conducted Monday to Saturday at 10am, 11am, 12pm, 1pm, and 3pm. Admission is $2 (including tastings; $3 more gets you a souvenir wineglass), and wines for sale range from $3.50 to $10 a bottle. *Note:* Most of the winery's product is exported for the European market.

Be sure to poke around a bit after your tour concludes, for Santo Tomás has more treasures to give up. The little modern machinery installed here freed up a cavernous space now used for monthly jazz concerts, and a former aging room has been transformed into La Embotelladora Vieja ("the old aging room") restaurant (see "Where to Dine," below). Across the street stands La Esquina de Bodegas ("the corner wine cellar"), former aging rooms for Santo Tomás. One of many pleasant cultural treats of Ensenada, the industrial-style building now functions as a gallery showcasing local art, with a skylit bookstore on the second level and a small cafe (punctuated by giant copper distillation vats) in the rear.

Ensenada's primary cultural center is the Centro Cívico, Social y Cultura (Blvd. Lázaro Cárdenas at Av. Club Rotario). The impressive Mediterranean building was formerly Riviera del Pacífico, a glamorous 1930s bayfront casino and resort frequented by Hollywood's elite. Tiles in the lobby commemorate "Visitantes Distinguidos 1930–1940," including Marion Davies, William Randolph Hearst, Lana Turner, Myrna Loy, and Jack Dempsey. Now used by the Rotary Club as offices and for cultural and social events, the main building is open to the public. Elegant hallways and ballrooms evoke a bygone elegance, and every wall and alcove glows with original murals depicting Mexico's colorful history. Lush formal gardens span the front of the building, and there's a small art gallery tucked away to one side. Through the lobby, facing an inner courtyard filled with the ghosts of parties past, is Bar Andaluz, which is still, though sporadically, open to the public. It's an intimate, dark-wood place where you can just imagine someone like Papa Hemingway holding cocktail-hour court beneath that colorful toreador mural.

**A NEARBY ATTRACTION**    South of the city, via a 45-minute drive along the rural Punta Banda peninsula, is one of Ensenada's major attractions: La Bufadora, a natural sea spout in the rocks. With each incoming wave, water is forced upward through the rock, creating a geyser whose loud grunt gave the phenomenon its name (*la bufadora* means "buffalo snort"). Local fishermen who ply these waters, however, have a much more lyrical explanation for this roaring blowhole. According to local legend, a mother gray whale and her calf were just beginning their migration from the safety of Baja's San Ignacio lagoon to Alaska. As they rounded Punta Banda the curious calf squeezed into a sea cave, only to be trapped. The groan that this 70-foot high blowhole makes every time it erupts is the sound of the stranded calf still crying for his mother, and the tremendous spray is his spout.

From downtown Ensenada, take Avenida Reforma south (Highway 1) to Highway 23 west. It's a long, meandering drive through a semi-swamplike area untouched by development; look for grazing animals, bait shops, and fishermen's shacks along the way. La Bufadora is at the end of the road, and once parked ($1 per car in crude dirt lots), you must walk downhill to the viewing platform, at the end of a 600-yard pathway lined with souvenir stands. In addition to running a gauntlet of determined vendors featuring the usual wares, visitors can avail themselves of inexpensive snacks at the sole restaurant located there, including the tasty fish tacos. Visitation is enormous, and there are plans to pave the dirt parking lots and build permanent restaurants and shops, but these long-standing plans have yet to become a reality.

## SPORTS & OUTDOOR ACTIVITIES

**FISHING**    Ensenada, which bills itself as "the yellowtail capital of the world," draws sportfishermen eager to venture out from the beautiful Bahía de Todos Santos (Bay of All Saints) in search of the Pacific's albacore, halibut, marlin, rockfish, and sea bass. A wooden boardwalk parallel to Blvd. Lázaro Cárdenas (Costero) near the northern entrance to town provides access to the sportfishing piers and the many charter-boat operators there. Open-party boats leave early, often by 7am, and charge around $35 per person, plus an additional fee (around $5) for the mandatory fishing license. Nonfishing passengers must, by law, also be licensed. Those disinclined to comparison shop the boats can make advance arrangements with **Baja California Tours** (© **619/454-7166**), which is based in San Diego. In addition to daily fishing excursions, they offer 1- to 3-night packages including hotel, fishing, some meals, and transportation from San Diego.

**HIKING**    Ensenada is the gateway city to the **Parque Nacional Constitución de 1857.** Located on the spine of the Sierra de Juárez, the park was once a heavily used mining area. Now, most of the mines are defunct. In contrast to the dry and sometimes desolate surroundings of much of the northern peninsula, the 5,000-hectare preserve averages about 4,000 feet in altitude and is covered in places with pine forests. The most idiosyncratic thing, however, is the sight of a good-sized lake in an alpine setting. The park has no developed trails other than a 6-mile one that circumnavigates the lake, Laguna Hanson, but there are endless opportunities for blazing your own. To get there, take Mexico Highway 3 south from Ensenada and exit at the graded dirt access road at Km 55. The park entrance road is gravel and generally well maintained, but can be really rough after a rainy year. It's 35km (22 miles) to the park entrance. If the entrance is manned you'll be asked for a modest entrance fee.

The Parque Nacional Sierra San Pedro Mártir is to Baja California what Yosemite is to Alta California. Almost 200,000 acres of the highest mountains on the peninsula have been preserved. The highest peak of all, Picacho del Diablo (Devil's Peak), rises to 10,154 feet. Views from the summit encompass both oceans and an immense stretch of land. Best of all, it's virtually unvisited, something that sets it apart from the normal National Park experience in Los Estados Unidos.

Farther south on Highway 1 from Ensenada, you'll come to a signed turnoff for the Park at Km 140, soon after you pass the little town of Colonet. The sign also says OBSERVATORIO. Fill up with gas in Colonet, as there is no more to be had until you exit this way again, and reset your trip odometer at the turnoff. In between it's entirely possible that you would put on 150 gas-guzzling miles of rugged driving. It's 47 miles to the park entrance.

What you'll find is a high alpine realm of flower-speckled meadows, soaring granite peaks, and year-round creeks. Official trails are few and far between, but anyone who's good with a map and compass or even just good at wandering off and finding his or her way back can have a great time hiking. Cow trails are numerous (yes, cows in a national park). Four year-round creeks drain the park and make great destinations. Picacho del Diablo is a difficult but rewarding overnight hike and long scramble. Always remember that you're in one of the most rugged and remote places in all of Baja, and it's quite likely that if you get lost or hurt nobody is going to come looking for you.

**SEA KAYAKING** The rocky coastline of Punta la Banda is a favorite first kayaking trip for beginning ocean kayakers. There are several secluded beaches, sea caves, and the scenery is terrific. Many kayakers use La Bufadora as a launching point to head out to Todos Santos Island. It's about 7 miles from La Bufadora to the southern and larger island of the two Todos Santos Islands. The first 3 miles follow a rocky coast to the tip of Punta la Banda. From here it's time to size up the wind, the waves, and the fog. If the coast is clear, take a compass heading and begin the 4-mile open-water crossing. Bring water and camping gear to spend a night on the pristine island. **Dale's La Bufadora Dive Shop** (© 6/154-2045) has kayak rentals and is open weekends or by prior reservation. **Southwest Sea Kayaks** (© 619/222-3616) in San Diego leads weekend trips to the island several times a year.

**SCUBA DIVING & SNORKELING**    La Bufadora is a great dive spot with thick kelp and wonderful sea life. Get underwater and zoom through lovely kelp beds and rugged rock formations covered in strawberry anemones and gypsy shawl nudibranchs. You may also spot spiny lobsters and numerous large fish. It's possible to swim right over to the blowhole, but use extreme caution in this area— you don't want to end up like that mythical whale calf. **Dale's La Bufadora Dive Shop** (© 6/154-2045) is located right on shore at the best entry point. They'll set you up with fills and advice.

Several dive shops in Ensenada, including **Almar,** 149 Av. Macheros (© 6/178-3013), or **Baja Dive Expeditions** at the Baja Beach and Tennis Club (© 6/173-0220), will arrange boat dives to Todos Santos Island, which sits at the outer edge of Todos Santos Bay. The diving here is similar to the diving at Catalina or the other California Channel Islands—lots of fish, big kelp, urchins, and jagged underwater rock formations. The visibility varies widely, depending on the swell.

## SHOPPING

Ensenada's equivalent of Avenida Revolución is crowded Avenida López Mateos, which runs roughly parallel to Boulevard Lázaro Cárdenas (Costero); the highest concentration of shops and restaurants is between avenidas Ruiz and Castillo. The street is filled with beggars, but the sellers are less likely to bargain—they're used to the gullible cruise-ship buyers. Compared to Tijuana, there is more authentic Mexican art- and craftwork in Ensenada, pieces genuinely imported from rural states and villages where different skills are traditionally practiced. Though from the outside it looks dusty and unlit, **Curiosidades La Joya,** Avenida López Mateos 725 (© 6/178-3191), is a treasure trove of stained-glass lamps, hangings, and other handcrafted curios. Piles of intricately designed glass lampshades lie side-by-side with colorful tiles and wrought-iron birdcages, the shop's other specialty. The shopkeepers here are stubborn about bargaining, perhaps because they know the value of their unusual wares.

You'll see colorfully painted glazed pottery wherever you go in northern Baja. Quality can range from sloppy pieces quickly painted with a limited palette to intricately designed and painstakingly painted works evocative of Tuscan urns and pitchers. The best prices are to be had at the abundant roadside stands lining the old road south of Rosarito, but if you're willing to pay extra for quality, head to **Artesanías Colibrí,** 855 Av. López Mateos (℮ **6/178-1312**). Here you can learn about the origins of this Talavera style—how invading Moors set up terra-cotta factories in the Spanish city of Talavera, and subsequent migration brought the art to the Mexican state of Puebla.

## WHERE TO STAY

**Estero Beach Resort** ℛ    Located about 6 miles south of down-town Ensenada, this sprawling complex of rooms, cottages, and mobile-home hookups is popular with families and active vacation-ers. The bay and protected lagoon at the edge of the lushly planted property is perfect for swimming and launching sailboards; there's also tennis, horseback riding, volleyball, and a game room with Ping-Pong and billiards. The guest rooms are a little worn, but no one expects fancy at Estero Beach. The beachfront restaurant serves a casual mix of seafood and other Mexican fare mingled with ham-burgers, fried chicken, and omelets. Some suites and cottages have kitchenettes, and some can easily accommodate a whole family.

Mail: Apdo. Postal 86, Ensenada, BC, Mexico. From Ensenada, take Hwy. 1 south; turn right at ESTERO BEACH sign. ℮ 617/6-6225. 106 units. Rates range from $95–$300; the average oceanview cottage for 2 runs around $100. MC, V. **Amenities:** Restaurant; tennis court; game room. *In room:* TV.

**Hotel Las Rosas** ℛℛ    One of the most modern hotels of the area, it still falls short of most definitions of luxurious, yet this pink oceanfront hotel 2 miles outside Ensenada is the favorite of many Baja aficionados, and does offer most of the comforts of an upscale American hotel (which doesn't leave room for much Mexican per-sonality). The atrium lobby is awash with pale pink and seafoam green (including a back-lit green-glass ceiling), a color scheme that pervades throughout—including the guest rooms, sparsely furnished with quasitropical hotel furniture. Some of the 32 rooms have fireplaces and/or in-room whirlpools, and all have balconies overlooking the pool and ocean. One of the resort's main photo-ops is the swimming pool that overlooks the Pacific and features a vanishing edge that appears to merge with the ocean beyond. If you're looking to maintain the highest comfort level possible, this would be your hotel of choice.

Highway 1, 2 miles north of Ensenada. Mail: Apdo. Postal 316, Ensenada, BC, Mexico. (℃) 6/17/4-4310. 48 units. $126–$190 double. Children under 12 $16; additional adult $22 extra. MC, V. **Amenities:** Restaurant, cocktail lounge; swimming pool; tennis and racquetball courts; basic workout room with mirrors (listed by the hotel as an added amenity!); cliff-top hot tub; tour desk; room service; massage services; laundry service. *In room:* A/C, TV.

**San Nicolás Resort Hotel**   Most rooms at this modern motor inn face the courtyard or have balconies overlooking the swimming pool—and the place is surprisingly quiet for being right on the main drag. The hotel also has a disco and branch of Caliente Sports Book where you can gamble on games and races throughout the U.S.

Ave. López Mateos and Guadalupe, Ensenada. (Mail: P.O. Box 437060, San Ysidro, CA 92073-7060). (℃) 6/176-1901. Fax 6/176-4930. 147 units. $48–$88 double; $130–$260 suite. Additional person $10 extra. AE, MC, V. Free parking. **Amenities:** Restaurant, cocktail lounge; swimming pool. *In room:* A/C, TV.

**Villa Fontana Days Inn**   This motel is notable for its out-of-place architecture—who'd expect a peak-roofed, gabled, New England–style structure in a land dominated by red-tiled roofs? This bargain-priced motel is otherwise unremarkable; well located and cleanly run by the Days Inn chain, it does have a small pool and enclosed parking. Most of the 65 rooms have showers, rather than tubs, in the bathrooms. Ask for a room at the back, away from street noise.

Av. López Mateos 1050, Ensenada. (℃) **800/4-BAJA-04** U.S., or 6/178-3434. www.villafontana.com.mx. 65 units. Summer $60 double; $115 suite. Rates are higher on holidays, lower midweek and in winter. Rates include continental breakfast. AE, MC, V. Free parking. **Amenities:** Pool. *In room:* A/C, TV.

## WHERE TO DINE

**El Charro**   MEXICAN   You'll recognize El Charro by its front windows: Whole chickens rotate slowly on the rotisserie in one, while a woman makes tortillas in the other. This little place has been here since 1956 and looks it, with charred walls and a ceiling made of split logs. The simple fare consists of such dishes as half a roasted chicken with fries and tortillas or carne asada with soup, guacamole, and tortillas. Giant piñatas hang from the walls above the concrete floor. Kids are welcome; they'll think they're on a picnic. Wine and beer are served, and beer is cheaper than soda.

Av. López Mateos 475 (between Ruiz and Gastellum). ℂ 617/8-3881. Menu items $5–$12; $20 for lobster. No credit cards. Daily 11am–2am.

**El Rey Sol** 🎇🎇 FRENCH/MEXICAN   Opened by French expatriates in 1947, the family-run El Rey Sol has long been considered Ensenada's finest eatery. Decked out like the French flag, this red, white, and blue building is a beacon on busy López Mateos. The country French ambience inside is punctuated by wrought-iron chandeliers and heavy oak farm tables, but the menu's prices and sophistication belie the casual decor. House specialties include seafood puff pastry; baby clams steamed in butter, white wine, and cilantro; chicken in a brandy and chipotle chile cream sauce; tender grilled steaks; and homemade French desserts. Portions are generous, however, and always feature fresh vegetables from the nearby family farm. Every table receives a complimentary platter of appetizers at dinnertime; lunch is a hearty three-course meal.

Av. López Mateos 1000 (at Blancarte). ℂ 6/178-1733. Reservations recommended for weekends. Main courses $9–$19. AE, MC, V. Daily 7:30am–10:30pm.

**La Embottelladora Vieja** 🎇🎇🎇 *(Finds)* FRENCH/MEXICAN   Hidden on an industrial side street and attached to the Bodegas de Santo Tomás winery, this find looks more like a chapel from the outside than the elegant restaurant it is. Sophisticated diners will feel right at home in this stylish setting, a former aging room for the winery now resplendent with red oak furniture (constructed from old wine casks), high brick walls, and crystal goblets and candlesticks on linen tablecloths. It goes without saying the wine list is exemplary, featuring bottles from Santo Tomás and other Baja vintners, and the "Baja French" menu features dishes carefully crafted to either include or complement wine. Look for appetizers like abalone ceviche or cream of garlic soup, followed by grilled swordfish in cilantro sauce, filet mignon in portwine-gorgonzola sauce, or quail with a tart sauvignon blanc sauce. If you're planning to splurge on one fine meal in Ensenada (or all of northern Baja, for that matter), this is the place.

Avenida Miramar 666 (at Calle 7). ℂ 6/174-0807. Reservations recommended for weekends. Main courses $8–$20. MC, V. Lunch and dinner; call for seasonal hours.

# Index

See also Accommodations and Restaurants indexes below.